Reynolds, Raschi and Lopat

Reynolds, Raschi and Lopat

New York's Big Three and the Yankee Dynasty of 1949–1953

SOL GITTLEMAN

McFarland & Company, Inc., Publishers
Jefferson, North Carolina, and London

LIBRARY OF CONGRESS CATALOGUING-IN-PUBLICATION DATA

Gittleman, Sol, 1934–
    Reynolds, Raschi and Lopat : New York's big three and the great
Yankee dynasty of 1949–1953 / Sol Gittleman.
        p.   cm.
    Includes bibliographical references and index.

    ISBN-13: 978-0-7864-3055-0
    softcover : 50# alkaline paper ∞

    1. Reynolds, Allie, 1915–1994.   2. Lopat, Ed, 1918–1992.
3. Raschi, Vic, 1919–1988.   4. Pitchers (Baseball)— United States—
Biography.   5. Baseball players— United States— Biography.
6. New York Yankees (Baseball team)— History.   I. Title.

GV865.A1G54   2007
796.357092 — dc22   2007010946
[B]

British Library cataloguing data are available

On the cover: Vic Raschi (*left*), Allie Reynolds and Ed Lopat (*right*), New
York Yankees, 1949–1953 (AP Photo)

Manufactured in the United States of America

*McFarland & Company, Inc., Publishers
  Box 611, Jefferson, North Carolina 28640
    www.mcfarlandpub.com*

To my big brother Melvin

Acknowledgments

Many people contributed their time and their memory to this book. Sally Raschi was always available to talk, and her candor informed every word I wrote about the lives and values of these men whom she knew so well. The early telephone conversations with Bobby Brown, Yogi Berra, Hank Bauer, Charlie Silvera, Phil Rizzuto and Jerry Coleman were inspirational. John Lopat shared his father's life with me. Mitje Raschi, Vic's daughter, was helpful in providing very special photos. The Oklahoma Heritage Association demonstrated infinite goodwill in locating information about Allie and Earlene Reynolds.

Zita Carno was a treasure of Eddie Lopat memories. Don Leypoldt, Jim Stern, Salvatore Salipante, Martin Oppenheimer, Don Gropman, Lou Mazza, Mike Singer and Phil Primack read text and commented freely. Tom Ling helped me deal with that techno-tool of the devil, my computer. Kyna Hamill is a research assistant I would wish on every author. Elizabeth Canny and Marcella Tanona in the Provost's office at Tufts University kept my finances and nerves in order; and it was Jim Lehrer, honorary degree recipient at a Tufts commencement, who told me: write that book about these three.

To those great baseball journalists and historians who preceded me, I give my gratitude: Harold Seymour, Roger Kahn, Peter Golenbock, Harvey Frommer, David Halberstam, Robert Creamer, Dave Anderson, Leonard Koppett and many others. Interviewers Dom Forker, Lawrence Ritter, Donald Honig, and Danny Peary traveled endless miles to capture the memories of hundreds of former ballplayers.

To my agent, Barbara Collins Rosenberg, I owe a special debt. Her father, a loyal Yankee fan, read the manuscript and urged her on to find a publisher. She gave time and energy to this project as only a loving daughter can.

To those Yankee players and especially the three pitchers who are the special subject of this book, thank you for five of the happiest years of my teenage life. I knew your uniform numbers, your birth dates and home towns; you have been in my memory for more than a half-century. Writing this book is a small gesture of thanks for those years. It was a labor of love.

Table of Contents

Introduction

"Professor Gittleman? I have your letter. This is Bobby Brown. I would be glad to talk to you." That was the first telephone call I received in reply to seven letters written to living members of the 1949–1953 New York Yankees. They are in retirement, celebrities in their own right, constantly dealing with requests for interviews and public appearances. Bobby Brown became president of the American League after a distinguished career as a cardiologist when his baseball days were over. His life is very busy. Within a week I had calls from Hank Bauer, Charlie Silvera, Jerry Coleman, and Yogi Berra. Why did they pick up the phone and call me? They all gave the same reply to that question: We didn't know *then* what these three meant to us. Tell their story now, please.

There have been many books written about the New York Yankees, mostly about the forty-one pinstriped notables who have been elected to the Hall of Fame at Cooperstown, a reasonable guarantee of baseball immortality. Babe Ruth, Joe DiMaggio, Mickey Mantle, Joe McCarthy, Casey Stengel, George Weiss and Jacob Ruppert command a library shelf all to themselves. Others, like Roger Maris, who broke Ruth's single-season home run record, Elston Howard, the first black Yankee, and George Steinbrenner, earn their place in the pantheon without benefit of formal election. They are, nonetheless, secure in their fame.

The subjects of this book are three Yankee pitchers who could easily disappear into the void of lost memory. Their names no longer appear on the ballots of the Hall of Fame's Veterans Committee. The more contemporary members of the Baseball Writers Association of America lack the historical context, and today's teenage admirers of Derek Jeter and Alex Rodriguez never heard of them. Such eminent baseball historians and statisticians of this generation as John Thorn and Bill James scarcely make a reference to them in *Total Baseball* and *The New Bill James Historical Baseball Abstract*.

They arrived in the Bronx late in the 1940s as products of the Great Depression at a special moment in American and New York City baseball history. Two were the offspring of European immigrants from Poland and Italy; the third was one-quarter Creek Indian. After World War II, former major leaguers had returned home to re-claim their place on the rosters of the sixteen major league teams, only to discover that a social revolution in the form of Jackie Robinson and Branch Rickey was about to shake the foundations of Organized Baseball, far ahead of the rest of America.[1] Within a year or two the big boy on the New York City scene seemed destined to be the Brooklyn Dodgers' juggernaut of Robinson, Campanella, Snider, Hodges, Newcombe, Reese, Furillo and Erskine. There was near-universal agreement by fans and media that the Dodgers were the next Big Apple dynasty, an epithet formerly reserved for the 1920s Yankees of Murderers' Row and the 1930s Bronx Bombers.

In contrast, the Yankees who returned to the House that Ruth Built had aged badly during the war, and even the sports writing New York City wise men said that the dynasty was over. Red Smith of *The Herald Tribune*, John Drebinger of the *New York Times*, Dick Young of *The Daily News* and every leading sports journalist in and out of the city declared that the Age of the Boston Red Sox and Cleveland Indians was upon us. As if to prove the point, the Yankees, who were not part of the pennant race in the two wartime years of 1944 and 1945, experienced a dismal failure in the first post-war season of 1946, coming in third behind Boston and a resurgent Detroit Tigers. Joe DiMaggio had his first under-.300 season, and the pre-war Yankees stars who returned seemed too old to compete. Expectations for the Yankee future were grim.

But between 1949 and 1953, five rather ordinary New York Yankee baseball teams won five *consecutive* World Series, an accomplishment that may never be repeated. *For those five years no New York Yankee led the league in any offensive category.* It was a time when the great DiMaggio's legendary skills were eroding and an ill-prepared kid from Oklahoma named Mickey Mantle was desperately trying to make his way against major league pitching and the temptations of the city. These five teams were held together by a crafty managerial genius who had failed in his first run in the National League and was considered a clown when he arrived in New York City; and by three older pitchers, two of whom had come to New York in trades as journeymen, at an age when they could look forward reasonably to only a few more years of competition; and the third who had been Yankee property for nearly a decade and did not have his first full season until he was twenty-nine years old. In this five-year period, the three won 255 games for the Yankees, exclusive of their World Series triumphs. The manager, Casey Stengel, knew enough to leave these three men alone with their pitching coach, a former major leaguer and Yankee veteran who had gone on to manage in the minor leagues, and now was coming back to New York. His name was Jim Turner.

One wonders if Stengel had any idea of the astonishing synergy that these three older men would generate — Allie Pierce Reynolds, an Oklahoman Creek

Indian; Victor John Angelo Raschi, from the Italian neighborhood of Springfield, Massachusetts; and Eddie Lopatynski, who found it easier as a kid on the streets of New York City to call himself Ed Lopat. They came from different worlds, shared a quiet and deep communion with each other, became lifelong friends, and over a brief span of five years re-wrote baseball history.

1

The Players of the American Game: Ethnicity and Race

In the summer of 1942, Johnny Pesky was a rookie shortstop for the Boston Red Sox. Somehow, word had gotten around the American League that his real name was Paveskovich. That was all Al Simmons needed to know. Simmons, who was finishing up a twenty-year career as a premiere home run hitter in the American League that would take him to the Hall of Fame in 1953, had been born Aloysius Szymanski in the Polish section of Milwaukee, Wisconsin.[1] Like so many Polish-Americans with an abundance of consonants, he found a name that fit better into the baseball box scores. Simmons was nearly six feet tall and weighed 190 pounds, comparable in size to another future Hall of Famer, Jimmie Foxx, whom other players called "The Beast." When Simmons took a look at the 5'9", 160 pound Pesky with the shortened name, it did not take long for the time-honored practice of abusive bench jockeying to begin. "You little dumb Polack, what the hell are you doing in that uniform?" Simmons badgered the rookie mercilessly, until he got want he wanted: a reaction. Pesky, enraged and thin-skinned, finally yelled across the diamond, "I'm no dumb Polack! *You're* the dumb Polack! *I'm a smart Croat!*" and challenged Simmons to a fight. Simmons laughed and shouted back, "You little son of a bitch, I'll send the batboy over and he'll beat the shit out of you!" This was the culture of the national pastime. Simmons, after two decades in the dugouts of a half-dozen major league baseball teams, understood the give-and-take of ethnic, even racial abuse and insult. This was the language of the game.

By the 1940s, it had been this way for nearly a century, since baseball ceased to be a game for gentlemen. For the first half of the nineteenth century, what passed for baseball was a game played in country fields and on college campuses, a leisure sport for the well-to-do. Before the Civil War it gradually moved to the cities, particularly of the East and Midwest. At one point, when it was still called "the New York game," baseball remained the activity for the Anglo-American urban leisure class. However, the entrepreneurial spirit got hold of a few wealthy businessmen who believed that people would pay to see someone hit a ball with a bat; by the early 1850s, some ballgames were charging admission, and after the Civil War, hundreds of professional teams began sprouting all over the country, and baseball had become, along with harness racing, the nation's leading spectator sport. It was inevitable that, when baseball moved to the empty lots of the city and the occasional green space parks, the children of immigrants and the urban poor would jump at the opportunity to play and to be paid for it. In overwhelming numbers, this meant first the Irish and the Germans.

The German immigration to America had commenced at the beginning of large-scale European settlement in the seventeenth century. Even by today's measurements, the Germans represent the largest single immigrant population in the United States. They started early as religious dissidents coming first to Philadelphia and then to eastern Pennsylvania. Their influence can still be seen today in names such as Germantown, Rittenhouse Square, Muhlenberg and Moravian College, and Pennsylvania Dutch, a corruption of "Deutsch," which referred to the followers of the Swiss-German Jakob Amman. Benjamin Franklin could not abide them or their language, nor did those earlier English, Dutch and French settlers particularly like them. It was thought that these humorless Germans would never assimilate, never learn English, and remain a people apart culturally and religiously. The first laws passed in the 1790s in Congress to keep out non–Anglo Saxons were directly aimed at the Germans, but the Supreme Court declared such laws unconstitutional.

The Irish, who came with the famine of the 1840s in Ireland, arrived in America as the first large Catholic immigration, and were hated and vilified. They were called vermin, maggots, too ignorant to learn, Papists and pariahs who would never get off the dole. By 1876, when the National League of Professional Baseball Clubs was founded — later and officially to be known as the National League — the rosters were peppered with names such as McGinley, McVey, Concannon, McLean, Cummings and Devlin, along with Gerhardt, Keck, Schaefer, Seibert, Snyder and Zettlein. For Irish and German youth, generally living in poverty at the bottom of the economic food chain in the United States, this new game could give them a living. Sports were a way out and up. It was to remain that way into the first decades of the twentieth century, when the giants of what was by then called the national pastime had names like McGraw, McGinnity, Mathewson, Wagner, Ruth, and a bit later, Gehrig, Heilmann and Duffy. (The pugnacious Irish took particularly to the boxing ring, where John L. Sullivan, Bob Fitzsimmons, Gentleman Jim Corbett, and Paddy Burns were the names on everyone's lips.)

With rare exception, these were not gentlemen at all. No sooner had professionalism entered the gates than gambling, corruption and drinking almost killed the sport. Baseball games were routinely fixed, cheating was rampant, and both players and spectators were more often than not in a state of inebriation. It took a generation of turn-of-the-century businessmen, many of them owners of breweries, to gentrify the game, to make it respectable. They accepted Theodore Roosevelt's optimistic progressivism, built green urban cathedrals for the games, and invited ladies to the ballparks. In 1901 a rival major league was announced and demanded parity with the National League. The newly named American League provided just the kind of competitive framework baseball needed. In 1903, the two leagues entered into a formal agreement that would become the bedrock of Organized Baseball. The owners eliminated the hard liquor and replaced it with their own malt products, and tried mightily — but failed — to isolate baseball from gambling and corruption.

However, the players, for the most part, remained the same. Occasionally, a college-educated baseball player would enter the professional game and make an enormous splash. Christy Mathewson of Bucknell University became an American icon, a model of clean-living American youth. (His addictive gambling was kept from the public.) Not so for the other Irish- and German-Americans who made up a significant percentage of the major league rosters. They took each other's ethnicity out of the neighborhoods and into the dugouts, along with their nicknames. If a player had a German surname, he was called "Heinie," "Fritz" or "Dutch" (the usual misuse of "Deutsch"). He might even be called "Germany." If a player's last name was "Wilhelm," he should be prepared to live with the nickname "Kaiser." The Irish were called "Mick," "Mickey" or just "Irish." The roughest portion was reserved for the exchanges across the diamond in the dugouts, when ethnic blasts were directed routinely at the opposing players; it didn't make any difference if opposing ballplayers were of the same ethnic group. Irish insulted Irish; Germans insulted Germans; everyone gave and took. Insult was part of the game, and a player's capacity to deal with it became part of the routine.[2] Some of the players had "rabbit ears" — they heard every word hurled at them and would react, which usually resulted in a fresh torrent of abuse or a brawl. Diminutive infielders such as John McGraw became accustomed to being described routinely as "you little Irish shit." McGraw, who was called "Mugsy" and did not like it, usually responded with flying spikes. The same could be said for "Wee" Willie Keeler, who took offense when his size or courage were called into question. Of course, overweight players could expect to be called "Tiny," "Hippo" or any variation of "Fatso."[3]

Meanwhile, immigration continued to swell. By the 1880s, there were hundreds of foreign language newspapers published across the East and Midwest, as far south as Texas and up to Milwaukee and Chicago. Germans, Irish, Poles, Scandinavians, people from nations throughout the world poured into this country. Although the newcomers fresh off the boats did not understand the culture of this strange game of baseball, their children readily did. The first generation born in this country took to baseball with an enthusiasm that often stunned and confused their foreign language–speaking parents. When pitcher "Rube" Waddell told his parents that he intended to make a living as a baseball player, his father threw him out of the house and did not speak to him for twenty years. Terrified immigrant parents would lock young daughters in their rooms if they were caught dating baseball players. Yet, these youngsters brought the language of the ghetto neighborhoods to the ballpark and particularly to the dugouts, conveniently out of earshot of grandstands where ladies were now invited to sit.

As Organized Baseball came to dominate interest in sports of the American public, the ethnic and educational mix was enriched. Even as the number of college-educated ballplayers increased in the first two decades of the twentieth century, rosters saw more ethnic diversity, although Irish and German names could still be found in abundance. (Lou Gehrig spoke German to his parents, even while he attended Columbia University.) Slavic names increased gradually. In the name of simplicity or to avoid the kind of abuse that John Pesky took, these names were often shortened and Americanized.[4]

Light-skinned Cubans had access to the game. "Redskins" were acceptable, but barely. John "Chief" Meyers, a Cahuilla Indian from California who attended Dartmouth and played in the majors from 1909 to 1917, said many years later, "I don't like to say this, but in those days I was a foreigner. I didn't belong. I was an Indian." [5] In almost every sense, the American Indians were the ultimate outsiders. Black Americans won at least legal enfranchisement with the Fifteenth Amendment in 1870 and women with the Nineteenth Amendment in 1920. For the American Indian, there was no defining moment when the vote was guaranteed until the Voting Rights Act of 1965. Individual states imposed different restrictions. In Oklahoma the legal language stated that the vote was extended only to "civilized persons of Indian descent." But, in an act of reluctant racial equality, members of all tribes were at least allowed to play in Organized Baseball. Other than that, almost from the moment men began to play for pay, baseball was a white man's game. Blacks were systemically excluded, although there was never a formal written declaration. Until the arrival of Jackie Robinson in 1946, Organized Baseball lived by an unwritten rule of racial discrimination that barred blacks. They were relegated to the Negro baseball leagues, which provided at least some opportunity for the many talented Afro-American baseball players, who were also able to create a dugout language no less abusive than the nearly all-white major leagues. During his time with the Kansas City Monarchs in 1945, Jackie Robinson was a "celebrity" bench jockey whose high-pitched voice carried across the diamond. The banter, insult and highly flavored racial and ethnic language of the Negro leagues rivaled anything that major leaguers could offer. The practice was expected, with players riding the back of the other team, hoping to find a "rabbit ear." Would this country have been able to deal with racial epithets in the American culture of the first decades of the twentieth century — with lynchings and Jim Crow laws— if baseball alone had integrated?[6] We will never know the answer; after *Plessy v. Ferguson* had been decided by the Supreme Court in favor of the "separate but equal" doctrine in 1896, the nation had to wait for Branch Rickey and Jackie Robinson fifty years later.[7] Even then, Rickey completely muzzled Robinson for two years; Robinson had to take the racial abuse, but he could not give it back. Those two years almost killed Robinson. His instincts were so competitive, his linguistic imagination so colorful, that Rickey's instructions to keep silent, while he took a stream of abuse, nearly undid him. Finally, in 1949, Robinson was unchained, and he became one of the most creative dugout orators in either league.

American Indians had to take their own particular kind of racial and ethnic abuse. "Blanket-Ass" was a regular descriptor; "Chief" was usually attached to a surname.[8] Like the Irish, it was assumed that American Indians could not hold their liquor, and that stereotype worked its way through the first half-dozen prominent American Indian baseball players of the new century. The first prominent baseball player of Indian heritage was Lou Sockalexis, who played for the major league Cleveland Spiders from 1897–1899. Everyone knew he was struggling with a drinking problem, and one of the local newspapers shared his troubles with its readers: "Sock swears by the feathers of his ancestors that he hasn't removed the scalp from even one glass of foamy beer since early last spring, when he whooped up a dance on Superior Street ... but the wiles and temptations of the big cities stimulated poor Lou's thirst and set him forth in search of the red paint."[9]

The new owners and their adherence to the principles of a progressive and idealized America loudly advocated the idea that baseball was America's game, and all Americans (except people with dark skin) would be given equal opportunity. In the December 6, 1923, issue of *The Sporting News*, the St. Louis–based newspaper generally accepted as the official voice of Organized Baseball, the editors ironically revealed more than they intended, when they aggressively responded to a charge circulating in newspapers that some baseball players were members of the resurgent Ku Klux Klan: "In a democratic, real American game like baseball, there has been no distinction raised except tacit understanding that a player of Ethiopian descent is ineligible. No player of any other 'race' has been barred. The Mick, the Sheeny, the Wop, the Dutch and the Chink, the Cuban, the Indian, the Jap or the so-called Anglo-Saxon — his 'nationality' is never a matter of moment if he can pitch, hit or field."[10] It was an act of deep faith that immigrants could become Americans by playing baseball. On the field, all one needed to have was talent, as well as the ability to accept and to give back the ethnic insults.

These took on a new dimension and challenge with the massive immigration of Italians and Jews—the editorial's Sheenies and Wops—that came to America starting in the 1880s. It was only a matter of time and one generation before the children of this last enormous European immigration—one Christian and scorned, one non–Christian and hated—made their way to the city playgrounds, empty lots and college campuses. When the Chicago White Sox brought up Francesco Pezzolo in 1911, he preferred to play under the name of Frank Bodie, taking his name from a town in California where he once lived. Bodie, who had the nickname "Ping," was one of the first Italian-Americans to make it to the major leagues, but a steady stream of players with names like Tony Lazzeri, Frankie Crosetti, and Joe DiMaggio in the 1920s and 1930s, playing under their own names, soon followed. Joe's brothers Vince and Dominic eventually joined him.

The earliest Jewish ballplayers in the major leagues also found it convenient to play under a name that would not attract ethnic attention. Sammy Cohen played as Sammy Bohne when he joined the St. Louis Cardinals in 1916. James Solomon became Jimmie Reese when he finally made it as a twenty-nine-year-old infielder with the New York Yankees in 1930, the same year that Hank Greenberg made his first appearance for the 1930 Detroit Tigers. Greenberg and DiMaggio became heroes to the Jewish-American and Italian-American communities in the 1930s and 1940s at the same time they routinely heard calls of "Jewboy" and "Dago" coming out of opposing dugouts. For DiMaggio, the term "Dago" didn't present any problems; his teammates called him "The Big Dago" to distinguish him from Frank Crosetti and later Yogi Berra, whom they called "The Little Dago." Greenberg, on the other hand, had a short fuse and heard every insult from the opposing dugout. "Not only were you a bum, you were a *Jewish* bum." When the Chicago White Sox one afternoon crossed a line in Greenberg's mind, he stormed into the visiting clubhouse after a game and challenged whoever was throwing around the insults to stand up and fight. Greenberg, who was 6'4" and 220 pounds of muscle, found no takers.[11]

This was a culture that remained constant into the second half of the twentieth century, by which time blacks were reluctantly admitted to the baseball fraternity. It was an American experience forged in the centuries before the Depression and World War II; it remained unchanged when the boys came back from the war. Ethnicity and race were as much a part of the American landscape as baseball, which preferred its anachronistic past. There was little political correctness in the attitudes that reflected this world, and baseball players, just like the rest of America, accepted this culture as part of the routine. When Rodgers and Hammerstein wrote their path-breaking musical drama *Oklahoma!*

in 1944, it was an Oklahoma without Native Americans, not even Indians just sitting on blankets. By 1949, with *South Pacific*, they could take a chance on the controversial song "You Have to Be Taught," which represents Broadway's first direct attack on bigotry. Of course, the producers wanted it removed, but the songwriters held their ground.

A more accurate reflection of American attitudes could be found in the motion picture industry. If baseball was the national pastime, then movies were the national obsession. From the moment the nickelodeons appeared in cities and towns, at about the same time that the two professional leagues formed their agreement in 1903, Americans by the millions flocked to this new entertainment. The moviemakers were not interested in creating public opinion; reflecting it was good enough and a guarantee that the audience would keep coming back. From D. W. Griffith's *Birth of a Nation* (1915) to Margaret Mitchell's novel *Gone with the Wind* and its Academy Award–winning 1939 film adaptation, the black American image was firmly fixed in the minds of the white audience. As for the Native Americans, John Ford's western trilogy *Fort Apache* (1948), *She Wore a Yellow Ribbon* (1949), and *Rio Grande* (1950) represented the culmination of fifty years of filmmaking that depicted drunken Indians murdering innocent women and children.[12]

If young Allie Reynolds was knocked out of a minor league game early, he could expect to be criticized in terms of race and hit with the stereotype that Indians could not stand the pressure.[13] Pitchers were expected to go nine innings, and if Reynolds could not, it was blamed on an implied lack of courage. It was a reputation he had to carry when he joined the Cleveland Indians in 1943, and it followed him to the Yankees. When he could not complete a game and needed relief help, reporters called him "the Vanishing American." Ed Lopat, who dominated the Cleveland Indians for his entire career in the major leagues, drove their manager Al Lopez to such fury after a Yankee victory that he called the laughing Lopat, "you Polack sonofabitch."[14] Here was Lopez, Cleveland manager and one of the few Latinos at the time in major league baseball, known to his players and rivals as "Señor," using language that players were accustomed to.[15] When Vic Raschi came to the Yankees in 1947, he was one of several Italian-Americans on the roster. "Dago" was used interchangeably to address Crosetti, DiMaggio, Yogi Berra, and Raschi. By 1950, three years after Jackie Robinson's breakthrough, there was an ethnic and racial census taken of the 382 major league ballplayers. Those who were prepared to say anything revealed there were nine blacks, four Jews (there were more, but they chose not to admit it), two American Indians, 69 Germans, 56 Irish, 47 English, 36 Scotch-Irish, 28 Polish, and 27 Italian. Higher education was not yet a high priority; only 28 had college degrees.[16] Some refused to give their ethnic background. There was no check-off apparently for Latino. There was also a preponderance of war veterans.

Reynolds, Raschi and Lopat were in many ways typical Americans and typical baseball players of their generation. They were born within a few years of each other toward the end of the second decade of the twentieth century. They spoke a second language other than English while growing up and experienced the full force of the American economic Depression before enjoying a professional career in the post–World War II prosperity. Yet, they grew up in hard times and were molded by the experience; they loved baseball, were raised in different parts of this country, and were destined to come together to share in a special moment of baseball history.

2

Getting There

When Lou Fette walked into the Boston Bees' dingy clubhouse at Braves Field in 1937, he thought, "I'm thirty years old, a rookie pitcher, and I finally made it." He looked around, wondering who the other rookies were. Baseball veterans were notoriously inhospitable to newly arrived first-year players. The Depression was still ravaging the country, but the minor leagues had not shut down completely. Rosters had been cut to the bone, sometimes containing just fourteen players, and there were still ten candidates at every position, waiting to take the job of any veteran player in the major leagues. Fette was a country boy from Missouri, a quiet, hard-working mature pitcher who had paid his dues in coming up through the low minors year after year, and he was ready. It was not unusual for players to labor for years in the minors, waiting for an opportunity, living on a pittance, separated from their families, working all winter at whatever job they could get. For most, that chance never came. Those with grit, luck, and talent stuck with it, and when a break came their way, they were ready. Lou Fette was going to make the best of it, as he looked around for any sign of a sympathetic face among the hardened veterans.

He found one. As he was putting on his spikes he looked up into a face that had seen as many or more seasons on the ball field. At first, he was pleased that one of the older Boston Bees had come over to welcome him. "I'm Jim Turner," said the voice with a southern accent. "I'm from Tennessee, I'm thirty-three, and I'm a rookie, too." They were about to make a little history for a perennial second-division team with little talent and few prospects.

In 1937, 33-year-old rookie Jim Turner, who had started in the minor leagues at the age of nineteen in 1922, and 30-year-old rookie Lou Fette each won 20 games, astonished the baseball world, and elevated the National League Boston team to a fifth-place finish. Turner had twenty-four complete games and a league-leading 2.38 ERA. Fette and Turner had five shutouts each in an age of dominant hitting, when only a few years earlier the last-place Philadelphia Phillies had a team batting average of .315 and a team ERA of 6.71.

Their rookie year of 1937 was destined to be the pinnacle of their playing careers. Fette won a total of 41 games in a five-year stint in the National League. Turner won 69 games, but got into two World Series with the Cincinnati Reds in 1940 and the New York Yankees in 1942. He finished up with the Yankees as a relief pitcher at the age of 42.

Fette returned to the minor leagues and then home to Missouri. Turner, who worked in the family dairy business in the off-season and was called "Milkman," had learned his craft well enough to make baseball his life for the next fifty years. He had been given some good advice by the new Boston manager in 1938, a crooked-legged former outfielder who had sat at the feet of manager John McGraw twenty years earlier and had learned the manager's craft. His name was Casey Stengel, and he saw in Jim Turner the patient maturity, intelligence, and internal fire that would make a great pitching mentor. He advised Turner to think about managing or coaching when his pitching days were over. Turner took the advice.

The pitching coach, Jim Turner: The first of the breed (photograph not dated) (National Baseball Hall of Fame Library, Cooperstown, N.Y.).

He coached and managed in the minors, reunited with Stengel when they both managed in the Pacific Coast League in 1948, and eventually came to the New York Yankees as pitching coach in 1949. General manager George Weiss had fired manager Bucky Harris as well as all three of Harris' coaches. Weiss knew that the future of the Yankees would to a significant degree depend on whether he could make the hard-hitting but defensively inept Yogi Berra into a reasonable facsimile of a catcher, so he brought back the great Yankee Bill Dickey to coach and to teach. There had to be someone to handle the infielders, and Yankee veteran Frank Crosetti was a popular choice. For the pitchers, Weiss had been watching Jim Turner's progress as a Pacific Coast League manager and wanted him. When new manager Stengel heard of Weiss' choice, he could not have been happier. No decision that Weiss and Stengel made together in their years with the New York Yankees was more important. While managing in Oakland Stengel had renewed his friendship with his former Boston hurler and then rival manager at Portland. When he joined the Yankees, Turner became the godfather for three veteran pitchers, who saw in this gentle but hard-nosed mentor someone who had experienced much of what they had lived through, respected their age, their work ethic and grim determination to win. Jim Turner proved to be another of Casey Stengel's legacies for baseball. Turner was the first of the authentic pitching coaches, the model for those who began to arrive in the 1960s with Johnny Sain and are epitomized by Mel Stottlemyre in this generation. Here was demonstrated for the first time the special chemistry between pitchers and coach, between three men who placed their confidence completely in Jim Turner, who in turn provided wisdom and support of a very special kind. When Turner met his three pitchers, he decided that they would be a team apart, even though he saw a dedication to winning and sacrifice that would always put the *team* first. Above all, he recognized the same individual ferocity of competitiveness that raged inside all four men. When he was with the Yankees as their pitching coach in 1952, Turner was speaking to a twenty-four-year-old reporter for *The Herald Tribune* named Roger Kahn, whom Raschi and Reynolds had intimidated during an interview with manager Casey Stengel. Kahn wanted to know why these two grim men were so hostile and uncommunicative with the members of the press before a game, and the soft-spoken and gentlemanly Turner told him "You have to keep this in mind, kid. Big-league baseball is not a fucking tea-party."[1] Jim Turner's experience in baseball — first the years of toil in the minor leagues, then as a thirty-three-year-old rookie, the need for off-season work and income, separation from family, pitching in pain while ignoring injuries — all of this was shared with his three veterans when they came together in 1949. Natural talent alone was not enough. There had to be an intangible quality, something that burned inside. Turner realized that he had a unique combination of personalities and temperaments that could lead to truly remarkable results; and he proved to be eternally grateful. Well into his nineties, Turner told a reporter, "Reynolds, Vic Raschi and Ed Lopat put me on the map. If I live to be a hundred years old, I'll never be able to repay these three guys."[2]

In the spring of 1937, when Fette and Turner were startling the National League, Allie Reynolds, a junior track and football star at Oklahoma A&M in Stillwater, was throwing a javelin on a practice field. He paid no attention to the man standing a few feet away, as Reynolds picked up the javelin, balanced himself, and sent off a 190-foot toss. The observer was Henry P. (Hank) Iba, the A&M athletic director, a near-mythic basketball and baseball coach in the annals of Oklahoma collegiate sports. The baseball team was practicing on an adjacent field, and Iba asked the javelin thrower if he would mind throwing some batting practice since all of his available pitchers had sore arms. "Warm up a little," Iba suggested. "I don't need any warmup," Reynolds replied. After striking out half the lineup, Iba told the fraternity baseball player that he was now a three-sport athlete at Oklahoma A&M. "Go get a baseball uniform." Allie Pierce Reynolds' baseball journey had begun.

His extraordinary athleticism had placed him on a path that could not have been foreseen and was not intended for the son of a Bethany, Oklahoma, Nazarene preacher. Allie, whose grandmother Eliza was a descendant of Creek Indians who lived in Alabama and Georgia until they were forced west into Indian Territory, was born on a reservation in what later was known as Oklahoma. She married a Scots Irishman from Tennessee who had moved to the Indian territory. They settled on Creek land, living among her people. Allie's father David was born in the Creek Nation and attended an Indian school before dropping out. He started third grade again in Bethany at the age of twenty-two, eventually graduated high school and was ordained a preacher in the Church of the Nazarene, one of the denominations that emerged out of the 19th century second Great Awakening in the Midwest.

This was a strict, God-fearing family into which Allie Pierce Reynolds was born on February 10, 1915.[3] There were neither movies nor dances at any time and definitely no activities on Sunday other than prayer and meditation.

From his earliest years it was clear that Allie was a gifted athlete. By the time he reached high school age coaches were already recruiting him. He kept the strict admonition against play on Sundays, but play he would during the rest of the week. He stood up to his father, told him he would run away if he couldn't play football, and the minister relented. Allie commuted to Capitol Hill High School in Oklahoma City and excelled at both football — quarterback as well as running back — and track, where he ran dash and threw the javelin. Allie's high school football team never lost a game in his final two years. At home in Bethany he played on the fast-pitch softball church team of his father's congregation, which still could not play on Sunday.

Allie and his parents expected a college education, but he needed scholarship help. At 145 pounds he was too light for the University of Oklahoma football program, but he was given a $20 per month stipend from Oklahoma A&M (now Oklahoma State) to run track, and in January of 1935 Reynolds became an Oklahoma Aggie on the campus of Stillwater. He started out as an education major and eventually graduated four years later, a dean's list student with a lifetime certification to teach in the Oklahoma public school system.

But, athletics came first. By May 1935, he had set three conference records

The "Superchief," Allie Reynolds, at his peak as a Yankee in 1952 (National Baseball Hall of Fame Library, Cooperstown, N.Y.).

with times of 9.8 seconds in the 100-yard dash, 21.3 seconds in the 220-yard dash, and a javelin toss of 197 feet. Here was a one-man team.

The same kind of resolute determination that Reynolds demonstrated in facing down his father brought him to a decision in the summer of 1935. During his Capitol Hill High School senior year, his younger brother, Denton, had been dating one of his classmates, Dale Earlene Jones, who had already won an award as the school's outstanding all-around female athlete. Older brother Allie exercised his prerogative and started seeing Earlene after she accidentally hit him in the head during a girls' field hockey game. It did not take him long to make up his mind, and apparently the sixteen-year-old coed had enough gumption to make it happen. That summer they became engaged and were married on July 7, 1935. For the next forty-nine years they spent as little time as possible apart from each other.

After summer work wielding a sledgehammer, Allie returned to Oklahoma A&M at Stillwater with his new bride. Athletics dominated his college career after Hank Iba got him committed to baseball as well as track and football. Reynolds excelled at all three while expanding his family. Their first child, Allie

Dale Reynolds, was born on June 8, 1936. They would have one more before he graduated, and a third soon after.

When Hank Iba took the javelin thrower under his wing, he was determined to make a pitcher-outfielder out of Reynolds. Of the three varsity sports that the collegian Allie Reynolds participated in, he was least schooled in baseball. Iba, who enjoyed a Hall of Fame career as one of the great college basketball coaches in the United States, saw in him a talent that could help the sorely depleted ranks of the Oklahoma A&M baseball team. There were just not enough players. Oklahoma was still staggering from the Dust Bowl and Depression. The state had lost more than 20 percent of its population. Iba needed the reincarnation of Jim Thorpe, an individual who could carry a school's entire athletic program. He saw in Allie Reynolds the kind of impact athlete — and indeed another Native American — who could take a second-tier Oklahoma college, living in the shadow of big-time University of Oklahoma athletics, and make a profound difference. What Thorpe did for the Carlisle Indians, Reynolds could do for Oklahoma A&M, thought Iba.

His protégé was thinking as well. He had seen a picture in the college newspaper of an eighteen-year-old Iowa farm boy who had just signed a contract with the Cleveland Indians for $10,000, an extraordinary amount of money in Depression-wracked Midwest America. The farm boy's name was Bob Feller. Baseball became even more interesting for Reynolds. No other sport could provide such money, and early in his collegiate career he saw clearly the need to support a growing family. When the college season was over, Allie signed on with the Stillwater Boomers town team, one of the hundreds of baseball clubs dotting the Oklahoma landscape. As popular as football was in the 1930s, it was the St. Louis Cardinals' "Pepper" Martin and ace New York Giants left-hander Carl Hubbell that were the icons for the young athletes. Martin was a native Oklahoman and part Osage Indian, and Missouri-born Hubbell was adopted by the neighboring state. When Reynolds was offered a chance to play summer ball for a Colorado coal company and get paid for it, two problems were solved: he could play baseball after the school year was over, and he had a summer job. Earlene and the baby stayed behind in Oklahoma while Reynolds barnstormed with the Colorado coal company semi-pro team in the rough and tumble world of company teams and make-shift professionals, some of whom provided his earliest racial education. Reynolds played against black barnstormers led by Satchel Paige and James "Cool Papa" Bell and became aware of the enormous talent pool that was not getting tapped. But, he had his own troubles to worry about. The first time the young ballplayer had been called "a gutless Indian," he was ready to punch out the lights of the offender. Like Thorpe, to whom he was inevitably compared, Allie Reynolds was growing into a physically formidable and intimidating athlete. The six-footer played football at 210 pounds in his senior year and found few opponents willing to take him on.

The second child arrived in May of 1938. By now Allie was earning $150 a month in the summer playing for the Stillwater town team; the salary plus his athletic scholarship kept the family going. Oklahoma A&M won the state conference baseball title with Reynolds' fastball and bat in 1938 and was ready to defend the next year, Allie's senior year. He was elected team captain. The football team during his years as a star running back could not get on track and never had a winning season. But, the young halfback attracted enough attention in 1938 to get drafted in the third round by the National Football League's New York Giants. Professional football was still in its infancy as a spectator game. All the Giants could offer this big and speedy halfback was $100 per game. That was still a great deal of money, if he could earn it every week of the football season. But, the young athlete had discovered his passion: he loved baseball more than any other sport. He asked Coach Iba for his advice and was told to wait for baseball.

Iba knew a Cleveland Indians scout, and Allie Reynolds signed his first professional baseball contract with a signing bonus of $1,000, more than the collective savings of several generations of the Reynolds family and as much as Reynolds would have earned teaching for the entire year in the public school system. By the standards of Oklahoma in the late 1930s, this was a great deal of money. Some of Allie's friends were working for a dollar a day.

Hot Plates and Campbell's Soup

Reynolds had a four-year minor league career, from 1939 to 1942. His family status kept him out of the draft, and all it would take would be one spectacular year to elevate him to the Cleveland Indians, who in 1942 were desperately looking for a replacement for their Navy-bound strikeout ace, Bob Feller. In June 1939, Reynolds arrived at Springfield, Ohio, the Indians' Class C farm team. Here he found some of the people who would become lifetime friends: a young Jim Hegan, later a great defensive catcher with Cleveland; Red Embree, who never fulfilled his promise as a pitcher with the Indians; and a strong-armed third baseman named Bob Lemon. Reynolds stayed with Springfield; he was wild and fast with an 11–8 record, 140 strikeouts and 107 walks in 155 innings. Local newspapers already referred to him as "Chief."[4]

In 1940 he was promoted to the Class B Cedar Rapids, Iowa team in the Three-I League, where he was 12–7, pitched 178 innings with 140 strikeouts and somewhat better control, walking 88, still enough to put him close to the top of the league in bases on balls. With the Depression-bruised roster reduced to seventeen players per team, when he wasn't pitching he played right field.

His athleticism could not keep him out of the lineup. In fact, the Cleveland brass suggested that Reynolds be shifted to catcher and made into an everyday player, but he had the determination to say no.

When he left in 1941 for his third year of minor league baseball at Wilkes-Barre of the Class A Eastern League, he was twenty-six years old, the father of three children, and needed to make progress. After only three appearances at Wilkes-Barre, he was shipped back to Class B Cedar Rapids; Reynolds was disappointed. Earlene and the children remained in Oklahoma, and Allie missed them terribly. He was a family man who hated to be away. He seemed to be going nowhere in his quest for the big leagues, and his pitching reflected his unhappiness. The newspapers complained that "the Chief" could not complete games.

The star of the Three-I League was a tall, skinny lefthander who threw four consecutive shutouts for Evansville: his name was Warren Spahn, and a friendship was forged in the low minors that would last a lifetime. But Spahn was glorified; Reynolds vilified. Spahn completed his games; Reynolds ran out of gas and seemed to lose interest. Spahn finished the season at 19–6 with an eye-popping ERA of 1.83. Reynolds finished the season with a 10–10 record and an ERA that ballooned to 4.63. Still, there were Reynolds' 153 strikeouts in 167 innings, albeit with 97 bases on balls.

Other events were now intruding into Reynolds' life. The Japanese attack on Pearl Harbor on December 7, 1941, was destined to have a profound impact on major league baseball. Detroit Tiger star Hank Greenberg had already gone into the service before hostilities had broken out. Reynolds, married with three children and an assortment of injuries from his football days, was not a prospect for either enlistment or the draft. Bob Feller enlisted almost immediately in the navy and spent four years as an anti-aircraft gunner on the USS *Alabama.* The major league rosters were going to be depleted, not because of the Depression — which World War II would end — but through the loss of a few hundred players to the armed forces.

When the 1942 season began, Reynolds promised himself that this was it: make it, or quit. At twenty-seven, he did not look forward to a lifetime career in minor league baseball. He had options, including teaching and entering the oil business back home. Allie had already made some connections with people who might help him start a new career. He yearned for his family. Earlene and the children did not like being away from home and preferred to wait for Allie in Oklahoma. He was confident in his ability and his education. But, he would give baseball one more try.

It paid off. In 1942 Reynolds was back at Wilkes-Barre in the Class A Eastern League for his final shot. Spahn was with Hartford. The Eastern League, although only Class A, was a stepping stone directly to the majors. With the minor leagues cut to the bone and rosters curtailed, players could move up faster than they had during the previous decade. The word around the league was that a 19-year-old prospect with Albany, Ralph Kiner, could make the jump because of his bat. He looked like a potential big-time home run threat. But Kiner, who led the league with fourteen home runs, was not the talk of the season. That role was left for the Indian who pitched for Wilkes-Barre, Allie Reynolds, who put together an 18–7 season, with eleven shutouts, an unexpected twenty-one complete games, a record-breaking 193 strikeouts in 231 innings, and an ERA of 1.56. Reynolds eclipsed everyone in the league, including his new buddy Warren Spahn, who finished at 17–12 with an ERA of 1.96.

They both got the word: Spahn was to report to the Boston Braves to finish the 1942 season, and Reynolds was called up to Cleveland. The first person he called with the news was Earlene. He was a big league pitcher, a twenty-seven-year-old rookie. Reynolds made two relief appearances for Cleveland in the last two weeks of the season, pitched five innings and did not give up an earned run, although he walked four. Reynolds, the big, strong fireballer from Oklahoma, became a top Cleveland prospect and a possible replacement for their star Bob Feller, who was in the Navy. At age twenty-three, Feller had already won 107 games and led the league in wins, innings pitched and strikeouts. Like Feller, Reynolds could be just wild enough to terrify hitters.

But in four major league seasons with the Cleveland Indians, Reynolds never fulfilled the promise that management hoped for. Even when the Cleveland teams were mediocre, Feller had performed miracles. Reynolds did not. His first full year in the majors was 1943. With Earlene and the children back in Oklahoma, the twenty-eight-year-old right-hander was still considered a rookie and stayed in the bullpen for the first half of the season. He did not start a game until June 20 and was knocked out in the third inning. He wound up with twenty-one starts and eleven complete games, threw 198 innings and had an 11–12 record. Cleveland manager Lou Boudreau thought he saw a unique ability in Reynolds to relieve between starts, a kind of resiliency that could be useful to the team. Six of Reynolds' losses came in relief. He may have been resilient, but it did not produce wins. The high points were a 2.99 ERA and a league-leading 151 strikeouts, the first time a rookie led the league. Not a bad first year; but not a Bob Feller year.

There were sensational moments. On July 2, he shut out the eventual World Series champion New York Yankees on three hits, beating them 12–0 in tiny League Park, Cleveland's home field when they did not play in cavernous Municipal Stadium, which held 80,000 spectators. Reynolds was overpowering. One Yankee reached second base. New York rolled out a series of relievers, and the final four innings were pitched by a forty-year-old journeyman whom the Yankees had picked up to bolster their depleted pitching staff. He saw something in this physically intense rookie, an attitude that was as overpowering as his fastball on this day. The Yankee pitcher's name was Jim Turner.

Allie started the 1944 season with high hopes. He was the opening day pitcher against Detroit and their ace, Hal Newhouser, who would win 29 games that year. Reynolds bested Newhouser in the opener, but little else went well for him during his sophomore year in the majors. He threw only 158 innings, although at 11–8 had the best won-lost record among the Cleveland staff. He completed only 5 of 21 starts, and complained of arm miseries.[5] His strikeout total plummeted to 84. He lost three more games in relief.

The 1945 season was Reynolds' best with Cleveland, even though he led the league with 130 walks. His record rebounded to 18–12 and his arm strength returned. He pitched in 44 games, threw 247 innings, continued to be used in relief between starts, got four saves, and won two games that he did not start, losing one.

When the war was over, everyone looked forward to the 1946 season at Cleveland. Feller was back, and the two aces of the staff took an immediate liking to one another. They became traveling roommates, shared baseball wisdom and values. Iowa and Oklahoma were not that far apart. This was another baseball friendship that would endure.

The 1946 season was yet another disappointment for Cleveland management and fans. Feller rose to the occasion in his first post-war season, going 26–15 with 348 strikeouts, an all-time record. Reynolds, who was 2–10 by the All-Star Game, started 28 games, only completed 9 of them, had as many walks as strikeouts, and ended the season with an 11–15 record, his worst with Cleveland. It didn't help any Indian pitcher that Cleveland's team batting average of .245 was the lowest in the league that year. Boudreau desperately needed a hard-hitting second baseman to put some punch in his batting order.

The New York Yankees had a dismal year as well, a third consecutive year without a pennant; they needed pitching. Their all-star second baseman, Joe Gordon, had returned from the war and produced a horrendous .210 batting average in just 112 games. He was expendable. Yankee general manager Larry MacPhail spoke to his team leaders Joe DiMaggio and Tommy Henrich. In off-season trade talks, Cleveland offered anyone on the pitching staff except Feller. They had given up on Reynolds. His 51–47 lifetime record was not what the Indians' management had expected. They were convinced that he was never going to be anything but an expensive .500 pitcher who would tire and lose games in the last few innings of a close contest. He even voluntarily fit the stereotype in what Roger Kahn called "baseball's chronic obsession with race," which suggested that Native American baseball players could not handle major league pressure.[6] Reynolds referred to himself as "one more scared Indian kid." The Yankees could have their choice. MacPhail wanted Red Embree. "Take Reynolds," DiMaggio said. Henrich concurred. Manager Bucky Harris put his blessing to the deal. On October 11, 1946, Joe Gordon was traded to the Cleveland Indians for right-handed pitcher Allie Reynolds, who was now a New York Yankee, with a reputation, in Roger Kahn's words, as "a thirty-one-year-old underachiever."

* * *

Everything in eighteen-year-old Vic Raschi's life was serious. He wore responsibility like an overcoat. Now that he was about to become the first member of his Italian-American immigrant family to go to college, he knew that he had to succeed for his parents, for his two sisters, and above all, for his brother, Gene, eleven years his junior. He remembered when his brother was born in 1930. No one expected a fourth Raschi child. The two girls, Celestina and Santina, were teenagers and Victor John Angelo, born in 1919, was mature beyond his years, a well-coordinated, strapping youngster who had brought fame to the Springfield, Massachusetts, Italian neighborhood by winning at the age of ten the state-wide marbles tournament. When Egyzia Raschi gave birth to a premature baby boy, no one thought he would live. Baptized Eugene, the baby survived but was stricken at three-and-a-half months with spinal meningitis; the doctors again gave him up for dead. There were no known drugs, no penicillin, so the mother did the only thing she had left. She prayed. "When the doctor go away I pick up my baby in my arms and I offer him to the Lord. I say, 'Take him if you want him.' And right after I pray, the baby, he start kicking."[7] A doctor declared the recovery a miracle, and the baby grew into boyhood with eyes weakened by the meningitis. Now, as Vic prepared to leave for college, his seven-year-old brother, already wearing heavy lenses in his glasses, was smashed in the eye by a batted baseball and suffered a detached retina.[8] Eugene was nearly blind. His younger brother's hardship only helped to knit a close family even closer together.

The five brothers of Massimino Raschi were with him when they left a farm village between Milan and Parma in Northern Italy to come to the United States. All six brothers settled around Springfield. Massimino—who called himself Simon—first settled in West Springfield, then after the birth of his third child and first son, Victor, moved to an old house in the Mt. Carmel parish of Springfield, with enough space so his wife could raise rabbits and chickens and grow vegetables. The senior Raschi worked as a carpenter for the New York–New Haven & Hartford railroad, but his health was never robust. The Depression, the stress of the premature birth of the unexpected baby, the near-fatal illness and blindness tightened the family bonds. As the ailing father grew less able to work, Victor assumed the responsibility of caring for his brother and providing for the family. College was the first step. As he set his sights on an education, he had been prepared to view life as a serious, no-nonsense business.

The temperament and personality that was to mark his professional baseball career were already in place.

It was Vic's extraordinary athletic ability that had gotten him this far. Even in elementary school he played everything well. He loved basketball most of all, but New York Yankee scout Gene McCann spotted a rawboned high school freshman throwing bullets in a scholastic tournament in Springfield. He saw a fluid motion, without stress, and with exceptional velocity. But, what could one do with a sixteen-year-old prospect just starting school? McCann knew his way around immigrant families, knew what mattered most. He spoke to Vic after a tournament game and asked to meet his parents. One evening he came around to the Raschi home at 35 Hickory Street and laid out a long-range plan. Vic would graduate from high school, he told the Raschis, and the New York Yankees would send him to college. There were two or three places where the team tried to locate their players, not too far away from Springfield. The Yankee organization would pay for tuition and even give some spending money, no matter how long it took Vic to get his degree.[9] After that, the Yankees had the first shot at him for a professional career, if they still were interested.

Other teams were interested, as well. The St. Louis Cardinals and the Cleveland Indians had approached Vic, and the Cleveland organization paid for a trip to Fenway when the Indians were in town. In a Cleveland uniform, the high school freshman threw fastballs that had the coaching staff looking until another teenager walked out onto the field and started throwing balls that exploded into the catcher's mitt. This young man, Bob Feller, was just seventeen years old. Vic Raschi decided that he wasn't interested in Cleveland.

The Cardinals wanted him immediately in their minor league farm system, but the Yankees had mentioned the magic word: college. This was a strategy that the Yankee organization would employ from time to time through the years. It offered an opportunity that the family could not refuse. At age sixteen, Simon Raschi, signing for his son, agreed to an arrangement with the New York Yankee baseball club. For the next twenty years, Vic's career would be tied to the Yankee organization.

There would be other opportunities. In his extraordinary athletic high school career at Springfield Technical, Vic excelled at football, basketball and baseball. Ohio State University was interested in him as a potential tight end. He was a high scoring, 6'1" center on the basketball team and was considered college material. But, once he signed with the Yankee organization, they would make the decisions for him and for the family. He was told that he could attend Manhattan College in New York City at the conclusion of his high school years. Everyone was delighted. It was a Catholic school and a basketball powerhouse. The Yankees had already told him, once his father signed the agreement, that his football days were over, so it made no difference that Manhattan did not field a football team. Basketball and baseball would be enough.

When young Vic went down to New York City to register, he was told that the class was filled. Raschi called McCann immediately. McCann said, "Don't worry, we've arranged for you to attend William & Mary College in Virginia. You're all set." In the fall of 1938, Vic Raschi arrived in Williamsburg, Virginia, on the campus of the College of William & Mary, compliments of the New York Yankees, who also provided him with $150 of spending money.

Vic threw himself into college life. He joined a fraternity, the Catholic society called the Gibbons Club, and went out for freshman basketball and baseball. He also got a part-time job waiting on tables in the dining halls. His basketball prowess got him selected to the an all-state team, and as soon as the Yankee organization heard about it, they informed Vic that his collegiate basketball career was over, and that he should concentrate on baseball. He started slowly on the baseball squad, but by his sophomore year Vic had turned around a mediocre program and led William & Mary to the conference championship. He had grown to 6'1", weighed in at 215 pounds, and was generally recognized by the press as the outstanding collegiate pitcher in the state.

He had also fallen in love. While waiting on tables in the freshmen dining room, he met a beautiful undergraduate named Sally Glenn. They waited until the war was over before marrying. Their union lasted until his death in 1988. Among the remarkable characteristics that bonded together the individuals in this book, a notable one was a sense of fidelity. Every marriage was for life. Not one of the twelve baseball players who were on all five of the 1949–1953 New York Yankee rosters ever divorced. The same could be said for the coaches, the manager and the general manager: Casey had his Edna and Weiss, his Hazel, both for life.

After the collegiate baseball season of 1941, the Yankees had seen enough. The twenty-two-year-old was overpowering against these amateurs, and they wanted to test his fastball against the pros. Now he realized what McCann had meant when the scout told the family that the Yankees would pay for Vic's education "for as long as it would take." Starting in 1941, Vic would be a part-time student, staying out of school during the professional baseball season and going back at season's end. After Raschi's enormously successful collegiate season in the spring of 1941, he was told to report to the Amsterdam (NY) Rugmakers of the Class C Canadian-American League. This was to be the end of his college eligibility. His professional career was underway. Raschi went 10–6 for Amsterdam, a good start.[10] He went back to William & Mary for the fall and winter term, then reported to the Norfolk Tars in the Class B Piedmont League. Pitching for a 57–79 team, his record plummeted to 4–10.

The war had broken out, and Vic knew that his draft number would soon

Vic, his wife Sally, and daughter Victoria, at his William & Mary commencement in 1949 (Raschi Family).

be called. The Yankee organization told him to get his military service over with. At William & Mary he had been studying for a degree in physical training, and when he enlisted in the army air force in 1942 at the end of the season, he was immediately selected as a physical fitness trainer for the cadets. He spent the next three years moving around the country from one air force base to another, rarely returning home or to Williamsburg, where he had left his heart. Sally Glenn was waiting also, and when Vic called her from Lowry Air Force Base in Denver, Colorado, it did not take her a minute to make up her mind. They were married in January 1945. Their first child, Victoria, was born later that year.

The war was over, and it was time to get back to the business of baseball. He was now a husband and father; he was also twenty-seven years old and had pitched only professionally as high as a Class B league. Vic needed to move up, and move up fast. The Yankees sent him in 1946 to Binghamton of the Class A Eastern League. He was wild, but struck out as many as he walked, and with two months of the season left he had a 10–10 record with an ERA of 3.16. That was enough to get him sent to the Yankees' top farm club at Newark in the International League. The Newark Bears were a storied minor league franchise; in the late 1930s the Bears routinely sent almost the entire starting lineup up to the big team. When Vic Raschi arrived with more than half of the season gone, he saw at least two youngsters who were hitting with a consistency that would get them to the parent Yankees very soon. One was the third baseman, a blond-haired college boy with a golden swing named Bobby Brown. The other was a squat, homely fireplug of a catcher who was a menace behind the plate and much safer in the outfield. He had to be in the lineup because he hit everything thrown near the plate. No one called Larry Berra by his christened name. Everyone called him "Yogi."

It also did not take Vic long to observe the extraordinary talent of the Montreal Royals' rookie second baseman, who was leading the league in hitting and stolen bases while tyrannizing pitchers with his bat and his speed on the bases. He was called many names. His given name was Jackie Robinson.

The Newark manager was an old Yankee hand, the future Hall of Famer Lefty Gomez, a pitcher who had won 189 games for the 1930s Yankees and six more in the World Series, where he never lost a decision. Raschi was given a start immediately, and after compiling a 1–2 record, with an ERA of 3.27, Gomez told the director of the Yankee farm system, George Weiss, that the burly righthander was ready for the big leagues. The call came in September, after the Red Sox has clinched the American League pennant. The Yankees also brought up the twenty-two-year-old golden-haired Stanford graduate with the magic bat, Bobby Brown, and the stumpy twenty-one-year-old catcher Berra. They played the last seven games of the season. Brown, who had already told the Yankee organization that he was planning to attend medical school, hit .333. Berra, who had come from the Dago Hill section of St. Louis that also produced Joe Garagiola, might have seemed as inarticulate as his teammate Brown was erudite, but his .364 batting average for that last week with two home runs got everyone's attention. These were two natural hitters, and they were going to be around for a long time; they would also become roommates and remain close friends for the rest of their lives.

Vic got two starts against the last-place Philadelphia Athletics, won both and went the distance each time. He, too, apparently had arrived, in spite of the late start in his career. He had won his first big league games at the age of twenty-seven and, finally, he thought, was on his way. When he returned for the off-season to Conesus, New York, where Sally had her home and they had settled, he was preparing himself mentally and physically for spring training and a career. Little did he know that the euphoria of September 1946 would lead to a crisis that almost drove him out of baseball.

When Raschi reported to spring training in 1947, he thought he had made the team on the basis of his late-season performance the year before. But manager Bucky Harris had turned the responsibility of his pitchers over to Charlie Dressen, an old-time National League infielder (and later manager of the Brooklyn Dodgers). Dressen thought he knew pitching and the mind of pitchers. It is difficult to find anyone who had a good word about Dressen's handling of any pitching staff.[11] He used Raschi exclusively as a batting practice pitcher during spring training, and before the season started, Vic was told to report to Portland of the AAA Pacific Coast League. His younger teammates from Newark, Brown and Berra, had made the team. Raschi was going back to the minors.

He was bitter and discouraged. Instead of reporting, he went home to Sally in upstate New York, ready to quit baseball. The Yankees called him twice, threatening eventually to banish him for life unless he reported. It was Sally, calm and deliberate, who saved him. "I've never seen Portland, so let's go."[12] She hated leaving her home in Conesus, New York, but Sally understood that Vic needed nurturing and her companionship to get past this crisis. It was the most important decision of their lives. They packed their bags and headed for the Pacific Northwest. After finding an apartment, Vic unpacked and went over to the stadium where the Portland Beavers played their games. He found the manager's office, knocked on the door, entered, and saw a tall figure coming toward him with an outstretched hand and a face he could trust. His name was Jim Turner. This was to be another friendship for life.

Whatever Dressen saw in the twenty-eight-year-old rookie, it was enough to believe that he wasn't ready for the big leagues. Jim Turner, consummate mentor of pitchers and the ultimate master of the mound, thought he saw something that could make the difference. It was obvious that Vic's "out pitch" was a formidable rising fastball. Turner studied Raschi's patterns, how he moved the ball around, his velocity, his curve, slider and change-up. This big, dour, earnest and mature pitcher had all the equipment necessary. Turner would work on all of Vic's pitches, and he could help him. But there was one ingredient missing. Turner would notice that in a critical situation, some .220 hitter would be sitting on Raschi's fastball and beat him. His pitcher needed to push these batters off the plate; in fact, Turner believed that a sense of fear needed to be instilled in every hitter, and Vic didn't do it. He didn't hate enough, and he would not throw inside. Turner was a quiet man, but he would lean over Raschi as they sat together in the clubhouse and in low tones communicate his philosophy to the often-frustrated pitcher: "You have to crucify those sons of bitches, Vic. Murder them, crucify them, kill them."[13] Turner came to understand Vic's terror at hitting a batsman. The tragic accidents that caused Gene's blindness left his older brother with a horror of hitting an opposing player in the head. But Turner wanted to overcome any inhibitions in his pupil.

He knew that eventually any major league hitter would catch up with a major league fastball, and that there was only one way to make certain that the pitcher owned the plate, not the hitter. That was intimidation, which meant "up and in." Jim Turner the teacher embarked on a course of hatred: hatred toward the hitter, toward anyone who came up to the plate intending to challenge his pupil. It was in this period at Portland that Vic's concentration led him to develop a terrifying scowl, a withering look that opposing teams, journalists, and even teammates came to appreciate — and fear. When they saw it, they stayed away. By the time Jim Turner was through with his course of instruction, no one would come near Vic Raschi on the day he pitched.[14]

By July, Turner had seen enough. He called general manager George Weiss and told him to get Raschi back. Weiss, who knew that Turner was one of the most astute evaluators of pitching talent, didn't waste any time. The Yankees were in the middle of an extraordinary winning streak, but they were running out of arms. Weiss recalled Raschi on the same day in July that he acquired forty-year-old American League veteran Bobo Newsom. They each started in a doubleheader, won both, and the Yankees went on to win nineteen consecutive games and lock up the 1947 pennant. Vic won the nineteenth game. At the age of twenty-eight, he was back in the majors to stay. When he walked into the Yankee clubhouse on that July day, he knew most of the faces from his brief stint at the end of the 1946 season. But there was one he looked for particularly, a veteran pitcher whom the Yankees had acquired over the winter who had the same pitching style and set of equipment. Even their wives had grown fond of each other. He looked for the big righthander with the rising fastball. His name was Allie Reynolds. They found each other in a corner of the clubhouse.

* * *

After seven futile years wandering through the low minor leagues, Ed Lopat was ready to chuck it and go back to New York City. He had told his wife Libby three years earlier, right after they had gotten married in 1941 when he was twenty-two years old, that he would stick it out for a while longer. Libby was by far the best thing that had happened to Ed Lopat in his wanderings through the backwaters of Organized Baseball. He met Mary Elizabeth Howell when he was assigned to Shreveport, Louisiana, in 1940. She came from nearby small-town Vivian, and the Polish-American baseball player married the Bayou girl. He convinced her that baseball, next to her, was the most important thing in his life. After all, this is what he had wanted for as far back as he could recall, when he was a ten-year-old running with the packs of kids on the streets of New York City's East Side. It was always baseball, always the New York Yankees, the same dream night after night. Some day the Lopatynskis would have a major league baseball player in the family.

Eddie was the second youngest of six children. He and his younger brother

Ted were the only ones born in the United States to a family that had emigrated from Poland with four children, seeking a new life in America. East 5th Street was a tenement neighborhood of Poles, Jews, Irish, Ukrainians, Russians, and any other ethnic group that could get a toehold. The Italians and Chinese were a few blocks away across Manhattan Island. The Europeans had come through Ellis Island, seeking the American dream. The Chinese had wandered eastwards when the great western railroads were completed and settled in Chinatowns in America's urban ghettos. Mr. Lopatynski, like 90 percent of his immigrant countrymen, had married a Polish girl from back home. And like so many of the New York City Polish community, he opened up a little shoe repair store, first on the Lower East Side, then, when his son, Edmund, born on June 21, 1918, was four, moved to East 98th Street and Madison Avenue with his wife and six children into a better storefront location and a five-floor walk-up flat. This was a neighborhood of parish churches, schoolyards, and occasional open lots, where kids could play ball and dream of their hometown New York Yankees. Eddie attended St. Cecilia's Catholic School, P.S. 71, and P.S. 172, all in the neighborhood. When it came time to choose a high school, he wanted one closer to Yankee Stadium. Eddie Lopatynski picked DeWitt Clinton High School in the Bronx. When he got to high school, he finally acquired his first baseball glove, a used first baseman's mitt. He was left-handed, and left-handers played first base; and he had an idol. The subway train on the way to DeWitt Clinton went right past Yankee Stadium, and on more than one occasion, Eddie could not resist the chance to see a somewhat larger left-handed first baseman playing for the Yankees. Lou Gehrig was the hometown hero for New York City's immigrant families. His parents barely spoke English.

DeWitt Clinton shut down many of its sports programs because of Depression budgets, and they did not field a baseball team. Eddie earned a reputation as a sharp-hitting, slick infielder with local clubs, and he hooked up with a city league that had a team from Radio City Music Hall. They gave him a job as an usher, and he played first base on the theatre team. It was then that he first thought of shortening his name so it could fit in the box score. It was as "Ed Lopat" that he appeared in 1936 at a Brooklyn Dodger tryout at Ebbets Field. He had one more year to graduate from high school, and he was ready to take his shot. Ed, with his beaten-up first baseman's mitt, took the hour-and-a-half subway ride from his home to Brooklyn and joined over a thousand self-identified prospects that would show their stuff to the Dodger organization.[15] For three days Ed Lopat made the daily trip to Brooklyn, while hundreds of other youngsters were sent home. The Dodgers gave sandwiches and milk to those who survived the daily cut. Finally, the prospects were reduced to forty, and they played some games. At the end of the session, Eddie was told that he would hear from the Dodgers the next spring, and he did. Now out of high school, he was sent a train ticket to Elmira, New York, where the Dodgers had brought together their outstanding tryout prospects from all over the country.

In 1937, there were twenty Class D leagues with more than 130 teams in minor league baseball. The Brooklyn Dodger organization had five D ball clubs. For $50 a month, they took a chance on nineteen-year-old Ed Lopat and packed him off to Greensburg of the six-team Class D Pennsylvania State Association, which by June was down to four teams when two went under. He hit .229 at Greensburg, and six weeks later he was sent to Jeanerette of the Evangeline League, another D level, but this time in Louisiana. Lopat, who had hardly made any trips outside of New York state, was shipped to Bayou country and was already beginning to worry about life in the minors. His stomach was bothering him, and he thought he might be getting an ulcer. But at Jeanerette he was destined to find someone who would make an enormous difference in his life before anyone knew what a mentor was. His manager was an old-time minor league pitcher named Carlos Moore. He saw Lopat, while getting ready for infield practice before a game, playing around the mound and throwing like a pitcher. Moore liked what he saw and told the young first baseman, "Get a finger glove and keep throwing off the mound, whenever you get a chance. I'm going to get you into a game as a pitcher." A few days later, in a game that was lost by the third inning, Moore waved his first baseman toward the mound. Ed Lopat had begun his pitching career with 6⅔ innings of shutout ball. For the rest of the season, Ed played first base and came in to pitch whenever Moore needed him.

He went home after the season and waited for the Dodger organization to make a move with him. They did. They didn't think he was worth the $50 a month investment, and Lopat was released. Jeanerette was able to hold onto a few independent players and Ed began the 1938 season on their roster as a starting pitcher. Minor league teams survived the Depression by selling an occasional player whom they kept on the roster outside the control of the major league parent organization. Lopat was 12–7 by mid-season with a 2.73 ERA when he was sold to Shreveport in the Class A Texas League, but was told to report to the Class C Kilgore Rangers in the East Texas League. By the end of the 1938 season he was with Shreveport. When the 1939 season began, his contract had been sold to the Longview club in the C East Texas League again, and he was back where had started. He was 16–9 with Longview with a 2.11 ERA, but no one seemed to notice a short, stocky left-hander who was developing into a finesse pitcher without a live fastball.

In 1940 he was still in the Class C East Texas League, without a contract authorized by any major league club, this time with Marshall. The modest move upwards was again to Shreveport, where he finished the season 0–3 with an ERA of 5.94. The only good news was that he had fallen in love with someone who was willing to put up with the miseries of minor league life. Libby Howell and Ed Lopat were married at the beginning of the 1941 season, and she followed him to Kansas, where he pitched well enough for the Class C Salina Millers to get sold to the Oklahoma City Indians, back in the Texas League.[16] At Salina he had little trouble with a left-handed hitting outfielder for the Springfield Cardinals who was burning up the league and had been called up to St. Louis. His name was Stan Musial.

Pack it up: that's all he could think of when he finished the 1941 season with Oklahoma City. He seemed to be stuck in the lower reaches of the game and was a minor league gypsy, wandering from hamlet to hamlet, living poorly and eating worse. The frustration and aggravation proved too much, and his stomach finally erupted. Ed spent six weeks in an Oklahoma City hospital being treated for acute gastritis and ulcers. He had to pay the $240 hospital bill himself. He had a wife, a lousy fastball, a worse stomach, and no future in baseball. It didn't seem to matter that he was able to examine the art of pitching from a very subtle angle. He studied hitters, crept inside their heads, anticipated their reactions to a variety of different pitches that he was slowly mastering. He also had been watching another left-hander in the major leagues, a New York Giant who "turned the ball over." Carl Hubbell had mastered the screwball, the curve from a lefthander that broke away from the right-handed hitter. Lopat had been working on his own screwball and was driving batters on both sides of the plate crazy. But what difference did it make? No one seemed interested in a slick but slow left-hander. He was no Lefty Grove or Lefty Gomez.

Libby convinced him to take one more shot. As miserable as Ed was, Libby knew her husband would be more miserable outside of baseball. In 1942, his contract was assigned once again to Oklahoma City, which was the highest Class A team he had ever started a season with. He was seen by a scout for the Southern Association Little Rock Travelers, who were in a pennant race in a league just ranked under the top minor league teams. Ed and Libby went to Little Rock, Arkansas, and Lopat helped the Travelers win the Southern Association title. The Lopats loved Little Rock and settled in over the off-season. He worked out all winter and was ready when the 1943 season began. Lopat had his breakout year, his seventh in the minors. With Little Rock that year he went 19–10 and led the league with a 3.05 ERA. The league president was Billy Evans, a former major league umpire and general manager. Evans took a liking to Lopat and began shopping him to several major league teams.

Yet, in spite of the war-depleted rosters, there were very few takers. Lopat was safe from the draft because of his terrible ulcers.[17] But, he just did not look robust enough to be a major league pitcher. He was short, short-armed, and lacked velocity. Finally, the Chicago White Sox, desperate for pitching, contacted the Little Rock organization and said they would take Lopat on a thirty-day trial. He was to show up at the White Sox' wartime spring training facility at French Lick, Indiana. At twenty-six, he was getting to the majors.

Ed and Libby Lopat in 1955: another marriage for life (National Baseball Hall of Fame Library, Cooperstown, N.Y.).

The thirty days turned into four reasonably happy years with the second-division White Sox. It was a team going nowhere, but Lopat held his own in the American League. He had learned his craft well in those seven arduous years. He would never blow his fastball by anyone. He saw pitching as an art form to be learned by a master who could confuse a hitter: never the same pitch twice, never in the same place twice, never the same speed twice. With that philosophy, Lopat put together two wartime seasons with 11–10 and 10–13 records, not bad for someone who had spent six years without emerging from the low minor leagues. Nevertheless, he was pitching against wartime players. How would his stuff stand up when the boys came home from the war?

In 1946, the twenty-eight-year-old Lopat received another great mentoring experience. Early in the season, after a dismal start, the White Sox fired manager Jimmy Dykes and handed the club over to veteran pitcher Ted Lyons, who at the age of forty-five was still on the player roster. Lopat, who studied every pitcher and batter, saw immediately that here was a twenty-year veteran of the major leagues who had won 260 games by changing speeds, angle of delivery, and by *not throwing strikes*. Lyons, who didn't strike out a lot of hitters and walked fewer, had most hitters swinging at balls *outside the strike zone*. Lopat was never shy about seeking help. "I wonder if you'll help me a little bit, like teach me to throw a slow curve."[18]

Lyons became a very willing teacher. In his two decades with the White Sox he had never reached 100 strikeouts in a season, yet with a perennial second-division team he ended his career with a respectable ERA of 3.67, which, along with his 260–230 record, earned him a place in the Hall of Fame in 1955. Lyons taught Lopat every trick he knew: throwing with a short arm, long arm, three-quarters, overhand, arm speed deception. Under Ted Lyons' tutelage, the legend that was to accompany Ed Lopat for the rest of his career was forged: Steady Eddie, the Junkman. Lopat did more than hold his own against the higher quality returning veterans. In 1946 he lowered his ERA to 2.73, although the best he could do with another hapless White Sox team was 13–13. In 1947 he repeated with a 2.81 ERA and a 16–13 record.

Ed Lopat had made it to the big leagues. What difference did it make that after four years his record was 50–49? He was making $14,000 a year, had an off-season job in Little Rock, Arkansas, where he and Libby were living. He was twenty-nine years old. Not a bad life. There was lots of fishing and hunting with good friends and other ballplayers. Then the phone rang.

On February 24, 1948, Ed Lopat was traded to the New York Yankees. His life was about to change forever. The New York City kid was going home, back to Yankee Stadium.

3

The Coming of Casey

Contrary to what many of the Yankee players thought, George Weiss was only human. He did everything he could in his first year as general manager to bring the 1948 pennant to the Yankees, and he failed. His efforts did not make him any more popular.

In 1948, anyone who had to do business with the new Yankee general manager knew him as a cold, humorless and uncommunicative administrator who could be perfectly brutal in his dealings with employees, which is what he considered the players. He begrudged them every nickel. Yet, he was a baseball man down to his very bones. All he ever wanted in life was to run a baseball club. Even while studying as an undergraduate at Yale he ran a semi-pro team that outdrew the Eastern League New Haven entry. He was a young entrepreneur who knew how to put fans in the seats. He would book his New Haven Colonials against barnstorming major league teams and pack the ballpark. After graduating Weiss bought the struggling New Haven franchise, made himself president and produced his first financial bundle at the age of twenty-four.

In 1932 he took general manager Ed Barrow's offer and became director of minor league operations for the Yankees. It was Weiss who built the Yankee farm system into a formidable nursery for the great 1930s Bronx Bombers and subsequent dynasties. Anyone who came up through the Yankee system had dealings with him. He created a much-envied network of coast-to-coast scouts led by Paul Krichell that produced a constant flow of talent onto Yankee farm teams: Joe Devine on the West Coast; Bill Essick in Southern California; Tom Greenwade in the Midwest; Gene McCann in New England and the Southeast. It was Weiss who made the deals that brought Joe DiMaggio, Tommy Henrich, Charlie Keller, Joe Gordon, Vic Raschi, Yogi Berra, Bobby Brown, and Mickey Mantle into the Yankee orbit. He was the single most important architect of Yankee success starting in the 1930s, and he was, in the eyes of most of the people he dealt with, a despicable human being.

Weiss was still farm director in 1946 with the war ended and big league baseball prepared expectantly to return to its pre-war quality. The Yankees did not. The rust produced by three years of inactivity reduced the team to a third-place finish behind Boston and Detroit. Joe DiMaggio had physically aged far beyond his thirty-two years and would never regain the heights attained in that extraordinary run between 1936 and 1941. The former all-star Yankees simply could not produce. To make matters worse, there was deep dissension in the front office. Ed Barrow had been forced out by the boozing and truculent Larry MacPhail, who became general manager in 1946 when he acquired joint ownership of the Yankee organization late in 1945 with two partners, Dan Topping and Del Webb. Topping, whose grandfather had been president of Republic Steel, was a New York sports personality and millionaire who had owned two football franchises. Webb had made his fortune in construction. He had built many of the detention camps used to concentrate Japanese-Americans during World War II. Webb and Topping had left the running of the team to MacPhail, who fired long-time manager Joe McCarthy thirty-one games into the 1946 season. The management was in chaos; the team veterans were not performing. The only bright lights were the rookies from Weiss's farm system who came up at the end of the season: Raschi, Berra and Brown. The New York Yankee franchise appeared to be on the slippery slope to mediocrity.

Yet, 1947 produced an astonishing and totally unexpected reversal. The baseball writers had overwhelmingly picked the Red Sox to repeat as American League pennant winners. The Yankees had hired a colorless veteran American League manager, Bucky Harris, who had led the Washington Senators to pennants in 1924 and 1925. Harris was a quiet baseball tactician, a very easy man to be around. With MacPhail—volatile and bibulous—running the club, events outside the lines commanded the public's attention. "The Great Experiment" had begun; Branch Rickey and Jackie Robinson were about to make history. So was Brooklyn Dodger manager Leo Durocher.

Durocher, always a headline grabber since his Gashouse Gang days in St. Louis in the early 1930s, was having a tabloid front-page affair with the still-married Hollywood actress Laraine Day, and the powerful Catholic church in Brooklyn and Manhattan did not like it. In the meantime, before the 1947 season had begun, MacPhail tempted Dodger coach Charlie Dressen away from Brooklyn, and the Dodger and Yankee front offices were blasting away at each other, to the delight of the New York City newspapers.

Just before the season began, Commissioner Happy Chandler dropped his bomb. Durocher was suspended for the season "for conduct detrimental to baseball." The Yankees and Dodgers were fined $2,000 "for engaging in public feuding." Robinson would have to experience his first big league season without his on-field champion Durocher, who was only interested in winning and saw immediately that Robinson's talent was going to put money in his pocket. Indeed, Robinson led the team in stolen bases, tied for the lead in home runs and led Brooklyn to its first postwar pennant. He was the first official Rookie of the Year.

But, the stunning surprise was in the American League. Ted Williams had a second Triple Crown season, but otherwise the Red Sox collapsed and finished fourteen games behind the Yankees. With a lineup filled with names like Williams, Pesky, Doerr, Dominic DiMaggio, Rookie of the Year Sam Mele and proven pitchers like Boo Ferris, Tex Hughson and Joe Dobson, all apparently at the peak of their careers, Boston began showing those signs of self-destruction that characterized the ownership of Tom Yawkey, who had a singular capacity to hand his team over to mediocre or self-serving managers and general managers, whose only virtue was that they were Yawkey's regular drinking buddies.

Was there really any such thing as "the Curse of the Bambino?" The Red Sox always seemed to get what they deserved. In one respect, the miseries of the 1940s and 1950s were sealed when Joe Cronin convinced Tom Yawkey in 1939 that the kid shortstop playing for Louisville named Pee Wee Reese was not up to major league quality. A year earlier general manager Eddie Collins had urged Yawkey to buy the entire Louisville franchise for $250,000 just to get Reese, who, he assured his boss, would be the shortstop of the future. Cronin, a shortstop player-manager pushing thirty-three and slowing down, but a drinking buddy of Yawkey's, was not interested in a challenge. Reese went instead to the Brooklyn Dodgers, who also had a player-manager at shortstop. But, Leo Durocher, one year older than Cronin, was interested only in winning and saw Reese as a potential franchise player. In 1940, he stepped aside and allowed the skinny kid from Louisville to take over, make a bushelful of errors in his first season, and become the engine that generated Dodger greatness for the next fifteen years. Say anything about Durocher: foul-mouthed, immoral, degenerate. But his will to win never had a rival. He let Reese have his shortstop job, and when he took a look at Jackie Robinson, he saw the color of money and not the color of his skin.

In Ted Williams, arguably the greatest left-handed hitter in baseball history, the Red Sox had a deeply flawed star with indifferent defensive skills and no team leadership capability. In 1948 he put up numbers that matched his 1947 season: a .343 league-leading batting average as well as the top figures in RBIs and home runs. But, when it came time to select a Most Valuable Player, the award went to Lou Boudreau of the Indians. The Red Sox management over the years— Yawkey, Cronin, Joe McCarthy in his sad decline, Pinky Higgins—could not sustain a winning team, even if it possessed over the years stars of the quality of Williams, DiMaggio, Pesky, Doerr, Vern Stephens, Mel Parnell, Jack Kramer and Ellis Kinder. After the seven-game heartbreaking loss of the 1946 World Series, a dismal third-place finish in 1947, the crushing last-day-of-the-season pennant losses of 1948 and 1949, the Red Sox slumped down into a general mediocrity with managers and general managers who took Tom Yawkey's seemingly endless supply of money and threw it away. The anticipated Red Sox Golden Age was over before it started. Instead, it was the beginning of the Red Sox story for years to come: twenty-five players, twenty-five cabs. After 1946, Williams never played in another World Series and he retired in 1960, a war hero who still refused to tip his hat to the fans.

And everyone would remain white. The Red Sox were forced by local politicians and journalists to give a tryout to Jackie Robinson in 1945, but nothing came of it. They sent someone down to look at a kid named Willie Mays in Birmingham, but the word came back that the seventeen-year-old outfielder did not have a great arm and couldn't hit a curveball![1] The Red Sox were the last team in major league baseball to bring a black ballplayer to the roster. The Yankees were not much better, but they were smarter.[2]

In contrast, the 1947 Yankees of the chaotic MacPhail and quiet Harris somehow built a team with remarkable chemistry out of what Roger Kahn called "shreds and patches." Years later, they were characterized by their rookie part-time third baseman, Bobby Brown: "There was never a mentally tougher team than the 1947 Yankees."[3] DiMaggio, old far beyond his years, managed just twenty home runs and did not drive in 100 runs, but he and the thirty-four-year-old Tom Henrich, along with thirty-eight-year-old veteran first baseman George McQuinn, provided the muscle and leadership. McQuinn, who had been picked up on waivers after being released by the lowly Philadelphia Athletics, had one final extraordinary year, hitting .304 and knocking in 80 runs. Rookies Berra and Brown contributed with their bats. No one really trusted Berra behind the plate, where he caught only fifty-one games, but he was an adequate outfielder. Veteran shortstop Phil Rizzuto rebounded and anchored the infield. But it was the pitching of first-year Yankee Allie Reynolds (19–8), rookie Frank Shea (14–5) and the unexpected and heroic relief pitching of Joe Page (seventeen saves, fourteen wins) that made the difference. When they floundered, MacPhail had Vic Raschi in Portland who joined the team in mid-season and won seven games. MacPhail also purchased forty-year-old veteran journeyman Bobo Newsom from Washington, and he delivered seven wins, as well. The Yankees won nineteen straight in mid-summer to put the season away and bury the Red Sox. Williams hit 9-for-36 (.250) against the Yankees. DiMaggio hit .388 against the Red Sox. They went on to win the World Series against Brooklyn in seven games.

Amidst the euphoria of an unexpected triumph and success, MacPhail resigned, his emotional instability becoming even too much for himself. He sold his partnership to Topping and Webb, who appointed Weiss general manager.

Now, in 1948, Weiss was furious at the third-place finish. Although the team was aging, his two old warhorses put together fine years. DiMaggio, finding strength somewhere, hit a league-leading 39 home runs with 155 RBIs, while batting .320, his last great year. Henrich drove in 100 runs with 25 home runs. Berra, while he lost his starting status as a catcher, knocked in 98 runs and hit .305. But, Weiss, who regularly hired private detectives to follow his players, knew that some were burning the candle at both ends, and he blamed Harris for not disciplining the night owls. There was little enforcement.

The pitching seemed extraordinary. Vic Raschi had his first full-time season as a Yankee and produced a 19–8 record. Allie Reynolds, in his second year in New York, went 16–7, but was walking too many and giving up home runs in crucial situations. He was still carrying on his back the burden that had followed him from Cleveland: the Indian couldn't take the pressure. Over the winter, Weiss had made his first trade, acquiring the left-hander he felt he needed in the starting rotation: Eddie Lopat, who produced a 17–11 season in New York, the best in his career. This was the first season that these three pitched together on the Yankee team, and they did not produce a pennant.

Joe Page, the star reliever of 1947, had discovered New York City nightlife and spent most of his time dodging Weiss's detectives, while failing in the bullpen; and the starting catcher, Gus Niarhos, did not hit a single home run. Weiss felt that there was still enough to produce a winner, and Bucky Harris did not deliver. In fact, he barely managed the club at all. The players, who were very fond of Harris, could see that he was losing his grip. Increasingly, he turned the day-to-day operations over to his deputy, Charlie Dressen, who thought of himself as a pitching coach among other things. The hurlers stayed as far away from him as possible. Weiss fumed; he could barely wait for the end of the season to fire both of them. The Yankees fell out of contention in the last week of the season, leaving the field to the Red Sox and Indians and their fateful playoff game.

The New York City writers began preparing their elegies about the fallen Yankee dynasty.

* * *

When Casey Stengel was managing the Boston Braves for six years in the late 1930s and early 1940s, his National League team finished the season fifth once, sixth once, and seventh four times. In the spring of 1943 he was accidentally run down by a Boston taxi cab and was unable to manage for the first two months of the season. Veteran columnist Dave Egan of *The Boston Record* voted the cabdriver "the man who did the most for Boston in 1943."[4] It was the same Dave Egan who wrote, after Stengel had been introduced to the media as the new Yankee manager at The Stork Club in New York City in early October 1948, immediately after the World Series, "The Yankees have now been mathematically eliminated from the 1949 pennant race."[5] Joe DiMaggio expressed the sentiments of most of the veteran players who were still loyal to Joe McCarthy: "They've hired a clown."

It was true. Casey Stengel's entire professional career as a player and manager had been characterized by behavior that Leonard Koppett described as that of "an overage juvenile delinquent."[6] He was a brawling, hard-drinking carouser as a player, and not much had changed when he "grew up."

How can anyone explain the hiring of Casey Stengel in 1949 by the New York Yankees, an organization that prided itself on its haughty dignity, corporate image and upscale clientele? The answer is as clear as it is improbable: George Weiss.

It was Weiss who had been impressed by what others failed to see. They met each other in 1925. Stengel was finished as a major leaguer, but he had accomplished two things during his career. He had sat, metaphorically, at the feet of John McGraw and learned the game. McGraw was a strategic and tactical genius who introduced platooning — he had used Stengel at the end of his career as a part-time thirty-three-year-old outfielder and got a .368 batting average in return when others said Casey was washed up — and emphasized defense, pitching and contact hitting to win. Stengel, who played for National League teams his entire career, spent years observing the McGraw strategy and soaked it up. He also saw McGraw the Impresario, part owner, part showman; Stengel emulated everything he saw in McGraw's style.

Stengel intended to make baseball his career after his playing days were over. This became possible when in 1923 he met Edna Lawson, daughter of a wealthy California family. He proposed two weeks later, and they were married the same year. She helped him focus an investment strategy in real estate and oil, and it was as a wealthy man that Casey played his last season for the Boston Braves in 1924, after which Judge Emil Fuchs, owner of the franchise, gave Stengel the opportunity to serve with his newly acquired Worcester franchise in the Eastern League as president, manager, and outfielder. Now McGraw was taking notice of Stengel and grabbed him to manage the Giants' affiliate in Toledo for the next six years. During that time, the owner of the New Haven franchise was a chubby, grim and still youthful Yale graduate named George Weiss. The wisecracking manager and the humorless owner most improbably became fast friends and talked baseball incessantly. Weiss realized that behind the clowning was a shrewd baseball man and an even shrewder money manager. Weiss could appreciate both talents.

Weiss left New Haven in 1932 for his first New York Yankee job running the minor league operations, and Stengel went on to a career of mediocrity managing second-division teams in the National League. He had managed the hapless Brooklyn Dodgers for a few years, so the New York City sportswriters knew him and delighted in the great copy that he provided. His mouth never

Casey Stengel: from baseball clown to genius (photograph not dated) (National Baseball Hall of Fame Library, Cooperstown, N.Y.).

closed, and the sportswriters could always be assured of a great quotation from Casey, even while his teams were playing dismally and finishing far down in the league standings. Stengel was managing Oakland to a league championship in the Pacific Coast League in 1948, and Weiss saw his chance. This strange Odd Couple — the prankster and the humorless front office man — were about to make history. No one — except perhaps Weiss— anticipated anything but laughs and losing. Leonard Koppett set the stage: "In New York, of course, Stengel was as firmly identified as a clown as the Statue of Liberty was as a statue. The Daffy Dodger managing the lordly Yankees? That would be a joke in itself. Publicity? Yes, the best. Victories? Never. But, it was no joke."[7]

Stengel and Weiss agreed that a specialized coaching staff would replace the old boys who hung around Harris. Most important of all was solving the problem of what to do with their young slugger, Yogi Berra. During the 1948 season his catching proved to be a continued liability, and he was moved to the outfield. The starting catcher, Gus Niarhos, while defensively very good, lacked any semblance of power that was required at his position. The answer to the problem was to get someone to make a catcher out of Berra, who, in spite of his awkward appearance, was a superb, intelligent and agile athlete.[8] The Yankees needed him in the lineup every day. They agreed that there was only one man for the job: Yankee stalwart Bill Dickey.

Stengel knew that pitching was not his pedagogical strength.[9] His three starters Raschi, Reynolds and Lopat had produced exceptional results in 1948, and the Yankees still finished in third place. A few more wins might have made the difference. Weiss and Stengel almost blurted out the same name simultaneously as someone who could get the most out of a pitching staff and also help a rough catcher with the nuances of his position. Stengel, who had him as a pitcher ten years earlier, watched him manage in Portland the year before. Weiss had followed his career for years. This man's name was Jim Turner.

The third coach was a tribute to psychology. Stengel and Weiss knew that Joe McCarthy might have been gone, but he was in no way forgotten by a key element of the team: DiMaggio, Henrich, and Rizzuto had played for him since the pre-war championship teams. Continuity for the Yankees was very important. Casey also knew that with rookie Jerry Coleman and part-time third baseman Bobby Brown potentially in the starting infield, he would need serious help. Who better than McCarthy-era veteran Frank Crosetti, the Yankee shortstop of the 1930s? As for the rest, no one knew more about outfield play than Stengel. Jerry Coleman said, "Stengel was a genius in using his outfielders."[10]

When Vic Raschi heard whom the new manager had selected as his coaches, he could not wait to call his closest friends on the team. These had not been lifelong buddies or minor leaguers who had come up together through the ranks. He had known Allie Reynolds only since the middle of 1947 when Vic returned to the Yankees in mid-season to stay. He met Eddie Lopat in 1948 after the trade with the Chicago White Sox brought the left-hander to New York. Yet, calling during the off-season now was not unusual for these three, because something very special had happened. From the first moment that they, along with their spouses, had met, it was clear that this was more than merely a baseball friendship. It was a friendship for life. Phil Rizzuto characterized it best: "Vic and Sally Raschi, Earlene and Allie Reynolds, Ed and Libby Lopat. Those six were like a family. A happy family."[11]

4

The Team Within the Team

"Reynolds, Raschi and Lopat were like his children."—Phil Rizzuto on Jim Turner

"Jim Turner treated his Big Three like they were his sons. I cannot tell you how they cared for each other, then and until Vic died. I understand how rare the magic was that the three pitchers and their coach shared. It was a society of four."—Sally Raschi

It really started with the wives, the idea of living close to one another. At spring training in 1948, the Raschis and Reynolds rented together in St. Petersburg. When the Lopats came south, they were soon invited to move close by. There were six of them, and their children: Earlene and Allie, Sally and Vic, and now Libby and Ed. When they came north, the Lopats took rooms in the Grand Concourse Hotel near Yankee Stadium. Vic and Sally had rented in Hillsdale, New Jersey; the Reynolds came to visit, and found a house for the season in nearby Ridgewood, near a golf course where Earlene, extraordinary athlete that she was, could beat up on the male players. Sally and Vic invited the Lopats over one evening, and Libby fell in love with the Hillsdale community. She saw a house that was being built near the Raschis, and within the year the Lopats moved out of their hotel, out of New York City, and next to their friends. Now, all six were living within a mile of each other. For the next five years they would babysit for each others' children, shop for each others' groceries, and drive to Yankee Stadium together. Only the Lopats bought and settled down permanently. Earlene Reynolds never felt comfortable away from Oklahoma any more than Sally Raschi did from the lake region of upstate New York. But, every spring they went south together and every baseball season they found homes near the Lopats in Hillsdale. What grew here, for these three families, was an enduring friendship that spread to the rest of the team, an emotional chemistry that meant a great deal to anyone who experienced it.[1]

Jim Turner saw it immediately. At Portland he had gotten to know Sally and Vic Raschi, had grown closer than any team manager normally did to a pitcher and his wife, and they reciprocated. He understood how to concentrate the pitcher's intensity. He knew that Raschi only wanted to find some object to dedicate himself to heart and soul, to bring all of his energy and intelligence to bear in some way. Vic, for his part, knew that this could be his last chance, and that Jim Turner was willing to share all of his wisdom with his pupil. Turner talked, and Vic Raschi listened.

Now, in 1949, they were reunited, and no one was happier than Vic Raschi, who had proved himself with the Yankees the year before with a superb 19–8 record. He had learned well. He gave up fewer hits than innings pitched — the only one of the three top starters to do so. He had struck out nearly twice as many as he had walked. Perhaps Jim could bring that extra wisdom that would take his comrades over the top, cut back on the number of walks for Reynolds and hits for Lopat, get Joe Page back on track, and help Tommy Byrne with his destructive wildness.

The moment Jim Turner met Allie Reynolds and Eddie Lopat, he knew something had happened. The planets had suddenly become aligned for him. These three pitchers, already close to each other in intelligence, maturity, concentration, fellowship, and above all a willingness to sacrifice, could become the instrument of leadership for any baseball team. What could this smoldering intensity do for the New York Yankees in 1949, a dynasty "that showed every sign of having crumbled before the start of the season"?[2]

The First and the Best: The Season of 1949

In spring training, it was Turner who spoke to Stengel about what he had observed in three of his starters. There was a fourth, to be sure, but he was different. Tommy Byrne was an exuberant, extroverted, fun-loving jokester, a graduate of Wake Forest, a fireballing left-hander with truly legendary wildness who was to lead the league in bases on balls allowed in 1949, 1950, and 1951.[3] He had won eight games in 1948, and Turner was certain he could improve his productivity; there was no hope in changing his personality. He had been pitching with futility and unfulfilled promise in New York since 1943, and owner Dan Topping could not stand watching a game in which Byrne was pitching: his nerves couldn't take it.[4] Byrne was twenty-nine years old, and irrepressible. Turner had heard about the "looseness" of the squad during the previous season and how Weiss had gotten private detectives to follow some of the players. Even Joe DiMaggio, now divorced, had showgirls on his arm regularly, lived in hotels, and enjoyed with Joe Page, outfielder Johnny Lindell and several others the New York City highlife. There had to be some new leadership.

"Watch the three of them run their laps," Turner told Stengel in spring training. Here were three veteran pitchers, Reynolds already thirty-four, Lopat thirty-one, and Raschi thirty. They invited a couple of the rookie pitchers to run with them. After three hours, the rookies were lying exhausted on the grass. Stengel saw that they were always talking to each other, holding a ball, facing an imaginary hitter. Lopat talked more than anyone, but each listened intensely. Then, Allie would go over to an exhausted rookie, give him a hand up, and tell him to start running again. A couple of infielders would come over and challenge them. Next Bauer or Woodling, and before long half the regular squad. Sometimes, one of the hitters would walk over with a bat in his hand and start talking, and then would listen as one of the hurlers spoke.[5] The three pitchers fed off each other, shared everything, and each had something to teach and sparked thoughts that other observant members of the team picked up. Bobby Brown, the medical student-turned-third baseman and pure hitter, could spot the synergy, realized that they did not behave like pitchers he had known. "There was no jealousy at all among the three of them, no competition, no Number 1, 2, or 3 starters. They were strong personalities with no egos when

Jim Turner, the pitching coach, and his boys. Pictured (left to right) are Allie Reynolds, Turner, Vic Raschi, and Ed Lopat (Raschi Family).

it came to each other."[6] They would do anything to win, and to win for each other. They communicated that same feeling to anyone near them.

Stengel was accustomed to dissention on ball clubs. He had seen bruising and bloody fights in the clubhouse during his career, cliques, cabals, and every sort of personality clash. It was the nature of the game when twenty-five individuals were together for a long season. Still, teams that had stars who never even talked to each other during a season — Ruth and Gehrig, Joe Tinker and Johnny Evers—could produce winners, as long as there was enough talent. Stengel was amazed when, in this first Yankee spring training camp, he observed a dedication, camaraderie, and discipline among rookies and veterans that were absent from any team that he had known. Older players would drill the rookies, challenge them to wind sprints, and then take them out to dinner. The will to win, to commit to the team, was there. But, was that enough? As he looked over his roster, Casey came to the conclusion that he would need some magic to get enough out of this Yankee team.

There were real problems. To be sure, this 1949 Yankees ball club was nothing like the dismal Boston and Brooklyn teams he managed in the National League. Yet, when he went over his roster, he understood why the pundits were proclaiming the end of the Yankee dynasty. George McQuinn had finally run out of gas and was released. There was no first baseman. Stengel would have to use Henrich at first when he could and then two light-hitting journeymen, Dick Kryhoski and Jack Phillips. At second there was an acrobatic rookie named Jerry Coleman who weighed about 150 pounds and chain-smoked. Stengel wasn't certain if he could survive the whole season. Rizzuto, now thirty-one, was coming off a sub-par year, had a weak arm, but would anchor the infield at shortstop. At third base he had a strong glove in Billy Johnson, who hit into too many double plays, and Bobby Brown, a great natural hitter possessed of what ballplayers call "stone hands." He accepted the good-natured ribbing from his teammates when they told him, "For God's sake, with those hands don't become a surgeon!"

The outfield had nothing but question marks. Rookie Hank Bauer had hit .180 in nineteen games at the end of the previous season. Weiss had acquired Gene Woodling from the Pacific Coast League, but Woodling had failed with Cleveland and Pittsburgh earlier in his career. Henrich was thirty-six and might have to play first base. Worst of all DiMaggio had reported to spring training with a spur in his heel and couldn't walk.

Behind the plate, the defensively reliable Gus Niahros created a power vacuum. Only Berra's maturing into a first-line catcher could settle things down, and that depended on Bill Dickey's talent as a teacher. Yogi had lost his confidence behind the plate. In the 1947 World Series the Dodgers stole everything in sight, and Harris finally had to get his distraught catcher out of there.

The 1948 season was not much better for him defensively. He needed help, and soon.

With all of this uncertainty, Stengel realized that he had one trump card that was unbeatable: his three pitchers. He sat down with Turner and hatched a plan. The Yankee team was a patchwork of aching veterans who might see only limited service, untried rookies, good fielders who could not hit for average and solid contact hitters who were uncertain fielders, and a great hitting catcher who couldn't catch.

But Turner had told the manager that the secret resided with these three pitchers. They are selfless. They will do anything to win. They will work with Dickey and with me, and they will make Berra into the catcher that the Yankees must have. Turner already had a name for it — "the Project" — and the first step had been taken. Carmen and Yogi Berra moved out of the Edison Hotel on West 47th Street in Manhattan to New Jersey, to be near his three project leaders. As for the rest of the team, they would mentor and discipline the rookies, keep an eye on the veterans' after-dark activities, and make certain that everyone brought the same level of maximum effort to the ball field. Stengel would not have to be the disciplinarian in his first year.

It worked. All the pieces fit together in Stengel's lineup mosaic. This was a team with only one regular player — Phil Rizzuto — who played in more than 128 games of the 154-game season. Henrich played sixty-one games in the outfield and fifty-two at first base and led the team with twenty-four home runs. No one drove in 100 runs. Only Rizzuto had more than 500 at-bats. Woodling, Bauer, Lindell, and second-year outfielder Cliff Mapes platooned with Henrich.[7] "We had no idea who would be playing any day. We'd get in and see what Casey had penciled in for the game. Other than Yogi and Phil, the only certainty was the pitcher," Hank Bauer remembered. Rookie Jerry Coleman stopped smoking, added twenty pounds, choked up six inches on his bat and played 122 games at second base, hitting a respectable .275 and creating the best double play combination in the league. At third base were the two complementary bodies: the sure-handed Billy Johnson and Bobby Brown, with the magic in his bat and rocks in his glove. Crosetti would hit hundreds of ground balls to Brown and Coleman each game day, right up to the first game pitch. They would never forget him.

No one realized how quickly Berra would learn, with what agility his squat body would respond. He had to be a quick learner. People were running out of patience. Milt Gross, writing in the *New York Post*, did not mince words when he described Berra's catching before the arrival of Dickey: "As a catcher, Yogi Berra is a hindrance to the pitchers. There is also the suspicion held by some of the Yankees' better thinkers that Yogi, living in constant dread and fear of basestealing forays against him, signaled for fastballs to get the drop on runners

Larry Berra, outfielder, in 1948: Many thought Yogi would never be a catcher (National Baseball Hall of Fame Library, Cooperstown, N.Y.).

when the situation clearly called for curveballs."[8] From the first day of spring training, Dickey started working with him. Dickey stressed positioning his feet correctly, moving closer to the batter, balancing while throwing, getting rid of the mask when chasing a pop-up, and improving his overall field generalship. He would leave the calling of the game and pitch selection for the time being to Turner and "the Project." But, Dickey did remind his student to study his pitchers, learn their tendencies, get inside their heads, study their habits, including what irritated them and what motivated them. The Yogi Berra of 1949 became a vastly different catcher than the insecure, awkward failure of 1947 and 1948. He was behind the plate for 109 games and would have caught twenty-five more had he not broken a finger that put him out of action for a month in the middle of the season. The metamorphosis did not happen overnight. In the last pre-season exhibition games before the 1949 season opened, the Yankees played a three-game series against the Brooklyn Dodgers, and Jackie Robinson stole four times against Berra. After the humiliation of the 1947 series, it was Robinson's way of reminding the catcher that he still had his number.

But the start of the makeover had been made. Berra would also sit for hours with Raschi, Reynolds and Lopat, talking about hitters in the league, individual team batting orders, strengths and weakness of every position player on every roster. Then, they would talk about each other, how they liked the sequence of pitches, how they threw in certain situations. At this stage and well into the season, they would not dare allow their apprentice catcher to call the pitches during the game. If he had runners on base, Berra would call for pitches that he could handle easily in the event of a steal. Each of the three, using a system of signals that they would change frequently, dictated what pitch would be coming. Gradually as the season progressed, Reynolds would say at the beginning of an inning, "Yogi, you call the pitches for a while." Eventually, he got completely on the same wave lengths as his two powerful right-handers. With Lopat, Berra's reflexes were so quick that he could adjust to anything that the left-hander threw. Over the course of the year, Lopat stopped giving signals, and so did Yogi. Berra proved to be not only a good listener but what every catcher must: the subtle psychologist and manipulator of his pitchers.

In this first season of his re-birth as a catcher, Berra listened and learned. Lopat could throw as many as twenty-four different pitches, from three different arm angles. Reynolds' fastball acted differently than Raschi's. One had a tighter curve; the other a sharper, quick-breaking slider. Allie loved to intimidate; he had no difficulty throwing inside, in pushing hitters off the plate. Vic made the hitters *think* he might throw at them, but he clearly felt less comfortable getting up and in. On the mound, Raschi and Reynolds literally hated the batter. Lopat, a more subtle pitcher, respected every hitter who came to the plate, even if it was with the intention of destroying the man who had the ball in his hand.

The clever southpaw saw a gleaming eagerness in the eyes of hitters who couldn't get to the plate fast enough to hit against him. He used what he called "the hitters' enthusiasm" to his advantage. When Lopat pitched, hitters thought they were in control. They walked away shaking their heads and not understanding why they hadn't smashed the soft offerings of this "junk man."[9] Berra realized in the endless conversations among the three pitchers that the two fastballers gradually understood Lopat's psychological warfare with the batter. They, too, became more subtle pitchers within their own styles. "The Project" was well underway.

No one laughed at the clown manager when the Yankees jumped out to a fast start with their patchwork team of platooned players. By the end of the season, no New York Yankee position player led in *any* league category, offense or defense. It was a team that did not care about individual statistics.

For the Boston Red Sox, 1949 would prove to be one of the great statistical highlight years in franchise history. They had everyone, and reason suggested that they would be the champions, finally. The year before they had acquired the best slugging shortstop in baseball, Vern Stephens, who was a solid enough infielder to move Johnny Pesky over to third base. Bobby Doerr was still at second, who along with Cleveland's Joe Gordon was the premier player at that position in the league. The outfield of Ted Williams, Dominic DiMaggio and the recently acquired Al Zarilla was all-star caliber from end to end. Stephens and Williams would finish the season tied with a league-leading 159 RBIs. Mel Parnell led the league in wins with 25, followed by teammate Ellis Kinder with 23. Williams also won the batting title with a .343 average.[10]

The defending world champion Cleveland Indians were almost as strong. With an infield of former batting champ Mickey Vernon, Gordon at second, perennial all-star Lou Boudreau at shortstop and Ken Keltner at third, the infield was rock solid. Larry Doby and sweet-hitting Dale Mitchell anchored the outfield. The pitching was superlative. Bob Lemon, Bob Feller, Mike Garcia and Early Wynn were four potential twenty-game winners. This was a team that could repeat.

Stengel knew that when it came to pitching as well as the subtleties of managing a staff, he would not second-guess his pitching coach. The only conflict came under the heading of "the Education of Yogi Berra." Berra became an instant favorite of Stengel's, and the novice catcher reciprocated. He found himself occasionally looking into the dugout for Casey's approval of a pitch call. The three pitchers, all of them fond of their new manager, nonetheless told him to stay out of "The Project"; they would handle Yogi. As Stengel saw the progress that Dickey and the pitchers were making with Berra, he told Jim Turner that the pitching staff was his, and that meant how they wanted to pitch to Berra. Turner took Stengel at his word.

It didn't take him long to get as close to his three aces as Sally Raschi later described. Turner had a capacity to win their trust and loyalty and to offer them an opportunity to *lead* a team that needed more than average commitment if victory was going to be at all possible. With a team of position players statistically unable to compete, it took a pitching coach to understand how Boston and Cleveland could be stopped, because the stoppers were the three men sitting in front of him in the clubhouse. In spring training he got out the 154-game schedule, bought a black book, and started laying out the starting assignments as far ahead as six weeks into the season. He maintained this program for the rest of the year, always with six weeks of scheduled starts.[11] The basic rules: Lopat pitches against Cleveland in every series; he owns them.[12] Whenever possible, put Lopat between Raschi and Reynolds. Be as flexible as possible and keep an eye on the opposing pitchers. Pitch Byrne against free-swinging, impatient and undisciplined teams with hitters who would swing at balls out of the strike zone. When Lemon, Wynn, Feller, Garcia, Parnell, or Kinder are pitching, set Raschi and Reynolds. If it's the Detroit Tigers, get Raschi and Reynolds against Virgil Trucks or Hal Newhouser. Match them against their aces, wear them down, grind them up. Turner sat them down, just the three of them. To Raschi and Reynolds he said, "You two are the intimidators. Show them that fastball under the chin. Tyrannize them. Terrify them. Eddie's soft stuff will drive them crazy. You will frighten them."[13]

Turner brought his strategic skills to the task as pitching coach. He would have to deal with contingencies. His first problem was what to do if Joe Page had another mediocre year. He watched and studied each of them. Raschi needed a long time to warm up and required long concentration to find his "game face," a fearsome countenance that left many a hitter shaken in the batter's box. He could not come out of the bullpen quickly and effectively. But he was stronger; he could pitch for extended periods of time on short rest. (In one stretch during the season he pitched on three days rest for ten consecutive starts.) Lopat's soft stuff was not appropriate for relief. Turner knew that late in the game and with fading light, an inside fastball was the proper purpose pitch, guaranteed to put fear into the mind of a hitter peering out into the oncoming darkness. He knew who would be throwing, if needed. During the first week of the season, in a close game with Tommy Byrne holding a tenuous lead and clearly tiring, Turner, who had been concentrating on his erratic southpaw, looked around the bench. Reynolds was gone. "Where's the Indian?" he asked. Lopat pointed to the Yankee bullpen, and he saw Allie throwing, loosening up. No one asked Reynolds to get ready in case he was needed. Even though he had started and pitched seven innings two days earlier, he knew that he could throw hard for another inning or two. Byrne got out of the jam and finished the game, but Turner looked silently at Stengel and they shared a thought: if needed, Reynolds in late innings, coming out of the bullpen, would make hitters faint.

When the season started, DiMaggio was not even with the team. His painful heel spur prevented him from putting any weight on his foot; he brooded in his midtown hotel room, not even coming out to the stadium for games. Veteran outfielder Charlie Keller was also hurt and out of the regular lineup. Stengel took a look at his talent and knew a platoon situation would work best. He used his six outfielders, had Henrich play first base as much as possible, had Woodling and Bauer in the lineup against the proper pitchers, put Bill Johnson at third when he needed defense, and placed Bobby Brown's bat into the lineup when he needed punch. He used McGraw's left-right platooning to perfection, and the Yankees took off.

Stengel instinctively knew that as a newcomer with a reputation he had to lay back as much as possible and let his players play. At the first team meeting in spring training he had confessed to his squad, "I know nothing about the American League. This year you will be on your own."[14] He also assessed as quickly as he could where the leadership on this team would come from. The McCarthy veterans were fading; the Yankee Clipper was nowhere in sight. Tommy Henrich was not a natural enforcer or disciplinarian; he did not use profanity and preferred a role as cheerleader. On the field, he was inspirational, a clutch hitter who played first base and outfield when necessary and became, in DiMaggio's absence, exactly what the Yankee broadcaster Mel Allen named him: "Old Reliable." Phil Rizzuto was another McCarthy loyalist, and, at 5'6" and 150 pounds, accepted the role assigned to the smallest player on the team; competitive, yes, but not ferocious. If anything, he needed protection when he was knocked down by opposing base runners.

Casey also looked for players who could show loyalty to him; he turned to his three aces for leadership. None of them had played for McCarthy. Stengel had already shown great judgment in bringing on Turner to replace the hated Dressen. The veterans responded. They helped the rookies. They passed endless hours with Berra, teaching him their pitching sequences, showing him how they liked to work, sharing their secrets. Their work ethic was inspirational, and they expected everyone to give 100 percent at all times. Raschi, Reynolds and Lopat became, in 1949, the leaders of Casey's team.

Early in the season, it was the pitchers who were the first to step up. Turner would have preferred a five-man rotation. He believed that pitchers, particularly older ones, needed to husband their strength. He had heard all the stories from Cleveland about Allie Reynolds, that he ran out of gas in the late innings. He had a plan to give Allie, at age thirty-four, as much rest as possible during the season, in effect to have him pitch seven- or eight-inning games. The key to this strategy was Joe Page, and the fun-loving left-hander responded to Turner's challenge to make him the emblem of the modern pitching staff in the second half of the twentieth century: the closer. By the time the season came to an end, Page had fulfilled all of Turner's hopes. He had appeared in sixty games, had saved twenty-seven (more than the combined total of the next three relievers in the league), with both totals representing records and league-leading numbers. He had won thirteen games without starting any. He pitched short and long relief, often as much as six innings.

He became the pitching alter ego of Allie Reynolds. Turner had asked Allie if he could take the journalists' jibes, if as a starter he were routinely lifted and allow Page to close out the game. Reynolds, after some reflection, thought it might be a good idea. In the heat of the game, he would be angry if he had to come out, but if there was a strategy behind it, fine. For the season, Reynolds started thirty-one games, and notoriously completed only four. As in the case of creating the concept of the closer, Turner convinced Stengel that complete games meant very little statistically if you had pitchers who could set up and others who could finish. As Turner predicted, the newspapers were all over him: it was the 1949 season that created "Allie Reynolds, the Vanishing American." But Lopat, who roomed on the road with Reynolds for seven years, told him that it would all pay off and extend his career. Allie might turn into a closer himself. Let the journalists write what they wanted.[15] Lopat was the Junkman. Vic wouldn't talk to reporters before a game he was pitching and would soon be voted the most uncooperative interview in the league. Allie lacked either stamina or courage.[16] Let them write whatever they want. But, the team was winning and the players knew why.

The 1949 season took on a context that looked like a Homeric epic, a struggle of titans. Joe McCarthy, the former Yankee manager from 1931 to 1946, so beloved by his players, now managed in his twilight years the Boston Red Sox, the new heirs-apparent in the American League. But, McCarthy was not the same man who had guided the Yankees. He would sit in the corner of the Red Sox dugout with a bottle of whiskey wrapped in a towel next to him, muttering about the great Yankee players he once had. He was a shell of what he had been.

In spring training, where the Red Sox appeared overwhelming, *Boston Globe* sports writer Harold Kaese predicted that Boston would win 124 games and lose 30. On Opening Day a poll of 112 writers covering major league baseball gave their season's predictions: the Red Sox received 70 first-place votes, the Cleveland Indians 37, and the Philadelphia Athletics 4. That left one lonely journalist who voted that the New York Yankees would win the 1949 American League pennant.[17] Red Smith picked them to finish fourth.

When the season started in Yankee Stadium against Washington with Casey Stengel in the dugout, DiMaggio was out of the starting lineup. The catcher,

Reynolds and Lopat in 1952: they taught each other (National Baseball Hall of Fame Library, Cooperstown, N.Y.).

after Berra's humiliation against Brooklyn and Jackie Robinson in the exhibition games, was Gus Niarhos. Berra was on the bench. Eddie Lopat started the opener. Berra pinch-hit in the seventh and knocked in two runs. Henrich hit a homer in the bottom of the ninth, and the Yankees won, 3–2. Next day, with Berra behind the plate and Coleman at second, Raschi threw a 3–0 shutout. Reynolds beat the Senators in the third game of the series for a sweep. Berra would not play a single game in the outfield the entire season.[18] Reynolds, Raschi, and Lopat would start 98 times and win 53 games. When including Tommy Byrne, these four started 128 out of 154 games.[19] The Yankees were in first place for all but four days. The sweetest season was underway.

There were two sequences of events that destroyed the Boston Red Sox during the 1949 season. The first took place in Boston, at Fenway Park, on June 28, 29, and 30, when, after missing the first sixty-five games of the season, Joe DiMaggio returned. The Yankees, in spite of major injuries that eventually would number 72 for the season, had taken the lead on Opening Day and held it. The Red Sox had gotten hot in mid–June, and when the Yankees came to Boston for three games, McCarthy's team had won ten of eleven and had cut the Yankee lead in half to five games. A sweep by the Red Sox would have them breathing down the necks of New York, and in Fenway Park, they were nearly unbeatable.

DiMaggio's return was dramatic. After months of pain in his heel that left him in a state of total frustration and close to an emotional collapse, he woke up one mid–June morning, put his foot down on his hotel room floor, and there was no pain. He ate, and immediately went up to Yankee Stadium to work out. The team was on the road. He blistered his hands into a bloody mess in batting practice and ran himself into exhaustion shagging fly balls in the outfield. Three months of cigarette smoking and coffee drinking had left him in terrible condition, and now he was in a frenzy to get back in the lineup.[20] A few days later he played in the Mayor's Cup exhibition game against the Giants and did not get the ball out of the infield in four times at bat. When the team left for the three games in Boston by train, DiMaggio stayed behind. Only on the afternoon of the first game, played at night, did he take a plane to Boston, still uncertain if he would play. He had a morbid fear of looking bad in front of fans. But, he went out to Fenway and put on his uniform. Stengel was talking to journalists, cautiously looking over at DiMaggio for any sign. (They never grew to like each other and did not communicate.) DiMaggio finished dressing, stood up, caught Stengel's eye, and nodded. He would play. In the middle of a sentence, Stengel interrupted himself and gave the word: the man can play and is hitting fourth!

Because the manager wanted to make certain that Lopat pitched against Cleveland, in this series Tommy Byrne would be sandwiched between Reynolds

The post-war DiMaggio. An old ballplayer at thirty-three in 1948 (National Baseball Hall of Fame Library, Cooperstown, N.Y.).

and Raschi, who had been penned into these slots six weeks earlier. In game one, the first of three complete sellouts in Fenway Park, Reynolds and Page combined for a 5–4 Yankee win. DiMaggio, who singled in his first time at bat, hit the game-winning home run in the third inning with Rizzuto on base. Next afternoon, Byrne was shelled early, and the Red Sox jumped to a 7–1 lead. In the fifth inning Red Sox starter Ellis Kinder walked Rizzuto and Henrich, and

DiMaggio hit a three-run homer. The game was tied in the eighth inning when DiMaggio came to bat. He homered for the second time, and the Yankees won, 9–7. Game 3 was the classic match-up of two aces. Raschi was 11–2, facing Mel Parnell, who was 10–3. Raschi gave up twelve hits and went the distance. DiMaggio hit another three-run home run in the seventh inning off Parnell, the margin of difference in a 6–3 sweep of the stricken Red Sox. He had hit four home runs, driven in nine runs, and scored five, while hitting .625. By the time July 4 rolled around, Raschi-Reynolds-Lopat had a combined record of 26–7.

The Red Sox showed true grit and did not collapse. After this horrendous weekend they finally found their game, played 44–16 ball and made up ten games on the Yankees. Berra had broken his thumb, and Yankee back-up catcher Charlie Silvera hit consistently over .300 while filling in, but the power numbers were absent. In the last days of the season, after being in first place since Opening Day, New York fell behind the charging Red Sox, who were in first place by one game when they came to Yankee Stadium for the final two games of the season, on October 2–3. They needed to win only one to clinch the pennant. The Red Sox finally had the Yankees' number. On the next-to-last weekend of the season the Red Sox had swept a three-game series in Boston and dropped the Yankees into second place. They were a confident crew as they took the field on October 2.

For Red Sox fans through the ages, this would remain one of those all-painful memories that seemed to endure. David Nemec, in *The Ultimate Baseball Book*, expressed the feelings of those Boston fans who were already savoring the taste of an American League pennant: "How could they miss? They had the two top winners in all of baseball (Note: Kinder and Parnell). They had four .300 hitters (Note: Williams, DiMaggio, Doerr and Pesky) and the last two men in the American League to knock in over 150 runs in a season (Note: Williams and Stephens). They even had Joe McCarthy! The Yankees, on the other hand, did not have a single batting title qualifier who hit above .287, and only one man who'd been healthy enough to play more than 130 games. No contest."[21] There was no question whom Stengel would hand the ball to in these two games: Reynolds and Raschi. There were 69,551 fans in Yankee Stadium for the Saturday game, announced as Joe DiMaggio Appreciation Day in honor of their hero. It was Reynolds against Parnell. Reynolds, who at times could be inexplicably wild when he was overthrowing, lost all semblance of control in the third inning. With the Yankees already down by one run he walked the bases loaded. Stengel could take no chances even this early in the game, and brought in Page, who walked two more, and the Yankees trailed, 4–0, before he closed the door — permanently. Over the next six innings, Page allowed one hit. The Yankees came back, and won the game 5–4 on Johnny Lindell's home run in the eighth inning. When asked who would pitch the next day, Casey said, "It'll be Raschi tomorrow, it'll be Reynolds tomorrow, it'll be Page tomorrow."[22] Everything rode on the last game of the season.

It was Raschi, 20–10, against Kinder, 23–5. It had been a long season, but the Yankees were more rested than the Red Sox. McCarthy had used his starting position players exclusively during the season and stopped pitching anyone except his two aces— Parnell and Kinder — through the final two weeks. In September they had started ten games and relieved in seven. Turner had told Stengel early in the season to forget complete games. Use Page; husband the strength of the starters, particularly Reynolds. Raschi was a horse and could pitch all day if he had to, but still he was not allowed to get to 300 innings for the season, a number not unusual for those times.

Raschi had on his game face. No one came near him while he dressed. Only Reynolds, Lopat and Turner were permitted in his proximity. Reporter Roger Kahn characterized his performance that day: "Raschi gave nothing away, no runs at all. Bulky, big-shouldered, glowering, black-browed, superb."[23] Going into the eighth inning, the Yankees were ahead, 1–0, and McCarthy lifted Kinder for a pinch-hitter. In the bottom of the inning the Yankees scored four more runs off Red Sox relievers. The score was 5–0 when Boston came alive in the top of the ninth, the last chance. A walk and a single with one out put two on base against Raschi. Bobby Doerr then hit a long fly to center field, which DiMaggio normally would have taken in stride. But DiMaggio, who played 76 games and hit .346 with 14 home runs after returning to the lineup, had been running on empty for the last month. He had lost eighteen pounds while suffering from an infection and fell down chasing Doerr's drive, which went over his head for a triple, scoring two runs and bringing the tying run to the plate. DiMaggio had embarrassed himself, and thinking that one more defensive slip could cost his team the game, called time and took himself out of the lineup. This was high drama, and the 68,055 fans cheered. Mapes moved to center, Bauer to right, and Woodling came into the game in left field. After a fly ball to Mapes, there were two down. Wanting to make sure that Raschi was not tiring, Tommy Henrich jogged over from first base to see if his pitcher needed a break. Berra was coming out to the mound from behind the plate. Raschi took a look at the two teammates about to gather around him and growled, "Just give me the damn ball and get the hell out of here!"[24] Both Berra and Henrich knew at that moment that the game was over. Red Sox catcher Birdie Tebbets lifted the first pitch in foul territory behind first base, and Henrich squeezed it for the final out.

For the second consecutive year, the Boston Red Sox, the overwhelming favorites in the spring, had lost the pennant on the last day of the season. In the final four games, three of which they lost, Ted Williams went 1-for-12,

Johnny Pesky 0-for-15, Birdie Tebbetts 0-for-12, Vern Stephens 2-for-10, and Dominic DiMaggio 3-for-17, thereby confirming their worst image of themselves. One of the games they lost in the final week, just before the fateful two games against the Yankees, was to the last-place Washington Senators, who to that point in the season had won only 49 games. They split a two-game series and beat Boston for their fiftieth victory.

No one was laughing at Casey any more. But, they did ask: how did he do it? This was a rag-tag team of part-time players whose only regulars were a pint-sized shortstop and an awkward-looking catcher who had undergone a professional Pygmalionization at the hands of Bill Dickey. Forty years later, the same question was asked of the team's then-rookie second baseman, Jerry Coleman. He didn't hesitate: "The Big Three made the difference."[25] The pitching staff as a whole led the league in shutouts, strikeouts, and saves. Tommy Byrne, with fifteen wins, was an important part. Page's contribution was enormous. But, the three aces, increasingly being called by teammates and press "the Big Three," contributed more than just statistics, important as they were.

Raschi, after his nineteen wins in 1948, produced the first of his three consecutive twenty-one-win seasons in 1949, going 21–10. He started 37 games, completed 21, with an ERA of 3.34, second to Lopat among the starters. In the eyes of the baseball writers, he was the ace of the staff. In his own mind, he was a part of the whole. The left-hander Lopat was 15–10, started 30 games, completed 14, and had an ERA of 3.27. Reynolds' year was, to outside view, a strange one. With only four complete games in 31 starts, he stuck out among American League starters as an example of what most saw as low stamina. Even his 17–6 record lost its luster because of the 4.00 ERA. No one outside of the team seemed to take note of his four relief appearances, during which he didn't give up a run. To the writers, he was perhaps the least reliable of the four starters, although Tommy Byrne, at 15–7, could always raise the level of excitement and uncertainty with his league-leading 179 bases on balls in 196 innings of pitching.

If there had been a Cy Young Award in major league baseball, it would have gone to Joe Page, the jovial reliever who put together his best career year, one that officially defined the idea of the premiere relief pitcher, the fire-balling closer with a rubber arm. Pitching in 60 games was truly remarkable, unheard of. Saving 27 games was the stuff of legend. Along with his 13 wins, Page was responsible for forty victories. He was also a traveling companion of DiMaggio's and spent time with the celebrity crowd at Toots Shor's restaurant in Manhattan, where the Big Apple's leading sports personalities hung out. Page loved the nightlife, loved basking in the reflected fame of the Yankee Clipper, and the 1949 season gave him his own center stage. DiMaggio didn't mind. He liked Page, and needed someone to be with after working hours.

In the clubhouse, away from the glare of sportswriters, it was a different story. Early in the season, when Berra did not run out an infield pop-up that was dropped, it was Lopat who walked up to him and asked, "Are you sick? Don't you feel well?" Lopat stuck his face in Yogi's until he got the answer that he wanted. After that, Berra ran out everything, and so did everyone else. With hard-working younger players who had the right work ethic, the pitchers used a different technique. When Jerry Coleman or Bobby Brown messed up a ground ball or a double play, Raschi, Reynolds or Lopat would tell them, "Don't worry, I'll get the next one for you." They watched Vic or Allie bear down and strike out the next batter, or Eddie tease a weak ground ball from a frustrated slugger. The feeling of relief for being "taken off the hook" by their pitchers was enormous, and their admiration grew exponentially.

The three veterans knew the sensitivity of their teammates. If Rizzuto were thrown out stealing to end a rally, Raschi would tell him, "Never you mind" and would make a point of shutting down the opposition totally in the next inning, which gave the little shortstop a distinct sense of relief. Phil never forgot what he considered this kind of thoughtfulness from all three of the pitchers. One evening after a road game early in the season, Reynolds went over to Bauer and Woodling and said, "Let's go out for dinner." Allie took all the rookies out for dinner. It became a tradition, handed down through generations of players: don't "ride" the rookies, bring them along, show them what a team should be, make them a part of us. Carmen and Yogi would join the three families for dinner during the season. The catcher grew closer and closer to his pitchers, his mentors, who eventually would watch their pupil grow into the premiere defensive catcher in the league. Discipline was handled, not by the manager or coaches, but by the three pitchers who communicated to the rest of the team what was expected. Eventually, after this season, others would take up the responsibility.[26] They were called by their teammates "the enforcers," and they did their work away from the glare of the writers and the public.

The World Series of 1949

"You never saw a guy pitch better against me. When I came up, he threw peas."—Jackie Robinson on hitting against Allie Reynolds in the 1949 World Series

It was to be a special time for Earlene, Sally and Libby. Earlene and Sally had sent the children home for school. Playing against the Brooklyn Dodgers in a subway series, they would go to all the games, sit together, bundled up against the autumn chill but still wearing white gloves, and thrilled that their husbands would be on center stage. The Raschis and Reynolds moved into a Manhattan hotel for the duration. The Lopats would often join them for dinner, along with Carmen and Yogi and Jim Turner and his wife. It was a wonderful time to be a Yankee and to have close friends sharing in the excitement.

It was also the World Series where Allie Reynolds shocked the baseball establishment, and Casey Stengel began taking on the aura of infallibility that accompanied him as long as he had his three aces up his sleeve.

The National League race had been as spectacular and tense as that in the American League. It also ended on the last day of the season, when the Cardinals lost and the Dodgers won, giving Brooklyn the pennant by one game. For the third consecutive season, St. Louis finished in second place; after that, they began a decline into mediocrity that was to last into the 1960s, when this most southern of franchises finally capitulated to the racial inevitabilities facing them.[27]

This was the first of the great Brooklyn teams, the Dodgers of Hodges, Robinson, Reese, Cox, Furillo, Snider, Campanella, Newcombe, Roe and Erskine. They had extraordinary balance, hitting 152 home runs and stealing 117 bases, to lead the major leagues in both categories. Over the season they outhit the Yankees in every department, had one of baseball's great infields, and a pitching staff anchored by twenty-three-year-old Don Newcombe, 17–8, Rookie of the Year and at 6'4" and 220 pounds the first domineering black power pitcher to make the big leagues. Next to him was the Dodgers' version of Lopat: Preacher Roe, 15–6, a slick, string bean left-handed off-speed pitcher who confounded National League hitters. Behind them came Ralph Branca, Joe Hatten, and a young Carl Erskine, who was 8–1 but showed an extraordinary "twelve-to-six" overhand curveball that dropped off the end of a table. The presence of Robinson, Campanella and Newcombe highlighted the fact that the Yankees were all white. It was to be a World Series where Rickey's muzzle had been taken off Robinson, and he was free to give as well as he got, which he did. His high-pitched voice could be heard in both dugouts, encouraging his teammates and insulting the opponents. This was baseball as he knew it. For many of the ten million viewers— the 1949 World Series sponsored by Gillette, was the first televised to a large national market — it was their inaugural taste of integration.

Stengel astounded the baseball world by announcing that Reynolds would start the World Series against Newcombe in Yankee Stadium. Why would Casey, who had managed so brilliantly during the season, pick someone to open the World Series who clearly had no staying power? Bets were being taken in the writers' section to pick the inning when Page would come into the game. No one thought that Allie would be there at the end. No one, except his two pitching buddies, the pitching coach, and the manager. This was what they had all been waiting for. Turner knew how to get Reynolds up for this big game. He sat with him as he dressed, going over each hitter in the Dodger order. Allie thought of the years of criticism about his stamina, his courage, his race.[28] He closed his eyes and saw the first fastball he would throw to Pee Wee Reese: up and in. Then, the first pitch to Jorgensen, Snider and Robinson. All fastballs, up and in. There were no nerves. He had pitched in a World Series before, won a game in 1947. But, this past 1949 season, when he had come out of 27 of his 31 starts without completing the games, he took a lot of abuse. Turner focused Reynolds' concentration, the heightened intensity that the other players could feel when they were around "the Chief" and he was ready for a big game. Berra came over, looked at his pitcher, looked at the grim determination even on the faces of Raschi and Lopat in this corner of the clubhouse, and knew he was in for a special day. To be sure, he had his own worries. The Dodgers would remember 1947, when they stole everything from Yogi except his glove. They would be running, again. But, this was a different catcher. Dickey had done his job well.

It looked like a potential mismatch. Newcombe had led the league in shutouts with five, was second in strikeouts and third in complete games, posted the most strikeouts per nine innings and allowed the fewest hits over a complete game. Reynolds was not in the top five in any category in his league. But, it was no mismatch. Instead, the first game of the 1949 World Series went down in history as one of the great classic confrontations of all time.

When he took the mound that day, Allie Reynolds was determined to demonstrate his mastery and to put to rest forever any doubts about his character. He had a fastball clocked in the high 90s and knew what to do with it. Rizzuto, at shortstop, was in the best position to view the drama: "We called it busting a fastball. If you ever encountered it on your high school team, you would call it a mixture of fear, nausea and the shakes. Reynolds' fastball was lethal. Campy [Dodger catcher Roy Campanella], a great bear of a man and a great classy guy, used to call it 'Jelly Leg.' Allie took their breath away, weakened their resolve, and if they did hit the ball, he made them feel that they hit it in self-defense."[29] As he worked his way for the first time through the Brooklyn batting order, Reynolds threw his lethal weapon up and in once to each hitter. He hit no one. He terrified all of them.[30]

The next day, Red Smith wrote in the *New York Herald Tribune*: "For eight and a half innings, nothing happened yesterday at Yankee Stadium. Reynolds and Newcombe would not allow anything to happen. There were no fielding plays of great distinction, no hits of special note. Humphrey Bogart and Lauren Bacall sat looking on, as silent as the 66,224 other witnesses. They have put on more spectacular battles themselves in El Morocco." Reynolds had struck out nine, given up two hits; Newcombe had struck out eleven and given up four hits. Their dominance was total. The hitters looked helpless. Most of the Dodgers who struck out went down looking. It was not just that their swing could not catch up to Reynolds' 97-mph fastball; the hitters were frozen at the plate, unable to get the bats off their shoulders. In the top of the ninth he looked as if he could pitch forever.

He didn't have to. On a 2–0 pitch in the bottom of the ninth inning, Tommy Henrich hit a leadoff home run into the right-field stands for a walk-off 1–0 victory. Reynolds had gone the distance in dramatic fashion. The first to throw his arms around Allie was Vic Raschi. He was as happy as if he had pitched himself.

The man who everyone expected to start Game One for New York started Game Two. In an astonishing repeat of the lowest possible score, Vic Raschi lost to Preacher Roe, 1–0. Jackie Robinson scored the game's only run in the second inning after getting on with a double. He moved to third base on an out, and danced down the line, threatening to steal home. Vic was sufficiently distracted to get a pitch up into Gil Hodges' zone, and he singled to score Robinson. He told historian Donald Honig: "Robinson was just about the best base runner I have ever seen. He could get away from a standing position in a flash. He had broken my concentration. I was pitching more to Robinson than I was to Hodges."[31] It cost Vic the game.

Stengel made his only judgment mistake in Game Three, when he decided to start his erratic lefthander, Tommy Byrne. He lasted into the fourth inning, giving up two hits, two walks, and left with the bases loaded. Stengel brought in Page, who gave up three hits the rest of the way in a 4–3 Yankee victory. The next day, Lopat went against Newcombe, who pitched on two days rest and was shelled out in the fifth inning, trailing 6–0. Into the sixth inning Eddie had given up two hits and was cruising. Reynolds and Raschi were sitting together on the bench, cheering on their friend. In the bottom of the sixth, Reese led off with a single; then Billy Cox pinch-hit and got an infield hit. Vic, a little nervous for his pitching comrade, got up to go to the water fountain, and when he came back, Reynolds was gone. Snider hit into a double play, but Robinson singled to knock in Reese. Stengel took his foot off the top step of the dugout, turned around and barked, "Where's the Indian?" Raschi replied, "He's already down there," and at the same moment their eyes went down the left-field line to the visitors' bullpen, where Reynolds was loosening up, fast. Hodges' single was followed by three more, for a total of seven singles and four runs. It was now a 6–4 game, and Stengel called time and waved for Allie. Raschi looked over at the Dodger dugout. They were cheering, but no one looked happy to see the Indian. They had every right to be apprehensive. Spider Jorgensen pinch-hit for the pitcher, and Reynolds struck him out on three fastballs. The rally was over; although no one knew it, so was the game.

Reynolds set down nine Dodgers in a row through the last three innings, striking out four without allowing a hit. It was an overwhelming relief appearance, even more dominating than anything that Page had shown. The Yankees had won Game Four, 6–4. Stengel raced out to the mound to congratulate his pitcher, and as he walked back with the jubilant Yankees, he looked up to the writers' section and sought out the face of veteran New York City baseball reporter Tom Meany, a close drinking friend of Casey's. He threw Meany a big smile and grotesque wink, one that said, "I told ya!" Meany looked down at Casey, smiled and nodded. They both recalled a conversation right after Reynolds had dominated the Dodgers and Newcombe in Game One. Casey, alone in his office with Meany, one of the favored writers he trusted, an hour after the game, was uncharacteristically pensive for a few moments, then turned to Meany. "What would you say if I was to tell you I'm gonna use Reynolds in relief for the rest of the series?" Meany answered, "I would say you are crazy, which I always thought anyway. Reynolds can't take it in the late innings. And Page is the best relief pitcher in baseball."

"What if I have to use Page over a long stretch one day and need some help the next day? Don't write it now, but Reynolds may not start another game in this series. There's nothing wrong with this fella's ticker, no matter what guys write. When I take him out, he's so red hot I can't go near him until he cools off. I know he's a fighter and he can go four or five innings in relief at top speed." From the beginning, Stengel had seen Reynolds' remarkable versatility as that rarest of pitching commodities, the starter who can also, in the clutch, relieve and close out a game.[32]

In Game Five Stengel gave the ball to Raschi with two days rest. Before the game, Vic sat alone in his corner, with Lopat and Reynolds keeping the players and reporters away from him. In these situations, he needed to be alone, to get on his "game face," to focus on the task at hand. In this mood, he was terrifying even to his teammates. "Vic was the gentlest man in the world, but on the day of a big game, you didn't want to be near him," said Berra. Turner visited Stengel in the dingy visiting manager's office in Ebbets Field. "The series ends today," he told Casey. "Vic will give you what you need."

And he did. Raschi pitched into the seventh inning, was relieved by Page, and the Yanks cruised to a 10–6 victory and a 4–1 World Series win, the first for Casey Stengel. Roger Kahn spoke for everyone: "After 1949 no one ever called Stengel a clown."[33] He had managed masterfully, but he knew enough to be grateful. He was completely generous to his team with the reporters. But, when asked if anything stood out in this triumph, he said something, for Stengel, uncharacteristically simple: Look at the pitching.

Stengel had won his first World Series with four pitchers. The most eye-opening performance was from Allie Reynolds, who threw 12⅓ innings, gave up two hits, struck out fourteen, won one complete game and saved another. With the 1949 World Series performance he ended all the negative mythology

Vic Raschi (1950): Teammates knew not to bother the intense pitcher on days he was scheduled to pitch (National Baseball Hall of Fame Library, Cooperstown, N.Y.).

that had evolved over the years. His ERA: 0.00. Raschi, Lopat and Page won one each. Collectively they held the best-hitting team in the National League to an average of .210.

Berra had been humiliated in the 1947 World Series. Reese stole three bases, Robinson two, and the Dodgers had a total of seven, all against Berra.

In 1949, he threw out the first three Dodgers who tested him. In the five-game series, Brooklyn stole one base. In all respects, "the Project" had proved to be a complete success. Berra hit a horrendous .063, 1-for-16 in the series, but his pitchers didn't care. In their eyes, he was a hero.

Even George Weiss, the silent and morose architect of this team, had made a late-season contribution. With a spot open on the roster, on August 22 Weiss purchased the contract of veteran thirty-six-year-old National League slugger Johnny Mize from the New York Giants. Mize was an unusual hitter: he had power numbers yet made excellent contact and struck out rarely. He had a .320 lifetime average and 315 home runs. He was slow afoot, but Stengel needed all the help he could get at first base. In the World Series, Mize had two at-bats, got two hits, scored two runs, and knocked in two, both in critical situations.

At the team celebration, Eddie Lopat, always the restless thinker, sat nursing a very weak Scotch and water, observing the happy festivities and going over some thoughts. Allie, his closest friend on the team and road roommate, came over and sat down next to him. "This is going to be an interesting team," Lopat said. "Yogi will hit, there's no doubt about it. But, look what the blond kid did." Bobby Brown had gone 6-for-12, hitting .500 as a part-time third baseman and spectacular pinch-hitter, with two triples and five runs batted in. "And the rookies, how the hell do you like them!" Woodling, Coleman, and Bauer had hit and fielded flawlessly. And their attitude was perfect: they were tough, demanding of themselves and others, and utterly selfless. What drove Woodling and Bauer to a rage was if they didn't play. Stengel platooned them to perfection, but either one on the bench was a seething inferno, giving the manager dirty looks and jumping on anyone who was not putting out 100 percent or more. "Even if some of the old guys fade, there is enough staying power. This was no fluke." DiMaggio, worn down and exhausted, hit an anemic .111, 2-for-18. Tommy Henrich remained reliable at age 36 but with questionable knees. DiMaggio had become an old man at 34. Rizzuto was still agile at shortstop. "Casey's team may have a future," Allie said.

Perhaps, but few pundits thought so. Even as they celebrated, the 1949 Yankees were still looked upon as a dynasty without a future.

5

The Education of Whitey

"Eddie Lopat was the only pitching coach I ever had."—Whitey Ford

The telephone was ringing on Casey's desk. It was a September afternoon in 1949, and Stengel was still in his shorts, getting ready to dress for the game. He had a lot on his mind, as he tried to figure out how to keep the Red Sox from closing on his wounded Yankees. DiMaggio was sick again, and Berra's broken thumb still hurt. He didn't want to talk to anyone, but he thought it might be Weiss, so he picked up the receiver. "Casey?" As soon as Stengel heard the accent, he knew it wasn't Weiss. Some goddam wise-ass New Yorker, he thought. He didn't know how right he was. "Who the hell is this?" he thundered, ready to hang up. "It's Eddie Ford at Binghamton. Our season is almost over, and I'm ready if you need me. Ask Krichell about me."

For one of the few times in his life, Casey was speechless. He knew about the slick twenty-one-year-old left-hander who some called an Ed Lopat clone. He was a street-smart New York City kid who had put together three impressive minor league seasons: 13–4 at Butler in the Class C Mid-Atlantic League; 16–8 in the Class B Piedmont League with Norfolk; now he was 16–5 at Binghamton in the Eastern League, with an ERA of 1.61. Here he was, calling the manager of the New York Yankees, because he thought he was ready to help the big club! Stengel told him he would see him at spring training.

The Season of 1950

"The Yankee victory in 1949 seemed like the last gasp of an aging warrior."[1]

With a World Series triumph tucked away, the Yankees returned to their homes to get going with off-season jobs. Average major league salaries were $11,000 a year, so most everyone did something extra to pay the bills. Allie and Earlene were back to Oklahoma, where he was already involved in oil drilling. (Eventually, Allie would earn more money in his oil business than he did from his baseball salary.) Vic finished up his undergraduate degree after twelve years, and Eddie barnstormed with other major leaguers around the country.

Over the winter, the families of the three men who sat together in the corner of the clubhouse were in touch with each other. Libby Lopat would call Earlene Reynolds and urge her to come to spring training in St. Petersburg. They would look for houses together; she had already spoken to Sally Raschi up in Conesus, New York, who was looking forward to a little warm weather and to seeing the Reynolds and Lopat children. Earlene loved her home in Oklahoma as much as she enjoyed the company of her friends. She just did not like to leave the familiar surroundings. But, in the end, she would go with Allie, and the friends would be united.

When the pitchers and catchers report in early February, the Lopats, Reynolds, and Raschis were together again in a cozy neighborhood a few minutes drive from the Yankee spring training site. Yogi and Carmen, now married a year, joined them with their first baby. Berra had spent the winter as a greeter in Ruggeri's Restaurant in St. Louis, taking advantage of his newly found celebrity status to make a few extra bucks in the off-season. When they greeted Jim Turner at the first pitchers' session, before the regular position players were scheduled to show up, no one minded that once again very few of the baseball writers were picking the Yankees to repeat. It was the awesome Boston Red Sox offensive power and the extraordinary pitching staff and balanced attack of the Cleveland Indians that grabbed the headlines. The Yankees, who didn't have a .300 hitter in the regular lineup the year before, were even picked by some to finish fourth, behind a resurging Detroit Tigers team that featured a deep starting rotation of Art Houtteman, Fred Hutchinson, Hal Newhouser, Virgil Trucks and Dizzy Trout and a hitting attack led by the youthful talent of George Kell, Vic Wertz, Hoot Evers and Johnny Groth.

They were loosening up on that first day in the Florida sun, stretching and lobbing baseballs back and forth, talking about off-season activities: Lopat's barnstorming with Bob Feller's black and white all-stars; Reynolds' success in getting started in the oil business; Raschi's completion of his college degree. Vic wasn't in camp, yet. He was one of seven holdouts who had sent back unsigned contracts to Weiss. Besides Vic, Berra, Byrne, Billy Johnson, Bobby Brown, Johnny Lindell and recently acquired outfielder Dick Wakefield were aggravating Weiss, who thought that players had no right to argue about salary. They certainly had no alternative other than to sign. The reserve clause in baseball, which gave a team total control over the players' employment, guaranteed that every player either eventually signed or sat out the season. Within a week, everyone was in camp, and Vic had gotten what he thought he was worth. Turner, who had been nearby with a group of rookie pitchers, walked over to his two aces, hesitated for a moment, and went up to Lopat. "Ed, do you see that blond kid, the little lefthander? His name is Eddie Ford, from New York City. He's sneaky fast, has two curves that he can throw for strikes at any time, and can change speeds. He can help us. Will you work with him?"

The next morning, Ford was shagging fly balls in the outfield, and Lopat walked up to him. After a few minutes conversation, Lopat thought that he was looking into a mirror that reflected himself ten years earlier: a street-wise Irish kid from the east side of Manhattan who thought he knew everything, brought up in the same kind of lower-income ethnic neighborhoods. They were both old and young enough to know the hardships of the Depression years. The Fords had moved to Astoria, where Eddie's father was a bartender. His mother worked in an A&P in Manhattan. Baseball was all he had cared about. When Ford got to high school, he commuted to Manhattan's School of Aviation Trades because it had a baseball team. Like Lopat, he thought of himself as a good hitter and started out as yet another undersized first baseman until a 1946 tryout at Yankee Stadium, when eagle-eyed scout Paul Krichell, who could recognize a live arm when he saw one, suggested that he try pitching. Ford had pitched in high school when he wasn't playing first, and after graduation became a sandlot pitching sensation in local New York City leagues. He was 5'8" tall, weighed 150 pounds. But, Krichell, who had discovered the diminutive Phil Rizzuto when Stengel with the Dodgers and Bill Terry with the Giants had laughed the pint-sized shortstop off the field, had an instinct that took little note of stature. He signed the eighteen-year-old Ford, who walked with a swagger, for a $7,000 bonus. The Dodgers and Giants, although they were interested, thought Krichell had lost his senses.

So, this was Eddie Lopat's pupil. The teacher could remember the early years in the minors, where he was begging for help but was ignored, and the enormous impact that Ted Lyons had in finally making him a serious pitcher. But, one look at the cocky blond who had enjoyed nothing but success in his three minor league years was all that Lopat needed to realize that he didn't have a willing pupil on his hands. After a couple of sessions, he went back to Turner and told him, "Take him back. He's too much for me."[2] But, after a while, Lopat saw that the arrogance was nothing more than the kid's terror at being in a big league camp. He broke through, and from then on, Ford became the acolyte that Turner had hoped for. Lopat would teach and Ford would learn. "You're going to see many of the same hitters year after year," Lopat preached. "Hitters change and you have to learn to change with them. You might get a guy out with a high fastball one year, but the next year he may start hitting that pitch and you have to switch on him. Move the ball around. High. Low. Inside. Outside. You have to get a book on these hitters. Who's looking for the curveball all the time? Who's a first-ball hitter?"[3]

Lopat poured his years of wisdom into this kid pitcher whose manager

Whitey Ford (1950): The kid from Astoria. Smart enough to learn (National Baseball Hall of Fame Library, Cooperstown, N.Y.).

the year before at Binghamton, Lefty Gomez, had called "Whitey." Within two weeks of spring training, Ford and Lopat were inseparable. Turner worked on Ford's mechanics; Lopat worked on his *head*: how to think like a pitcher, especially a crafty, undersized left-hander who needed every trick of his trade to outsmart the man with the bat in his hand.

By the end of spring training, the teacher was both pleased and worried. When it came to learning his trade, Whitey Ford had shown himself to be a very intelligent, willing and quick-witted student, mature beyond his years. Lopat had told Vic and Allie, "This kid will be back and will help us make money." Turner already knew it.

But, Whitey was not like the three older pitchers, who had settled down into a kind of hard-nosed seriousness in learning their craft and in dedicating themselves to it. Not a small part of this stemmed from their stable marriages and responsibilities as parents. The three of them became adults very quickly in life, and that discipline carried over into their profession. They had found spouses who shared these values. Ford, on the other hand, was not yet twenty-two years old, had been brought up in a tavern, knew how to drink and have a good time. In this his first major league spring training camp, he found another twenty-one-year-old rookie, a fast-talking infielder from Berkeley, California, who reminded him of some of the tough kids he had grown up with around Precious Blood Catholic Church in Astoria. He had a big nose, quick fists, and a willingness to use them. They had a couple of beers together, and became friends for life. His name was Billy Martin.

Martin was a street-fighting brawler, charming, quick-witted, with an explosive temper and enough natural ability to battle his way out of the ghetto. His nervy aggressiveness even frightened his new buddy. Martin would ask veteran boozer and team celebrity Joe Page to go out for a drink with them. Page, always accommodating, would bend a few with the youngsters. He liked the hero-worship and didn't mind treating them to a beer or a boilermaker (a beer with a shot of whiskey). Martin saw how Page hung around DiMaggio and terrified Whitey when he walked up to the Yankee Clipper and introduced himself, something no rookie in his right mind would have dared. But, DiMaggio, generally aloof and suspicious, took a liking to the tough kid from California and let him into his inner circle.

Casey kept an eye on these two sharp youngsters and knew that they would be around for a long time. He didn't need to keep Martin right now, but he had taken an instant liking to the rookie with the big mouth ever since he had him at Oakland in 1948 and left him on the roster when camp broke. In fact, with Coleman hurt, Martin started on Opening Day and in an enormous Yankee uprising late in the game up in Fenway Park, he singled and doubled in the *same inning*, setting a record for a rookie debut. But, Rizzuto and Coleman had proven to be a superb double play combination, and Stengel had infielder Snuffy Stirnweiss as backup. On May 15, Stengel yielded to Weiss and sent Martin down to Kansas City. He packed, then before leaving the stadium, Martin bolted into Weiss' office for a farewell. "I'll make you pay for this! I'll get even!" he exploded at the Yankee general manager, and then slammed the door behind him. One wonders if Weiss, not accustomed to such outbursts from underlings, tied a knot in his memory to remind himself some years later that he would take care of Billy Martin in his own way. As for Ford, a little more seasoning with the top Triple-A minor league team at Kansas City in the American Association was all he needed. He could be spared for the time being. The starting pitching, under Jim Turner's tutelage, let Stengel sleep at night. Nonetheless, by the end of June, both Martin and Ford were back with the Yankees.

The three veteran pitchers had turned Berra into a solid defensive catcher and strategist during the previous campaign. The manager had to accept their very special role, all worked out with Turner and Dickey. At the beginning of the 1949 season, Stengel knew that Reynolds, Raschi and Lopat would not allow Berra to call the pitches. They had worked out a system of signs that informed Yogi of what to expect. They were in charge, and they didn't even allow Casey to intrude. Stengel one time early in the year yelled at his catcher to look over to the dugout where he was signaling what pitch to throw. As soon as Allie saw what was happening, he shouted at Berra from the mound, "Yogi, if you look toward the dugout, I'll cross you up! Keep your damn eyes on me!" But, Stengel was yelling at Yogi to look over, and the poor catcher was getting desperate. In the dugout, Lopat and Raschi were laughing into their gloves. Finally, Jim Turner walked over to Casey, who by this time was waving dollar bills at Berra, indicating the fine that he would pay if he didn't pay attention to his manager! Turner told Casey to lay off, to let the three of them work it out with Yogi if you want the catcher you hope to have for the next ten years. Stengel turned to look at Bill Dickey, sitting on the bench. The catching coach gave a short, affirmative nod of his head; Casey put the money back in his pocket and sat down. Reynolds, Raschi and Lopat were left in charge of the education of their catcher.

This was a mighty concession, for the Casey Stengel of 1950 was not the same manager who meekly told his team a year earlier at spring training that he was the new boy on the block and would defer to the veterans. When he showed up at spring training after winning his first World Series, he had been named Manager of the Year by those same skeptics who had mocked him a year ago, and now he was ready to take charge. The old McCarthy men did not like what they saw now: an arrogant, vain showman who publicly criticized his players and thought he knew everything.[4]

Not everyone shared this almost palpable hostility, which veterans like

Rizzuto and DiMaggio now carried sullenly as chips on their shoulders. They were professionals, gave 100 percent, but they did not like their manager. Tommy Henrich, another of the old-timers, had developed a deep and enthusiastic admiration for Stengel's knowledge of the game and strategic decision-making. For the younger players who had watched the bow-legged magician the year before, there was no doubt about Casey's role: he was their leader. Berra worshipped him, and Stengel reciprocated by announcing to all who would listen that "Mr. Berra is my assistant manager." The platooned outfield couple of Hank Bauer and Gene Woodling were hard-nosed and competitive. They were friends, but each wanted to play regularly. From time to time, one of them would shoot off his mouth at Stengel, who would laugh to himself, because he loved their competitive and combative attitude. Casey also knew that his three veteran pitchers belonged body and soul to Jim Turner and left them alone. He did not even sit in on the pre-game strategy meetings with Turner and his pitchers. In his endless conversations with the press, Stengel only had words of praise for his Big Three. They never felt his barbs. They reciprocated by giving him, during their time with the New York Yankees, their total loyalty and admiration. There was never a word of criticism spoken by Allie, Vic or Eddie about their manager. For his part, Stengel knew what he could expect from the three of them — and what he owed them.

As camp broke for the trip north in 1950, Stengel again had a team with problems. He still had no first baseman. Mize and Henrich, both thirty-seven, were increasingly immobile around the bag. Mize's shoulder was still sore, and he would have to go to Kansas City to work into shape. There was a twenty-eight-year-old rookie, Joe Collins, who could play both outfield and first base and might help. Casey was always looking for ballplayers who could play multiple positions. Charlie Keller, one of the links to the McCarthy era and the great teams of the 1930s and early 1940s, was gone, victim of a herniated disc in his back. Frank "Spec" Shea, the great rookie right-hander from the 1947 world champions, continued to have sore arm miseries. Joe Page hadn't shown anything in spring training. Would he straighten out once the games meant something? He had a tendency to alternate great years with mediocre years. He was great in 1947 and 1949. He was awful in 1948. What could Stengel expect in 1950? His golden boy hitter, Bobby Brown, never even made it to spring training because of his medical studies. Worst of all, DiMaggio looked old. At thirty-five, years of chain smoking and coffee drinking had taken their toll. He had ulcers, did not sleep, and had lost a significant amount of his confidence: "I don't go up to the plate feeling that I can hit any pitcher who ever lived." The writers, on the eve of Opening Day, had made their choice: Boston, Cleveland or Detroit.

There was a routine in place when the team got back to New York City.

The single men and a few of the married couples took apartments in hotels that the Yankees preferred: the Grand Concourse, the Edison or the Biltmore. The Yankee wives as a group formed an unusual bond, a remarkable female camaraderie, very much like the team itself; but the three best friends among all the Yankee wives were Earlene Reynolds, Sally Raschi, and Libby Lopat. They had found their comfortable enclave in nearby New Jersey and moved from the togetherness of spring training to the neighborhood familiarity of the regular season. The Lopats had bought; the Reynolds and Raschis were renting just a few blocks away. Opening Day found them coming to the stadium together, sitting together, watching Vic start the season. The year before it had been Eddie. There never was a thought of jealousy on who would have the Opening Day assignment. The wives projected the same sense of selflessness that marked the relationship between the three pitchers.

During the 1949 season the Yankees were out of first place for a total of four days. By the end of the first month of the 1950 campaign, they had only been in first place for twenty-four hours. For most of the month they chased Detroit, Cleveland and Boston, making the sportswriters appear visionary in their predictions. Stengel kept Joe Collins with the team and sent Mize down to Kansas City in May to get his shoulder in shape. Mize's bat was sorely missed. Henrich tried heroically, but his knees and back were beyond treatment. He played sparingly and retired before the season was over. DiMaggio got off to an awful start and was hitting near .200, although knocking in runs. At one point early in the season Stengel, now flexing his authority, even moved DiMaggio out of the cleanup slot and made him hit a degrading fifth, behind Berra. The humiliation reached its peak when Stengel put the now weak-armed Yankee Clipper at first base for one game, but DiMaggio refused to go back there. It would be center field, or nowhere. Now the discord between the two came out into the open: the easily insulted DiMaggio would not even talk to Stengel and sometimes would sit in the bullpen rather than share a bench with his manager.

Weiss, always supporting Stengel, decided it was time to clean house of some of McCarthy's loyalists. In May, veteran outfielder Johnny Lindell was sold to the St. Louis Cardinals, thereby easing the job of Weiss' private detectives. In June former regular second baseman George Stirnweiss went to the Browns; and as if to tell the world that Yogi had officially come of age, Gus Niarhos was sold to the Chicago White Sox. Now, there clearly was no other starting catcher but Berra, who went on to catch 148 games that season.

Of all the concerns at the beginning of the 1950 season, the greatest was the ineffectiveness of Joe Page. He was getting shelled in relief, blowing save opportunities one after another. Reynolds, who showed that he could go the distance anytime it was necessary in the Game One World Series victory in

1949, could no longer rely on Page to close out wins for him and was increasingly pitching into the late innings as well as completing games, although a lack of hit support cost him several wins. The journalists no longer wrote about a lack of stamina or staying power. Still, Earlene Reynolds, herself a great athlete who understood the importance of pacing, wanted to make certain that Allie and Jim Turner knew how many pitches her husband was throwing, and she began keeping a very careful pitch count at every game he started.[5] The husband and the pitching coach eagerly used her stats. Without an effective Joe Page, the starting pitchers— Raschi, Reynolds, Lopat and Byrne — now had a greater burden on their shoulders and responded. They were 36–19 as the season moved toward the halfway mark.

The biggest surprise of all was Rizzuto, who was tearing up the league and fielding brilliantly. After an early season slump, he picked up, out of desperation, a thirty-six-inch bat used by Johnny Mize. It looked bigger than Phil, even choking up three inches, when he walked up to the plate for the first time, but he started lining hits all over the field, and for the rest of the season he never parted from Mize's thick-handled war club. He had not hit .300 since his rookie year, and here he was, not only hitting near .350, but also making plays that no one expected from a thirty-two-year-old shortstop who no longer had a shortstop's arm. His range was great, but his instincts and ability to read the pitcher's selection and location gave him a one-step jump on groundballs. His anticipation and quick release — the ball seemed to leave his hands at the instant it arrived — astonished his teammates. Rizzuto knew the limitations of his throwing arm from deep shortstop. He perfected a play with Billy Johnson, who had a cannon up his right sleeve. If Phil had to race into the hole to backhand a ball hit wide of third, he would flip the ball to Johnson, who would make the rifle shot to first in time to get the startled runner. Vic Raschi, who had little patience with post-game questions by reporters, called a few over after one particular win and volunteered, "My best pitch is anything the batter grounds, lines or pops in the direction of Rizzuto."[6]

Detroit was hot from Opening Day and stayed in first place once they got there. The pitching and Rizzuto kept the Yankees close, with Cleveland and the always expectant Red Sox staying in contention. Boston management was falling apart again. Joe McCarthy's drinking got out of control, and he quit as manager in late June. Third-base coach Steve O'Neill took over, and the Red Sox took off, going 56–25 for the rest of the season and posting individual statistics that were staggering. At the end of the season the Red Sox would post a *team* batting average of .302, twenty points higher than the Yankees, and led the league in every offensive category, except home runs, where they were second. Parnell, Kinder, Dobson and sophomore Chuck Stobbs gave them a solid pitching rotation. Yet something was missing, an ingredient that could be found in great abundance in the Yankee clubhouse.

When the All-Star game selections were made at mid-year, Allie and Vic were furious. Stengel, as manager of the World Series victor from the previous year, selected the pitching staff for 1950. He included Tommy Byrne, but left Lopat off the roster. They were happy for Byrne, but did not like the slight to their other teammate. Both Reynolds and Raschi had made the 1949 All-Star team and now had been selected again. They knew that fastball pitchers got much of the glory, and they did not want to have the one teammate overlooked who, both agreed, had helped them more than anyone understand the art of pitching.[7]

Eddie Lopat was already becoming a legend among power hitters. Ted Williams was not the only one to sing frustrated praises of the chunky left-hander. American League veteran Dave Philley expressed the feelings of the many hitters who could not figure out the mysteries of the Junkman. "He didn't throw hard enough to mash your finger, but you go back to the bench talking to yourself."[8] Reynolds and Raschi wanted respect for their friend.

A few years later, when Hank Bauer made his first All-Star team, he was fuming because Gene Woodling had not been chosen, as well. For their entire careers with the Yankees, their names were most often used in tandem; and in their personal relationship, they demonstrated the same selflessness that they had seen in the three pitchers, who had already selected these two for a special role.[9] Born within two weeks of each other, Woodling and Bauer had been anointed as the next generation of enforcers, those teammates who by temperament could be counted on to keep the pressure on everyone to play at peak performance. They described themselves as "red asses," baseball players who knew only one way to play the game and were not afraid to stick a chin in the face of a moody teammate who was thinking more of himself than the team. It took a certain type. It was neither Rizzuto nor Berra, both of whom possessed genial and sunny dispositions. It was not the moody DiMaggio, who selected his friends carefully and preferred privacy. Bobby Brown had the fire, but it burned with an intellectual's flame. Bauer and Woodling: they would "do."

On the long train rides during road trips, Allie, Vic and Eddie the year before had invited Bauer and Woodling into their hearts card game, which they set with the smallest stakes, yet played with the same intensity that they brought to the ballgame. Turner would stand nearby, laughing while he watched the three pitchers and the rookie outfielders, both older beyond their years, furiously battling over a five-cent pot. Reynolds had told him about Gene Woodling, whom he had known since their days together at Wilkes-Barre, and again it was family as well as attitude that drew them together. In that minor league life, Betty Woodling would babysit for the Reynolds during a rare night out. The pitching coach saw what was happening. Woodling and Bauer only wanted to play to win, whether it was a five-cent card game or a ballgame. They had the same fire burning that Turner had seen in his three pitchers. The two outfielders brought a kind of disciplined, yet raging intensity that Stengel loved and exploited when he platooned them. Eventually, he would get them both into the lineup.

The pitchers were expanding the nucleus. The energy generated would be critical for a team that fundamentally was made up of parts that had to move together. This was the special character that made the Yankees greater than these individual parts. But what made the enterprise successful was the leadership provided by the three pitchers.

Once Detroit took over first place in May, they gave no indication that they would relinquish their hold. The starting pitchers matched the Yankees win for win and were 38–18 at mid-season. Their bats were much more potent. Kell, Evers, Groth and Wertz were pounding the ball. Cleveland also had the talent to run away with the pennant. The pitching of Feller, Wynn, Garcia and Lemon certainly seemed to the writers the strongest in the league. (Three were destined for the Hall of Fame.) Rookie Al Rosen was leading the league in home runs and hitting over .300. Larry Doby was off to his best start ever, hitting over .350, with power. With Luke Easter and Ray Boone hitting for average and driving in runs, the Indians looked unstoppable. The Yankees went 15–17 in June and were falling back in the race. Tommy Byrne, the erratic left-hander, stopped winning. They needed a shot in the arm.

On June 25, Communist North Korean forces crossed the Demilitarized Zone separating the two Koreas, and the United States was again at war, although it was officially called "a police action." Two days later, the call went out to Kansas City. Whitey Ford was to report to the Yankees. He was destined to have his moment in the Bronx sun before being called up to active duty. Before the war was over, Ford, Jerry Coleman, Billy Martin, Bobby Brown, Detroit Tiger ace Art Houtteman, Ted Williams and dozens of major leaguers would be out of baseball for one or two years. Many saw combat, and every player held his breath, wondering if the game would go on. The Yankee organization, to show its patriotism, stopped hoisting a red flag to designate a home game loss (blue was for victories) and shifted to white.[10]

With Ford, Mize and Martin now back, Stengel gradually began taking matters under control. Martin didn't play much, but kept the bench alive with his over-the-top aggressiveness. Jerry Coleman, in his second year, played 153 games at second base and was just as acrobatic as he had been in his rookie year. He and Rizzuto gave the Yankees the best up-the-middle defense of any infield in the American League, and with a matured Berra behind the plate,

Stengel had his strength where he wanted it. Only in center field did Stengel feel inadequate. DiMaggio had slowed, both in the field and at bat. In the heat of the late July doldrums, Stengel took the unprecedented step of benching the Yankee icon. "He needs a rest. We'll need him down the stretch." DiMaggio fumed, and sat. With Mize now hitting in the cleanup spot, the Yankee bats came alive. Mize went on a rampage that resulted in 25 home runs with 72 RBIs resulting from just 76 hits in a total of 72 games. DiMaggio, out of the lineup and limelight, sat and fretted. He also rested and recharged his batteries.

On August 13, Reynolds went the distance against the Athletics to even his record at 10–10, leaving the Yankees three games behind Detroit. Mize was hitting fourth; Woodling and Bauer were both in the lineup. Ironically, Allie had been pitching better than at any other time during the past three years. This was his tenth complete game of the season, two less than Vic and one behind Eddie, who were winning with their usual consistency. Raschi was again the steadiest, the meal ticket, starting with a relentless regularity; he never missed a turn in the rotation in spite of shoulder miseries. Lopat was not far behind in complete games and wins. They lost rarely, and with Page ineffective, they pitched deeper into the games than ever before. Reynolds was also working double duty. In mid-season, Weiss picked up veteran Tom Ferrick from St. Louis, who appeared in thirty games for the Yankees, saving nine and eventually going 8–4 for the year. But, in tight situations against the contenders, Casey knew he could turn to his Chief, and he didn't have to ask him. Reynolds relieved six times during the season, recorded two saves and rarely was scored on. Tommy Byrne was winning in the first half of the season, but he still gave owner Dan Topping ulcers on his way to another league-leading 160 bases on balls.

However, the biggest lift came from Eddie Lopat's tow-haired pupil from the streets of New York. Whitey Ford was 6–3 at Kansas City and was ready for the call when it came. But, there was concern in the front office. Stengel wanted Billy Martin back for the pennant race, and got his way. Weiss did not like the chemistry between Martin and Ford and told Stengel. Casey loved Martin's big mouth and didn't mind his occasional carousing. He reminded the manager of his own wild oats, and Stengel would tolerate some fitful bad behavior from Martin. Besides, Martin hustled, fought like a tiger, and the veterans did not seem to mind him. Martin and Ford were both kids, Stengel reasoned, and they would be scared enough to stay out of trouble. But, one day Casey saw Ford leaving the stadium with Joe Page, and that really worried him.

Weiss was now concerned; Stengel had to make certain that the prized rookie pitcher did not get off on the wrong foot. At first, they thought that rooming with Yogi would be a good idea. Although Yogi was married and a father, they were almost the same age, and anyone could tell that they hit it off immediately. But, on one of the early road trips before an afternoon game in Chicago, Berra, always an early riser, got up at 6:00 A.M. and was soon ready for breakfast. Ford, who was pitching that afternoon, told his roommate to let him sleep and to wake him before he left for Comiskey Park. Ford was still in bed when the phone rang at noon and Turner asked him where the hell he was. The game was a 1:15 start! The rookie leapt from his bed, dressed, got a cab, and arrived at the ballpark fifteen minutes before game time. While he warmed up, Whitey could feel the eyes of Lopat, Raschi, Reynolds, Woodling and Bauer burning into him. Fortunately, he went the distance and won the game. When he asked Berra, "Why didn't you wake me up before you left?" his roommate answered, "I forgot."

As much as Berra and Ford got along, this was not a good rooming situation. Something had to be done. Ford and Martin were already being scouted by baseball "Annies," young girls who hung around the players looking for a good time. The two rookies were sure to reciprocate. Casey asked Jim Turner for a suggestion. "He's a cocky kid who thinks he knows everything, but he's scared to death of the Chief. Let Reynolds do it." Turner asked Reynolds to room with Ford on the road. He knew that Lopat was working on the kid's pitching smarts; now it was time to terrify him a little. This would also keep Ford away from rooming on the road with Martin, or worse yet, Page. "Give him some class," Turner said.[11] Even Martin, who had little respect for his elders, buckled down. Ford told writer Joe Durso, "We were afraid of the older guys. You know, Vic Raschi or Eddie Lopat or Allie Reynolds would say something, and we'd listen."[12] Lopat treated Whitey like a long-lost younger brother; Allie was the formidable father figure. "He was a chief in more ways than one. He was the boss. Everybody looked up to Reynolds."[13] As Lopat was teaching the rookie the tools of his trade and giving him the vast accumulation of knowledge gathered over the years, Reynolds taught him what respect meant, how to dress when going to a hotel dining room. For all his street smarts, Ford didn't even own a tie when he came up to the Yankees and borrowed one from Allie.

They all knew, however, that they had something special, maybe the perfect fourth man in the rotation. He was young, looked even younger, so this was a new experience for the three friends, whose age and temperaments helped them share so much. They had succeeded with Berra, and Whitey Ford could prove just as valuable. Turner was placed in charge of his game appearances, and they would be managed carefully. A few days after his late–June call-up, Ford went into a game in Boston to relieve. He got shelled. Lopat and Turner, on the bench, looked at each other: Turner puzzled, Lopat with a grim, sardonic smile. He had spotted it immediately. They waited until the next morning to take the somewhat chastened rookie over to the Fenway visitors' bullpen.

Eddie told him to throw from the stretch position with men on base. Ford threw alternative fastballs and curves. Then Lopat told him.

When Ford was throwing his fastball, he would lay the inside of his wrist flat against his stomach. When he threw his curveball, the *side* of his wrist was against his stomach. Any first base coach could pick up what Ford was telegraphing. Whitey stayed in the bullpen until Lopat was satisfied the problem had been corrected. He made his first start a week later in New York against the last-place Philadelphia Athletics, and with every living relative and friend from Astoria looking on, pitched creditably, but was not involved in the final decision. Next, he faced the fifth-place Washington Senators, another under-.500 club, with no decision again. Finally, on July 17 Ford got his first major league win, 4–3, over the hapless Chicago White Sox, who were already thirty games out of first place. Ferrick relieved him in the eighth inning with the bases loaded and two out to preserve the win. Turner was bringing his rookie along slowly, against second-division teams. By mid–September Ford was 6–0, all against the bottom teams in the league.

He was learning his trade from two of the smartest teachers in baseball. Turner worked with Ford routinely between starts on his mechanics. Before each game, the veteran Lopat and the rookie Ford sat down and went over each hitter, each sequence of pitches, every detail of the hitters' strengths and weaknesses. During the game, with Whitey working the hitters with the deliberation and cunning taught him by Lopat, he still would occasionally seek advice. He and Eddie worked out a system of communication from mound to bench. Ford could ask, in silence, "Is this the right pitch sequence for this guy?" With a series of signs, Lopat would answer him. It was a special kind of conversation.

In spite of the last-day Armageddon of the Red Sox in the previous two seasons, two weeks into September both Las Vegas and Broadway bookmakers established Boston, sitting in third place, as the 7–5 choice to take the American League flag.[14] All of the statistical leaders were with Boston, Detroit or Cleveland: Walt Dropo, Vern Stephens, Vic Wertz and Al Rosen in home runs and RBIs, and Billy Goodman, George Kell, Hoot Evers, and Dominic DiMaggio had the top batting averages.

Meanwhile, the Yankees had closed on the Tigers and came into Briggs Stadium on September 14 for a three-game series, now a half-game behind Detroit. The final September charge came when DiMaggio returned to the lineup at the beginning of the month and exploded offensively. The bench rest had paid off. For the rest of the season he hit at a near .400 pace, smashing home runs and batting in a torrent of runs, taking out his anger at Stengel on the opposition. It worked for DiMaggio just as it did for Woodling and Bauer. The angrier they got, the better they played. The Yankees and Detroit split the first two games, with Raschi beating Newhouser in the opener. Byrne, ineffective and wild even for him, started the second game, was shelled. Stengel brought in Reynolds, who had gotten hot since getting his tenth victory in mid–August, but had been starting and relieving to the point where he was getting arm weary. In a rare letdown, Allie took the loss in relief. This was the rubber game: the winning team had first place and the momentum for the final two weeks of the season. Turner, who had been watching Ford like a hawk during his starts against weak teams as he built his winning streak, asked Lopat what he thought. Eddie, who the day before had beaten Cleveland for the *sixth* time in 1950, and was almost a second pitching coach as well as a starter, had no doubts. "He's ready. He has the guts of a burglar." Turner then told Stengel: we start Ford in the third game against Detroit. Casey, as always trusting his pitching coach, went along.

Some 56,548 screaming Tiger fans stuffed themselves into Briggs Stadium to see their beloved Tigers win this critical third game of the series; they had a rookie pitcher going against them who had not yet faced a contending team, and veteran Dizzy Trout was on the mound for the home team. But Turner and Lopat knew what they had going for them, and Whitey did not disappoint. DiMaggio, still on a raging streak, put the Yankees in front 1–0 with a towering home run in the sixth inning. Ford made the slimmest of leads hold up until the eighth, when Wertz and Kell hit back-to-back leadoff doubles to tie the score. This looked like the end for Ford. With Joe Page virtually useless by this time, Reynolds had run down to the bullpen in the seventh inning and was heating up. There was a runner on second, nobody out, the crowd was on its feet screaming for blood, and Stengel called "Time!" to talk to his twenty-one-year-old rookie. Ford looked past his manager into the dugout and saw Lopat and Raschi on the top step. He could read in their eyes: you can do it. Casey came to the mound, but did not take the ball away from his pitcher. He asked Ford, "Are you tired?" and Whitey said no. Stengel looked hard into the gray eyes of his pitcher, then turned around and walked back to the dugout. The next three batters hit ground balls to Rizzuto at shortstop, and the danger was over. In the top of the ninth inning, with the score still tied at 1–1 and Ford leading off, everyone in the ballpark expected Mize would hit for him. Instead, Casey told him to take a bat and get to the plate. Ford walked, and the Yankees exploded for seven runs. With Ford going the distance, the Yankees won the critical third game, 8–1, and took over first place. They never relinquished it.

This was the moment that the three veteran pitchers knew they had a fourth in their group. As good a contributor as Tommy Byrne was over these two years, he was too wild, casual and unfocused when he took the ball. He would chat with the hitters, distract his infielders. Ford, on the other hand, was so much like Lopat. He threw harder, but it was his cunning on the mound that made him, as a rookie, as cool as a veteran. He was always around the plate, hitting the corners, getting strikes on swings when the ball was out of the strike zone. Lopat's hours of teaching paid off. What they didn't know was it would be another two years, after his army service, before the kid pitcher would join their ranks again, and then only for the final year of their extraordinary time together.

Detroit did not crumble. They kept the blistering pace set now by a New York team whose bats had come alive. With ten games left in the season, the Yankees and Tigers were tied for first place; the Red Sox were moving fast, having won twenty-three out of twenty-eight games. They were two games back of the leaders, with two crucial series about to take place. The Red Sox came into Yankee Stadium on September 23 for games on Saturday and Sunday. Detroit had to face the faltering but still dangerous Cleveland Indians in a three-game set. Before 63,998 fans, it was the Red Sox ace Mel Parnell against Eddie Lopat. DiMaggio, hitting in his favorite clean-up spot, homered in the first, Mize drove in two, and Jerry Coleman tripled in the ninth with the bases loaded. Lopat completely closed down the Red Sox hitting machine with an 8–0 shutout, on a five-hitter. Ted Williams got one harmless single. The next day, with Raschi on the mound, the Yankees pounded Red Sox pitching for sixth runs before the fifth inning and went on to a 9–5 win to sweep the Red Sox, with Vic getting his 21st victory for a second consecutive year. Meanwhile, Detroit lost all three games to Cleveland. With eight games left in the season, the Yankees now had a 2½ game lead.

Ford and the Yankees kept on winning. He was 9–0 until the last week of the season, when he lost his only game against the lowly Philadelphia A's, in relief of Lopat, who was looking for his 19th win. Stengel and Turner learned something that day: Ford would not be an Allie Reynolds, who could start and relieve. Without Page available and with Reynolds showing signs of occasional weariness, they thought that perhaps Ford could, in between starts, pick up the slack. But Whitey was inconsistent as a reliever. He needed the pacing of a full game to get his rhythm. The Athletics tied the game in the seventh and won it in the ninth, when Ford surrendered a home run.

For the third consecutive year, the American League pennant race would go down to the last week. DiMaggio, rejuvenated and still boiling at the public insult he suffered, had now hit in nineteen straight games and for the final six weeks whacked away at a .370 pace. Rizzuto, with the big Mize bat, had nearly 200 hits, and Berra had already more than 120 RBIs. Reynolds, Raschi and Lopat, getting a second wind and an extra day's rest with Ford now in the rotation, relentlessly went after the contending teams and beat them into submission. Finally, Detroit and Boston folded. With two days left in the season, the Yankees clinched a tie when they beat Philadelphia in a game where Rizzuto got four hits and won it with a single in the tenth inning. As if to let everyone know that the world was in its proper order, Reynolds won in relief of his friend Vic Raschi, pitching three shutout innings. When Detroit lost, the Yankees, for the second year in a row, were the unexpected American League champions.

They closed out the season with two meaningless games against the vaunted Boston Red Sox. On the last day, the Red Sox pummeled two rookie New York pitchers in a 7–3 win. The headline in *The New York Times* about this meaningless game was "Williams Stars."[15]

There had been some genuine offensive heroics on this team. The diminutive Rizzuto, who would be named the league's Most Valuable Player, had 200 hits while batting .324. Mize and DiMaggio put together a second-half of the season that carried the offense. DiMaggio even got his average up to .301, and his 32 home runs passed Vern Stephens for third most in the league. Berra had his first 100+ RBI year, knocking in 124 and hitting 28 home runs to go with his gaudy .322 batting average. But, what really had Casey shaking his head were his catcher's *twelve* strikeouts in 597 at-bats, a truly phenomenal demonstration of contact hitting. Still, the Red Sox, Tigers, and Indians had more impressive numbers up and down their batting order.

Stengel and Turner really knew what made the difference. They understood why each of the contenders faded away toward the end of the season: three Yankee pitchers had systematically crushed them.

Again, Vic Raschi was the stalwart, with a 21–8 record and a league-leading .724 win-loss percentage. He was third in strikeouts with 155. Eddie Lopat finished 18–8, fourth in league ERA with 3.47 and single-handedly eliminated Cleveland from contention. Allie Reynolds, doing double duty as a starter and reliever, was 16–12, second in the league in strikeouts with 160; the three of them defeated the contending teams a total of thirty-three times. Joe Page's ERA had ballooned to 5.07; he was through as a Yankee, released at the end of the season.

The World Series of 1950

As tense as the American League race had been, the struggle in the National League was heart-stopping. The Dodgers, heavy favorites to repeat, found themselves in a battle with the New York Giants, now improbably managed by Leo Durocher, and a bunch of determined youngsters on the upstart Philadelphia Phillies whom the press dubbed "the Whiz Kids." The Giants fell away in the last week of the season, but the Whiz Kids would not let go even after giving up the lead they held for much of the season. No adversity seemed to get them down. They had lost their twenty-one-year-old lefty pitching ace Curt Simmons, who was called up by the Korean War draft board on September 10, after posting a 17–8 record. They still had a workhorse in twenty-three-year-old Robin Roberts, who would have his first of six consecutive twenty-game seasons while throwing a league-leading 304 innings. The pitching staff was held together by a bespectacled former school teacher who had been a journeyman National League pitcher for a few years. Now at the age of thirty-three, Jim Konstanty appeared as a relief pitcher in an unprecedented 74 games! He was not a power pitcher, but led the league with 22 saves to go with his 16 wins and steadied the kiddie corps of pitchers. Konstanty, who would win the National League Most Valuable Player award, was the most important reason that the Phillies came down to the last day of the season with a chance to win it all. The Phillies' bats had enough potency all year. Del Ennis, Willie Jones and veteran Andy Seminick provided the power, and Richie Ashburn, at age 23, had already established himself as one of the league's best leadoff hitters. This was a franchise that had not won a pennant since 1915, but good fortune seemed to bring everything together for them this year. For the final game of the season, what could have been better than a duel to the death in front of 30,073 wild Dodger fans crammed into cozy Ebbets Field? Roberts was starting his third game in five days, and the ferocious Don Newcombe, Brooklyn's iron man for the past two years, opposed him. Hard-luck Newcombe, who was to carry unfairly the stigma of being a big-game loser for his entire career, went into the tenth inning tied 1–1, and lost the game on a three-run homer.[16] The Phillies were in their first World Series in thirty-five years.

Both teams had been going all out right down to the wire as the season ended. Raschi's shoulder hurt, but he had not missed a start. He did not miss a start in five years. Lopat was aching, and Reynolds was arm-weary. The teams had three days to get ready, which, everyone assumed, would mean that Robin Roberts would start Game One. But Phillies manager Eddie Sawyer had not yet announced his choice. Stengel had his mind made up: whenever Roberts pitched, Reynolds would pitch. This was the match-up he wanted. He knew that he had three aces and that Raschi had been the consistent mainstay for the past three years, even before Stengel took over. He pitched on three days rest, never came out of the rotation, in Stengel's mind had more courage than any pitcher he had ever had. Casey never forgot Vic's gutsy performance in the final winner-takes-all game of the 1949 season. Also, Stengel, as harsh and often brutal as he could be with his players once he had settled in as Yankee manager, had a very soft spot for many of them, particularly the family men. If he heard that someone's child was ill, Stengel would give him the day off and send him home.[17] He knew about Raschi's blind brother, Gene, and how Vic cared for him. Reynolds and Lopat would smile whenever the manager put his arm around the bearish shoulders of his big right-hander, almost as if he sensed vulnerability in this otherwise ferocious-looking competitor. "Years later," reporter Harold Rosenthal reminisced, "Casey was to single out Raschi as the best pitcher he ever had with the Yankees. Why? 'Because,' said Stengel, 'he had it here, here and here.' Casey touched first his arm, then his head and then finally placed his hand over his heart."[18] True, Casey also placed Allie on that same pinnacle. He made it clear to Roger Kahn, who wrote, "Stengel spoke a paragraph I have never forgotten: 'The greatest two ways, which is starting and relieving, the greatest *ever,* and I have seen the great ones, Mathewson and I seen Cy Young.'"[19] Stengel also had a sense of Reynolds' relentless, almost perverse delight in facing the best of the opposition and never giving in. The performance against Newcombe in the 1–0 World Series opener the year before showed him that Reynolds *loved* the combat with the best of the enemy more than anyone. It would be Reynolds against Roberts, no matter what Sawyer did.

When Sawyer finally announced his opening World Series starter, the press and public were stunned: it would be Jim Konstanty, who hadn't started a game in three years. Sawyer figured that he needed one more day of rest for his ace Robin Roberts. He also hoped that Konstanty's off-speed breaking balls would be enough to confuse the Yankees, who feasted on fastball pitching. But, Turner and Stengel knew what they were doing, as well. They handed the opening game ball in Philadelphia to Vic Raschi.

The World Series was, for the second consecutive year, a coast-to-coast event, in spite of the two eastern teams. CBS, NBC, and ABC shared the nationwide television coverage. In spite of having all the games starting at noon, more than 35,000,000 viewers were on hand for the first pitch, the largest television audience in history to that time, and seventy million more tuned in on the radio.[20] The first game was played on October 4. The final game was played on October 7. Each of the four games was closely contested; none was decided until the final out. The Yankees won them all.

A few years later, after Whitey Ford had returned from his military service and moved back into the starting rotation, Branch Rickey—who had seen every great pitcher, from the legends of the Deadball Era down to modern times—told reporters, "Allie Reynolds, Vic Raschi, Eddie Lopat and Whitey Ford are the best balanced pitching staff in the history of baseball."[21] An astute observer and historian might have thought that Rickey's judgment began evolving as early as the 1950 World Series.

Only once before in World Series history had there been such total pitching dominance. One had to go back to 1905, when it was another Philadelphia-New York contest, but in reverse. The National League Giants defeated the American League Athletics in five games, and incredibly each game was a shutout. Christy Mathewson threw three shutouts and his teammate Joe McGinnity had one. The A's Chief Bender won Game Two for Philadelphia with yet another shutout. The Giants used three pitchers, with Red Ames throwing one inning of relief. The team ERA was 0.00! The Athletics were similarly unbelievable. They also used only three pitchers and had an ERA of 1.47. The winning New York Giants hit .203 for the five games, the A's, .161. But, the low batting averages are somewhat deceptive. One game was a 9–0 blowout; in another the Giants got ten hits.

The 1950 World Series demonstrated much more mastery on the part of the pitching staffs. The Phillies' Konstanty, Roberts and even journeyman left-hander Ken Heintzelman were heroic, combining for a 1.73 ERA. They held the Yankee hitters to an anemic .222 batting average. But, facing the historic performances of Raschi, Reynolds, Lopat, Ford and reliever Tom Ferrick, the Phillies' offense was smothered. In Game One, Raschi retired the first thirteen Phillies, gave up singles to Willie Jones and Andy Seminick in the fifth inning and faced only thirteen more batters after that, giving up no more hits, striking out five, and walking one. Konstanty was nearly as good. He gave up four hits in eight innings before being relieved, but in the fourth a double by Bobby Brown — a World Series phenomenon during his entire career — and two fly balls produced a run, knocked in by Jerry Coleman. Raschi went all the way for a 1–0 win. For the second time in two years, a Yankee pitcher had shut out the opponents 1–0 in the opening game of the World Series. After the game in the clubhouse, Vic walked over to his catcher and spoke to him softly: "Yogi, you called a perfect game. I didn't shake you off once. Thank you." Berra never forgot this consummate praise from one of his mentors.

In Game Two, it was Roberts versus Reynolds, just as Casey had foreordained. The Yankees scored one in the second; the Phillies tied it with their first run of the series in the fifth. It stayed that way until the tenth inning, when Joe DiMaggio, having produced thus far four feeble pop-ups to the infield, hit Roberts' first pitch on a line into the upper deck in left field for a one-run Yankee lead. Allie shut down the Phillies in the bottom of the tenth inning to seal the victory.[22] Reynolds gave up seven hits, struck out six, held the 3–4–5 Phillies hitters Sisler, Ennis and Jones 0-for-14 and went the distance in the 2–1 win over the Phillies' valiant ace. Game Three moved the next day to Yankee Stadium, and it was Eddie Lopat's turn. Eddie pitched the way he did when he did not have his best repertory. He gave up nine hits in eight innings, but walked none, struck out five (Ashburn, the Phillies' best contact hitter, three times), and left the game tied at 2–2. The Yankees won it in the bottom of the ninth, with Tom Ferrick getting the win.

There had been three games and a total of nine runs produced by both teams. This had been a study in offensive futility and pitching mastery, on both sides. The fourth — and final — game was a tribute from the student to his teacher. Rookie Whitey Ford was given his first start in a World Series and pitched the way he had been taught all year. He went into the ninth inning with a 5–0 shutout, having spread out five hits, striking out seven and walking one. But, in the ninth inning he tired. After giving up a leadoff single, Ford hit Ennis with a pitch. Two on, none out. Stengel was fidgeting in the dugout. His eyes wandered restlessly out to the Yankee bullpen in deep right field, and he saw something stirring. Someone was moving around; a catcher was getting ready to warm up a pitcher, although neither Casey nor Turner had given the sign. Neither had to. They both knew what was happening. It was the Indian getting ready, if he was needed. Sisler bounced to Coleman, who got the force at second. Runners on first and third, one out. Now shortstop Granny Hamner struck out, and Ford was one out away from his shutout and the Yankees from a four-game sweep. Andy Seminick hit what looked to be the final fly ball out to left field, but in the October late afternoon haze of smoke-filled Yankee Stadium, Gene Woodling lost the ball as it descended, and it hit him in the leg for a two-run error. That made it 5–2. Ford still was safe, until the next batter singled, which put two men on base and the tying run coming to the plate. That was enough tension for Stengel. While Casey came to the mound and was being greeted by more than 60,000 people screaming at him to let the kid pitcher finish, he had only one thought: Get this over with. Gimme the Indian. He took the ball from Ford and waved to the bullpen.

It was the kind of moment that Stengel had come to understand when he fully realized what a unique force he had in Allie Reynolds. As a big-game starter, he was superb; as a late-game relief pitcher, with the kind of high-and-hard buzz on his fastball that he preferred to throw in and around the uniform letters at nearly 100 miles per hour, he was simply unhittable. Casey had said it last year: "When he puts his leg over the bullpen fence, batters will faint."

Pinch-hitter Stan Lopata said he never saw any of the four pitches that Reynolds threw that hazy afternoon. He knew he had to get out of the way of the first one, which threatened his life. The next three may have been for strikes, he did not recall. He swung at them, missed, and the 1950 World Series was over.

That evening, there was another team celebration in the Bowman Room of the Biltmore Hotel. It showed all the over-the-top playboy style of Dan Topping, with 500 guests; it began at 7:00 P.M. and ended at four o'clock in the morning. Guy Lombardo brought his entire orchestra to play. The reigning king of television, Milton Berle, performed his nightclub act; Yankee broadcaster Mel Allen served as master of ceremonies.[23] George Weiss, amidst the general gaiety and high spirits, blunt and humorless as always when speaking in public, made a speech informing the gathering that, because the series ended in four games, the owners did not make any money, so people should not think about salary increases for the 1951 season.[24] Weiss was not happy. The average baseball salary for all of the major leagues was $12,500, but the Yankee payroll swallowed up 20 percent of the $2.75 million American League salary budget, around $500,000. DiMaggio's $100,000 accounted for one-fifth of the total. Too many of his players were making more than $20,000, and Weiss resented it. Berra, who was only twenty-six, would probably hold out for $30,000, Weiss fumed. Hall of Fame catcher Bill Dickey had never made more than $28,000. "There is too much complacency here," he would complain a few years later.[25] Few of his players would agree.

As the gathering tried to rebound from the cold water of Weiss' remarks, Allie and Earlene were standing near the edge of the dance floor when Eddie wandered over to them and spoke quietly into his friend's ear. "Allie, with Henrich gone you gotta be the players' representative. You're the only one Weiss respects; and you've got enough money not to care."

6

Eddie's Year

"It looks like he throws wads of tissue paper. Every time he wins a game, fans come out of the stands asking for contracts."—Casey Stengel

"The hitters' mouths used to water while they waited to hit. When they came back, they were foaming at the mouth."—Allie Reynolds, on hitting against Eddie Lopat

Libby was helping her husband pack. "Will you get a place for us in Phoenix?" she asked. She had not yet called Earlene and Sally to find out what living arrangements they would make for spring training. She would be the first of the wives to arrive.

Eddie had gotten off the phone with Casey a week earlier. The Lopats had returned to their New Jersey home after another barnstorming trip organized with a few other major leaguers. Allie had also barnstormed this year, in Oklahoma, where in three weeks he made enough money to sit for the rest of the off-season. Besides, his oil wells were already producing. Earlene preferred to spend the winter months enjoying the off-season and watching the kids grow. Allie, now a celebrity in Oklahoma, attended a few dinners honoring the state's outstanding athletes. At one he met a young, shy Yankee minor leaguer from small-town Commerce who at age 19 had hit .388 for Joplin in the Class C Western Association and had just been named Oklahoma's outstanding minor league player. The Yankees had signed Mickey Mantle for $1,000. He could barely utter a sentence in public; Allie liked him. Sally and Vic were back in New York State, visiting family and getting to know the physical education faculty at the local state college. There was still a month before anyone would have to get ready for the trip they thought would be to St. Petersburg, Florida.

One phone call from Stengel had changed all their plans. Casey had asked his left-hander and the most natural teacher of all his pitchers if he would come early to the new spring training site in Phoenix. Eddie was startled. "Phoenix, Casey?" Stengel then told him that the Yankees had traded places, for one year, with the New York Giants and would go to Arizona, where Del Webb could show all of his buddies that he really owned a baseball team. So, still deep in the January darkness, Eddie Lopat packed his bags to join Jim Turner, Casey, and a handful of selected coaches to work with around forty of the best prospects that Weiss had assembled. Eddie and Libby saw this as a special opportunity. He had already decided that, if it worked out, he would stay in baseball when his pitching days were over. To be asked by his manager to help with the young prospects was Stengel's validation of Eddie Lopat's very special capacity to teach and to coach. Jim Turner knew this, as well. They handed Whitey Ford to him, and Lopat did not disappoint. But, Ford was gone, drafted two weeks after the end of the 1950 World Series. They would not have him back for two more years.

In giving Lopat this unique role in the first rookie camp, Stengel knew what he was doing. He had seen Lopat transform an instinctive power pitcher like Allie Reynolds into a smart, manipulative thinker on the mound. Casey would watch the two of them when they stood for hours in the outfield, sat in the dugout or in the hotel dining rooms. They roomed together on the road, and they talked. Stengel wondered what the hell they could be talking about; they were so different from one another as pitchers. One day during the 1950 season, at Yankee Stadium while watching Reynolds pitch, a light went on in Stengel's head. Power-hitting Cleveland Indian Al Rosen batted four times, got ahead of Reynolds 2–0 each time, a hitter's count. Rosen knew that the pitcher would have to come in with a strike. Each time Reynolds, whose control was steadily improving, put a fastball on the outside corner of the plate, tempting and hittable, and Rosen would hit a ball 400 feet to center or to right-center field, where DiMaggio or Bauer would haul it in. In cavernous Yankee Stadium, a 400-foot fly ball to center field was just a long out. The Indian bench was all over Reynolds, saying each time at bat, "You lucky blanket-ass. Al just missed that one. Next time it will be outta here!" Reynolds, unperturbed on the mound, just kept racking up the 0-for-4 against the Cleveland power hitters and their long fly ball outs. Even the reporters wrote that Reynolds was hit hard and had good fortune. They had no idea what was happening; Stengel did. He had watched Lopat use the power of the big hitters against themselves, tempting them, leading them on as they lunged toward a pitch that looked like a watermelon coming up to the plate and left them walking back to the dugout wondering how this lucky "goddamn Polack" got so many long fly ball outs. Now, his friend Allie Reynolds was doing the same thing, using finesse, location and intellect to defeat the enemy. Eddie could teach anyone. He taught Allie to be a swindler, and the hitter had no idea.

The pre-spring training instructional school was just another of Stengel's innovations. Within a decade almost every major league club had a similar camp. Most of the prospects were between twenty and twenty-two years old.

The stars of this first camp were a big, raw-boned right-handed pitcher from California, Tom Morgan, who Lopat worked with, and Gil McDougald, an awkward-looking infielder who had played a tremendous second base for Beaumont in the Double-A Texas League and could hit. Crosetti, who worked with the infielders at the instructional camp, said that McDougald had the arm and range to play third or shortstop.

Then there was Mantle, a shortstop who was throwing balls into the stands, but who hit towering home runs as a switch-hitter and outran everyone in camp in getting down to first base. Stengel had Henrich, no longer on the playing roster, as an instructor in the camp and told him to make Mantle into an outfielder.

Casey was thinking of the coming season with Page and Ford gone from the pitching staff; with Martin and Brown likely drafted; and with his center-field icon Joe DiMaggio so diminished in skills as to be a liability. Not even the extraordinary finish the Yankee Clipper put on the end of the last season could erase the image in Stengel's mind of the first half, when DiMaggio was barely a shadow of himself. Casey was convinced that DiMaggio would fold in 1951. He was right.

The Season of 1951

> *"That's does it, if they don't win the pennant this time, they ought to give it up."*—Tigers manager Red Rolfe, on hearing that the Red Sox had acquired two more experienced pitchers before Opening Day.

The consensus among the writers was that Allie Reynolds was finished. He had not thrown a ball all spring training; the bones chips in his elbow would require surgery. At age thirty-six, he was through. The Yankees looked lousy. DiMaggio could not get the bat around on a fastball. As usual, there was no one to play first base; this year Mize was nearly forty and almost glued to the bag. Ford and Martin were gone, and Bobby Brown would probably be gone soon. The other two Yankee mound stalwarts, Raschi and Lopat, were being shelled in spring training and weren't getting anybody out. Vic, who had banged up his knee in a home plate collision against Cleveland the year before while beating them 1–0, could barely walk. The writers saw that Stengel was looking more and more at his rookies; this was a team that would have a hard time challenging in the American League. Besides, who could overcome the extraordinary pitching of the Cleveland Indians? As powerful as the Boston Red Sox looked (again), Cleveland could throw Feller, Garcia, Wynn and Lemon at the opposition all week. Who needed relief pitching with these four? As spring training broke, the consensus of the experts was that Cleveland and Boston would battle it out. The Yankees? With everyone's other managerial genius, Paul Richards, taking over the Chicago White Sox and after Detroit's terrific run for the pennant the previous year, New York could conceivably finish in fifth place.

When they headed east from Arizona after exhibition games in California, Stengel looked like he might have three rookies in his starting lineup, even though Weiss, former minor league Yankee boss and a believer in appropriate seasoning, was not thrilled. He had a special eye on the teenager from Oklahoma who had writers and veteran players gasping. Mickey Mantle kept on hitting monstrous home runs left-handed or right-handed, ran like the wind, and, once safely put in the outfield, proved to have a powerful arm which showed much more accuracy when throwing from a distance instead of shortstop. Weiss looked at Mantle with narrow, strategic eyes and knew he had his problem solved. Mantle would help avoid bringing black ballplayers to the Yankees and at the same time remain competitive.

Weiss was too good a judge of talent not to notice the impact that Robinson, Campanella, Newcombe, Larry Doby and Monte Irvin with the New York Giants were having. These were not genuine rookies. Only Newcombe was under twenty-five when he came up to Brooklyn. Weiss wondered how many young Robinsons were out there, teenage black ballplayers who hit with power and had leg speed good enough to be a formidable base-stealing threat? He had to go back to the Deadball era and perhaps Rogers Hornsby to find that combination of talent. Weiss knew about a rookie that the New York Giants had signed from the Birmingham Black Barons, a twenty-year-old kid named Willie Mays. Weiss had a chance to sign Mays to a Yankee contract in 1949, but passed.[1] One of the few baseball people whose judgment on talent Weiss respected was Leo Durocher, and Durocher publicly stated that this prospect was going to burn up the National League. Weiss knew that soon every team, even reluctantly, would be mining the fields for black talent that eventually could leave the Yankees at a disadvantage. Yet Weiss had no intention of bringing black athletes to the Yankees. Not now, not as long as he was associated with the team.[2]

The answer to Weiss' dilemma was Mantle. He was white, but he "played black." Weiss believed that with Mantle properly prepared, he would have an athlete who could "protect" the Yankees for years to come from the need to sign black ballplayers.[3] But, he did not want to rush Mantle and told Stengel that the young Oklahoman, who had only played as high as Class C, would be shipped out. Besides, Mantle had become the center of an unforeseen controversy. With the Korean War raging, he had been declared 4-F because of a life-threatening bone infection from a high school injury. Osteomyelitis almost cost Mantle his leg. He was now in remission, but the 4-F classification did not sit well with fans and patriots who saw him run like the wind. Weiss sent him

George Weiss, ca. 1950: A brilliant, ruthless, and cold baseball genius (National Baseball Hall of Fame Library, Cooperstown, N.Y.).

back to his Oklahoma draft board for re-classification, secretly hoping that he might be able to serve, and mature as well. But, the army doctors re-examined the damaged leg and were not going to take a chance on him; Mantle returned to the Yankees. Weiss prepared to send him to Kansas City in the American Association.

Casey had his own ideas. He looked at his team and decided he needed Mantle. Weiss, seeing a roster that appeared significantly weakened from the previous year, capitulated. When Opening Day came, there were *four* rookies in the starting lineup: Mantle in right, McDougald at third, a young California phenom and Rose Bowl football hero named Jackie Jensen in left, and — demonstrating the disastrous condition of the Yankee pitchers — Tom Morgan on the hill, the starting pitcher, a *rookie*. Stengel had said it to everyone within earshot: "I can't win with my old men. We have to rebuild."[4] For once, Casey was wrong.

Raschi started at home against Boston and shut the Red Sox out, 5–0. Lopat went the next day, won 6–1, and began the season with a personal streak of eight consecutive wins. Reynolds, who was barely able to lift his arm during all of spring training and still had bone chips floating in his elbow, got his first win, a complete game on May 3. Reynolds pitched the first of his two 1951 no-hitters on July 12, by which time he had won ten games and thrown five shutouts. The rebuilding was over. The Big Three Old Men were back, and the race was on.

Page was gone, and there was no replacement in the bullpen. Allie, at age thirty-six, with bone chips grinding, told Casey he could relieve whenever he was needed. By mid–June he had thrown his third consecutive shutout, had thirty-five innings without walking a batter and twenty-nine consecutive innings without giving up a run. He had already saved three games in relief. His catcher, Yogi Berra, summed it up: "I think Allie was pitching the best ball of his career, and Casey used him in relief in crucial spots. You never heard Reynolds gripe, not even with the bone chips rattling around in his elbow. He'd pitch two days in a row, good weather, bad weather, day game, night game, anything to help us win."[5]

Lopat, Raschi and Reynolds, once the gun went off to begin the season, were in control. Byrne was no longer a factor and would soon be gone. The three were 32–13 by the All-Star break, with their usual dominance of each challenging team. The surprising Chicago White Sox jumped off first, and one trade made all the difference. Eight games into the season, they acquired from Cleveland a black Cuban baseball player who, regardless of his Caribbean origins, would never have been permitted to play during the Jim Crow baseball days.[6] Orestes "Minnie" Minoso was traded for Gus Zernial, a big, lumbering home run hitter who was a *bona fide* long ball threat for the White Sox, but so slow afoot on the bases and in the outfield as to be a liability. Minoso totally transformed the Chicago offense and would eventually lead the league that year in triples and stolen bases. He was fast, hit with sufficient power, had a rifle arm from the outfield, where he covered the expansive space in Comiskey Park with ease. When he played third base, he anchored the infield, which featured a Venezuelan named Alex "Chico" Carrasquel, who was playing the most elegant shortstop in the league.[7] Zernial, who led the league in RBIs with 129 and home runs with thirty-three, also led in strikeouts, with 101. He managed two stolen bases.

The Detroit Tigers never got started. What occurred was a total team collapse of pitching and hitting. After their terrific second-place finish and near miss of 1950, they were never a factor in the 1951 race and finished under .500, a dramatic drop of twenty-one games in the standings.

The Chicago White Sox were running as fast as Minnie Minoso, with a 25–4 streak in May and early June. They could not beat the Yankees, but they beat everyone else. On June 8–11 they hosted the Yankees in a four-game series at Comiskey Park. New York took three out of four. The winning pitchers: Vic

Raschi, Eddie Lopat and Allie Reynolds. The White Sox held on to a two-game lead, but would soon run out of gas. They played 13–15 baseball into July, when the resurgent Red Sox took over. At the All-Star break in the second week of July, Stengel, again the manager of the American League squad, demonstrated how he understood the psychology of his three bulwark pitchers and close friends. He selected one New York Yankee pitcher: Eddie Lopat. His friends Vic and Allie beamed. None of them had as many wins nor as low an earned run average as Eddie, who was racking up victories and complete games while giving up fewer runs than anyone else in the league. It was his year to shine.

The Yankees went into the All-Star break losing three in a row to Boston and five of six overall. They needed a lift, and Reynolds gave it to them. On July 12, he pitched a demoralizing 1–0 no-hitter against Bob Feller, who had thrown his own no-hitter on July 1! Gene Woodling's solo home run was the difference. Reynolds' domination of Cleveland in 1951 equaled that of his pitching partner Lopat. The Indians managed two runs all season in thirty-six innings against their former teammate. In this no-hitter he retired the last seventeen Cleveland batters in a row.

By July 20, four teams were in a virtual deadlock for first place in the American League: Boston, .598; Chicago, .596; New York, .595; and Cleveland, .593. There was no doubt what kept the Yankees in contention: three pitchers. Only Rizzuto and Berra were playing every day (and eventually would be the only regulars to have more than 500 at-bats for the season). DiMaggio was having an abysmal year, barely hitting .250. Mantle, who started the season like a hurricane, was now striking out with extraordinary regularity and eventually would be sent down in mid–July to Kansas City, to return on August 24 after re-discovering his batting eye. Stengel had to bench the slumping Jerry Coleman, Mize was struggling around .250, and Rizzuto was fifty points under his MVP year. Only Berra, rookie Gil McDougald, and the tandem of Bauer and Woodling hit consistently. But, Stengel was platooning with genius, and his three pitchers were relentless. Casey moved the versatile McDougald, who had been platooning at third base, back to second and inserted golden boy Bobby Brown with the bad hands and wonder bat into the lineup at third base, and he immediately started chewing up opposition pitchers. In the next twenty games, Brown hit in eighteen and the Yankees went on a 17–3 rampage. Through the month of August, Boston gradually gave way, and it looked as if it would come down to a September battle between the Yankees and Cleveland.[8]

Eddie was worried. He knew that Allie had gone off to see Dr. George E. Bennett at Johns Hopkins Hospital. Bennett was an orthopedic surgeon. After finishing a game the week before with a save two days after a complete game win, Reynolds could not raise his arm enough to put his hand in his pocket. Lopat also knew that Raschi's knee was bothering him. They routinely would run for hours in the outfield between starts, and for the first time in memory, Vic begged off one of their training sessions. The three of them prided themselves on their training regimen. Lopat's shoulder was also aching, but he was winning with such consistency that it didn't seem to matter. They kept their miseries to themselves, sharing problems only with Jim Turner. Vic more than anyone wanted no one to know about his knee, thinking that opposing teams would start bunting on him if they knew about his limited mobility.

Little escaped George Weiss. He came first to his midtown office every day, then arrived at his Yankee Stadium office just before the start of the game, going up to his private box overlooking the field in the first or second inning. He watched his employees perform and made occasional notes, often picking up his personal phone to make a call. It became very clear to him by the middle of the season that this New York Yankee team would rise or fall on the backs of his three warhorse pitchers. Lopat, at age thirty-three, was winning with extraordinary consistency. Raschi, thirty-two, who gave him the most trouble at contract time, hadn't missed a start since his permanent arrival in 1947; again, this year he was on the mound every fourth or fifth day, beating the contenders with relentless regularity. He checked his data sheet. Reynolds had his thirty-sixth birthday back in February. Stengel was using him as a starter and reliever. How long could this go on? These men were not spring chickens. Before the trading deadline of June 15, Weiss traded three players to the Washington Senators for left-hander Bob Kuzava, a twenty-eight-year-old journeyman who had bounced around the American League, from Cleveland to Chicago and now to Washington. He could be a spot starter and long reliever, if necessary, and Weiss thought he could help.

Weiss was not through. He had a special gift for finding National League castoffs who could help the Yankees in the final month of the season, especially at first base, where there always seemed to be a problem. Stengel, a National Leaguer all his life, knew the talent in the other league, as well. Veteran John Mize came in 1949, already thirty-six and not part of Leo Durocher's rebuilding program for the New York Giants; thirty-four-year-old Johnny Hopp was picked up from Pittsburgh in September, 1950. Both could still hit and proved invaluable.

But, this year Weiss was not looking for offensive help. He was convinced that there was enough left in the Yankee bats to carry them on. What worried him was the durability of his three titans. Could they be given some help during the final month of the season? He spent hours examining the rosters of National League teams, then went over his own minor league possessions and prospects. Late in August, he reached for the phone again. He wanted to talk to Casey about a pitcher he had managed when he was with the Boston Braves.

On August 29, the Yankees announced that they had purchased the contract of thirty-three-year-old veteran right-hander John Sain from the Boston Braves. The deal included cash and Yankee pitching prospect Lew Burdette, who was 14–12 with San Francisco in the Pacific Coast League.[9] Sain looked like he had lost his effectiveness. He had a dismal 5–13 record for the season so far, and all seven National League teams waived the opportunity to claim him. When Turner told his three charges that Johnny Sain was joining the team, they immediately opened a spot in their corner for him. They had all bounced around the minor leagues together, had known each other, and understood each other's work ethic.

Sain started his first American League game on September 3 against the Philadelphia Athletics. The night before, Lopat, at Jim Turner's suggestion, invited the newcomer to join him for dinner, and they talked for three hours. At this stage of his career, Sain was a right-handed version of Eddie. He threw several different curveballs from almost any direction at various speeds, none of them fast. His fastball, once a formidable weapon, was gone, and he treated batters now to the same cunning menu offered by his new teammate Eddie Lopat. He even threw a screwball, the reverse curve. Jim Turner knew what he was doing in handing Sain over to Lopat, who had driven the Philadelphia hitters to distraction. They had the American League batting champion, Ferris Fain, a .340 left-handed hitter and tough "out"; he would have to be pitched to carefully, along with outfielder Elmer Valo, another .300 contact hitter who swung from the left side. Lopat suggested that Sain's "out" pitch against these two should be the screwball, a pitch that the right-handed Sain could break away from left-handed hitters. The same was true for Dave Philley, a switch-hitter who would hit left-handed against Sain. The rest of the Philadelphia lineup could be handled. They were free-swinging right-hand bats: Gus Zernial, Eddie Joost, and Hank Majeski. Sain was satisfied that he was now inside the heads of the team he had to debut against, and that Lopat had put him there. He threw a complete game, winning 3–1.

The next day, Allie told his manager that he would go to the bullpen for the rest of the season, if needed, but could still start. The Yankees were ready for the final run.

In July and August, the Indians went 44–19 and made their charge. But, with Reynolds starting and relieving, Lopat dominating Cleveland, and Raschi putting away the other contenders, the Yankees stayed close. Then, while the Indians split twenty-four decisions, New York won seventeen of twenty-six. Raschi, Lopat and Reynolds went 12–5, and Sain chipped in two wins.

Four games stand out in that streak. On September 16 Cleveland came into New York for an abbreviated two-game Sunday-Monday series, with a one-game lead and momentum in their favor. The Yankees had just lost four of five to the lowly St. Louis Browns and the collapsed Detroit Tigers. They had made four errors in one game and looked terrible. On the Saturday before the Cleveland series Sain had given up four home runs to Detroit in a 9–2 drubbing. Now came the league leaders. The two-day match-ups had been planned for weeks: Feller and Lemon for Cleveland, Reynolds and Lopat for the Yankees. Feller was rested; at 22–7 he was the league's best pitcher. Reynolds, used in relief two days earlier, had a 14–8 record. Las Vegas money was on Cleveland.

A crowd of 68,760 came to share the drama. With Mantle hitting leadoff, Berra fourth, and a somewhat rested DiMaggio relegated now permanently to the fifth spot in the batting order, the Yankees knocked Feller out of the box in the fifth inning. Reynolds threw a complete game five-hitter; the Yankees won 5–1, tying Cleveland for first place. Boston also won and was now two games behind the leaders.

The next day, Monday, more than 42,000 people showed up at Yankee Stadium, the largest non–Opening Day workday crowd of the year in the major leagues. Lemon was 17–12; Lopat, 19–8 and looking for his first twenty-win season. He was already leading the league in earned run average. The Yanks drew blood first, when Bobby Brown, by then an M.D. and still a formidable hitter, doubled with one out in the fifth inning and was driven home by Rizzuto's single. The Indians tied it in the top of the sixth with an unearned run on a rare Rizzuto error. Lemon and Lopat shut down the opposing hitters after that. Through nine innings, Eddie had given up three meager singles. In the bottom of the ninth inning, DiMaggio scratched out an infield hit that bounced off third baseman Al Rosen's glove with one out. Gene Woodling singled to right, just past the outstretched glove of second baseman Bobby Avila. DiMaggio, at the end of his career, aching in every limb of his body, still had the instincts necessary to get a jump start and to go from first to third on a single. He was a consummate professional to the end and took ultimate pride in doing what had to be done on the baseball field. In this particular instance, he knew he had to go from first to third on a single to right field, and he did. *In his entire thirteen-year career as a Yankee, DiMaggio had never been thrown out going from first to third.*

Now Cleveland manager Al Lopez had to make the wheels whirl. With Bobby Brown coming to the plate and Rizzuto behind him, he ordered Lemon to walk the more dangerous Brown, filling the bases and making possible a force out at home plate.

On the bench, Eddie was sitting next to Vic Raschi. Even though he had pitched a complete game the day before, Reynolds had gone down to the bullpen. Lopat, who always kept a very calm exterior but whose stomach churned, looked casual as he watched the drama unfold. Bases loaded, one out, bottom of the ninth, against the team that had to beat you. "Allie beat them yesterday; I have to beat them today." Strike one. Then Eddie saw something that made his heart almost leap out of his chest. Rizzuto stepped out of the batter's box and started arguing about the strike call. At the same moment he held his bat at both ends, with his left hand on the narrow knob and his right hand on the end of the barrel. The message exploded on all eyes in the Yankee dugout: Rizzuto was giving the sign for a squeeze bunt. In a blink Lopat, without moving his head, looked down at third base, where DiMaggio had taken off his hat to smooth his hair. This was the recognition sign; he had seen Rizzuto flash the squeeze. So had Casey, who had nothing to do with his two veteran players putting on a play at this most dramatic moment in the game. Cleveland pitcher Bob Lemon had been a third baseman before switching to the mound and sensed the threat from Rizzuto, who everyone acknowledged was the best bunter in the league, maybe in all of baseball. But, Lemon thought, not with DiMaggio on third. Joe was barely looking at Lemon. He was casually chatting with third baseman Al Rosen no more than a step from the bag when Lemon went into his windup.[10]

The next five seconds were explosive. As soon as Lemon started his motion, the languid DiMaggio, in mid-sentence conversation with Rosen, broke for home. Rosen immediately charged, two steps behind him. Lemon, now with his arms raised above his head, saw out of the corner of his eye the streaking figure of a base runner racing down the line. He knew exactly what to do: throw an unhittable pitch that the catcher could handle and then tag the runner out. Rizzuto was short, this would be easy, and he sped up his motion and threw a fastball right at the batter's head. Rizzuto reacted twice, simultaneously. He dived out of the way of the menacing pitch, with his feet leaving the ground. At the same instance Rizzuto threw his bat at the ball and laid down a perfect bunt that rolled down the first base line halfway between the pitcher and the foul line. DiMaggio touched home plate a second after Rizzuto sprung to his feet and started running to first base. He didn't have to, but he wanted the hit, anyway! Lemon, who had been the only Cleveland player able to reach the ball, held it in his hand while he watched the winning run score. He looked at the baseball in his hand, then heaved it furiously into the roaring crowd at Yankee Stadium and walked off the field. The Yankees were in first place, and they would remain there. Lopat's three-hitter was his fifth victory over Cleveland that year. He had his twentieth win. Before Raschi and Turner ran out to greet the two Yankee heroes, they hugged their beaming pitcher.

That ended the season series with the Cleveland Indians. The Yankees had won fifteen of the twenty-two contests.

On Friday, September 28, the Yankees had a doubleheader against the Red Sox at Yankee Stadium. There were five games left in the season, and the Yankees need one win to tie, two to clinch. The Red Sox could only play the spoiler, because they had already been eliminated. But Boston would not role over; Mel Parnell, their ace with eighteen wins, would go in the opener against Allie.

Lopat knew that his friend was upset. They had driven to the stadium from New Jersey in silence. Allie was worried about Earlene, not the Red Sox. As he was getting ready to leave the house, she collapsed on the floor in a faint. Libby Lopat came right over and called a doctor. Allie stayed as long as he could, but felt he had to get to Yankee Stadium. It was also American Indian Day across the country, and he was to be the center of the celebration before the game. He left Earlene before the doctor had arrived. She had complained about dizziness for the past week, and Allie now was distraught.

How he got through the first two innings, without giving up a hit, he couldn't say. He kept glancing over at the empty seat where his wife normally sat, with pen in hand and sheets of paper, tracking Allie's pitch count. But, when he went out to the mound for the top of the third and looked over to the wives' section, there was Earlene, waving to him with her pitching charts! (The doctor diagnosed an inner ear infection and let her attend the game.) A charge of energy went through Reynolds, and he went about his business with a happy vengeance. The Yankees were hammering Parnell and had built up an 8–0 lead going into the seventh inning. Allie had walked three, but had not given up a hit. As the game progressed, he threw harder and harder; he was throwing another no-hitter into the final inning.

With two out in the ninth inning, he knew who was stepping into the batter's box: the most feared left-handed hitter in the American League, Ted Williams, whose ego as a hitter knew no limits. Making the final out in a no-hitter would serve as a total humiliation, and he was not about to permit it. Williams always set himself perfectly with a picture stance and smooth stroke. It would be master against master, except the Yankee pitcher was not alone on the mound. Allie had instructed Yogi: no fastballs on the first pitch to Williams, then heat. Lopat had told him before the game that the only way to work Williams was to start him with low breaking stuff, then surprise him with the unexpected. Williams was always thinking, always playing mind games with the opposing pitcher. He could out-think anyone, except "that fucking Lopat." Eddie, standing with one foot on the dugout steps next to Stengel and Turner, was thinking along with Allie. Williams took strike one, on a hard biting curveball down and away.[11] Williams thought: Lopat would try to sneak that goddam pitiful fastball past me now. The Indian has been keeping me off him with breaking stuff all day. Now he'll try to get the fastball past me, and I'll be waiting. Williams dug in. Reynolds got the sign from Berra and threw a 100 mile-per-hour fastball up on the letters of the Red Sox uniform, right in the power wheelhouse of Ted Williams. Williams had no more than a second to react. His extraordinary eyes picked up the rotation and location of the ball instantly, and he began to bring the bat forward. But, this was not Lopat's sneaky fastball; Reynolds' fastball that day was near to being unhittable. Williams ripped at the ball, and sent a soaring pop-up into the air between home plate and the Yankee dugout along first base. Berra threw off his mask and looked up at the speck. Hitters like Williams could drive a pop fly literally out of sight. Berra, at this stage of his career, was an agile, accomplished catcher who could handle all aspects of this challenging position, pop-ups included. He picked up the speck, watched it grow larger, camped underneath it and was ready to make the catch, when a gust of wind blew the ball back over his head. Yogi lunged for the ball — and it bounced off the edge of his catcher's mitt, falling to the ground.[12] The crowd groaned. "Give Williams a second chance? My God! What have I done?" Berra was rubbing his throwing hand. Allie had come over to help with the pop-up if necessary, and when he saw Berra stagger, Reynolds accidentally stepped on his hand and spiked him. Berra, heartsick at having lost his friend's no-hitter, tried to apologize, but Reynolds beat him to it. "Don't worry, Yog. We'll get him again."[13] He sensed the misery of his catcher.

Williams stepped back in. He had been given a reprieve and was determined to make the best use of it. There was no way he would tolerate being given *two* chances to break up a no-hitter! He was grinding the handle of his bat menacingly. The usually conversational Berra, who loved to distract Williams with chatter behind the plate, squatted in a deep despair, believing he had cost his teammate a no-hitter. Now it was the always profane Williams who was talking to Berra, waiting for Reynolds to get set: "You son of a bitch. You had your chance. But, you blew it!" Berra looked out at Reynolds, thinking about what pitch to call. Then, he saw a signal familiar from the earlier "Project," when Allie was calling the pitches for his catcher. No, Yogi thought, not that, Allie! But, Yogi knew that the look on Reynolds' face said it all. Reynolds started his motion.

Whatever Williams was expecting from the pitcher, the last thing he thought he would see would be the exact same pitch, thrown in the exact same spot, with, if possible, more velocity. There was simply no time, not even for a hitter who believed he was the world's greatest, to react. Reynolds unloaded another screamer across the letters of Williams' uniform. Again, with his extraordinary reactions, Williams got the bat moving faster than any other human might have. But, on this pitch, he was facing something superhuman. He made contact, but barely, and Berra saw immediately that it was another pop-up, as a catcher can detect instantly, in almost the same spot. Yogi ripped off his mask and threw it away, then caught sight of the dot just as it reached its apex, hovered for a split-second, and then descend. He glued his eyes on that dot, getting gradually bigger. Berra knew he was drifting closer to the Yankee dugout, but he didn't care. If he fell in, he would fall in; he was not going to take his eyes off that ball. He heard coach Tommy Henrich yell out, "Plenty of room, plenty of room!" Yogi camped under the dot, watch it become a ball, pounded his catcher's mitt, and squeezed the third out. When he looked down, he was less than a yard from the steps. The Yankees in the dugout were closer and were the first to hug the catcher, delighted that he had gotten his second chance. But, no one was happier than Allie, who had been right next to Berra when he made the catch, in case he could help. Reynolds hugged his catcher and delighted in his salvation.

Reynolds' second no-hitter of the season clinched a tie for the American League pennant. The Yankees jubilantly raced into the clubhouse to celebrate and to talk to the press between games. Stengel was ecstatic. He told Allie, "You can have the rest of the season off." Then he gathered the press around him in his office and kept up his praise of Reynolds: "There is one of the greatest pitchers of all time. Starter, reliever, day or night the great competitor. Imagine Reynolds pitching a no-hitter for the clincher, even though he's handicapped by that bunch of bone splinters in his pitching elbow. It's without parallel."[14]

There were smiles all around, except in one corner of the clubhouse, where Vic Raschi was getting on his game face. Allie had clinched the tie. Vic was preparing to clinch the title, and no one went near him. Even the reporters, hungry for interviews amidst the general mayhem and congratulations, stayed away from him when he had that "look" on his face. Reynolds, knowing that his friend would want space and privacy, deliberately moved away from his locker next to Vic and gave his interviews on the other side of the clubhouse. Vic sat alone, smoldering and internalizing, while the players got ready for the second game. Reynolds, in one of their many conversations since coming together, had told Vic, "You have to learn to despise hitters." As Vic Raschi sat alone, with dark visage, preparing himself for this ultimate test, he was hearing his friend's advice. Allie and Eddie knew enough to protect him at times like this. One flashbulb popping off would have sent him into a growling fury. Reynolds had to deal with the reporters, but Lopat stayed near Vic, and made certain that no one, who might not have known better, approached him. Then, twenty minutes before the game was scheduled to begin, Jim Turner walked over to the hunched-over bear of a man sitting on a chair in front of his locker, and whispered quietly, "Vic, it's time." Raschi looked up into a face that reflected as deep an understanding of his feelings as anyone in his life. Jim, Eddie and Allie: they know me. "OK, Jim. Let's go."

The Yankees scored seven runs in the second inning. Later, DiMaggio hit a three-run homer, the last of his career during the regular season. Vic struck out seven, walked one, and pitched a complete game victory, winning his twenty-first game, 11–3. The Yankees had won their third consecutive pennant, against the odds. Raschi and Reynolds, for the eighth time that season, had beaten the Red Sox.

New York finished the season five games ahead of Cleveland. No regular position player hit .300. No one drove in one hundred runs. No one hit thirty home runs. In fact, Berra was the only Yankee to hit more than fifteen. DiMaggio finished with the lowest batting average of his career, .263, having played in only 116 games. The nineteen-year-old Mickey Mantle hit .267 in only ninety-six games and still managed to lead the team in strikeouts with seventy-four. Berra was the offensive leader, with twenty-seven home runs and only eighty-eight runs batted in. There were several more potent offenses in the league. The Yankees averaged barely four runs a game for the last month of the season. There was little doubt why this Yankee team prevailed.

Lopat and Raschi each won twenty-one games; Reynolds won seventeen, saved seven more (to lead the club), threw seven shutouts (to lead the league), and pitched two no-hitters. But, for the first time in their seasons together, Lopat bested both of his teammates in lowest earned run average. Eddie's gaudy 21–9 record was accomplished with a frugal 2.91 ERA, better than Vic's 21–10, 3.27, and even Reynolds' 3.05 to go with his 17–8 won-lost record. But, they didn't care about individual records. They shared in each other's pride and success. One could find few more graphic examples in modern baseball history of a team with relatively ordinary talent and dependency on just three pitchers. They were responsible for more than half of all the innings hurled by the Yankee staff.

The National League race in 1951 had already become the stuff of folklore.[15] In August, the Giants trailed Brooklyn by 13½ games. New York proceeded to win sixteen straight and went on to a 37–7 streak over the last six weeks of the season. Charlie Dressen's Dodgers, looking over their shoulders, could manage only a 26–22 record over the same stretch. From Labor Day to the end of the season, Brooklyn was 14–12, and the Giants won 19 of 24. The season ended in a tie that forced a three-game playoff, with each team winning one, until Thomson's "Shot Heard 'Round the World" gave the National League pennant to the New York Giants and broke hearts all over Brooklyn.

Eddie Lopat watched very carefully when he attended all three of the Dodger-Giant playoff games.

The World Series of 1951

There was a unique intimacy in this World Series. The two stadiums were literary in sight of one another: the Polo Grounds on Coogan's Bluff in Harlem, and Yankee Stadium in the Bronx, separated by a small river and a gorge.

Although the dramatic playoff and anticipated "Subway Series" produced enormous excitement in New York, both teams entered the series with exhausted pitching staffs. Durocher had gone the final six weeks using three starters exclusively: Sal Maglie (23–6), Larry Jansen (23–11) and Jim Hearn (17–9). Stengel, without the luxury of a genuine relief pitcher, used Reynolds in double duty, with or without bone chips. The Giants' hitting was formidable. Seven of their starting eight position players had home run totals in double digits. The biggest bat was held by Negro league veteran Monte Irvin, who broke into the majors in 1949 at age thirty and now two years later was having his breakout year with twenty-four home runs and a league-leading 121 runs batted in. One of the additional causes of excitement stemmed from the fact that the Giants had three black starting position players: besides Irvin, there was Rookie of the Year Willie Mays, whose twenty home runs, sixty-eight RBIs, and .274 batting average eclipsed the Yankee's phenom, Mickey Mantle. Mays also opened eyes with his play in the outfield. He had extraordinary speed and range in the wide-open spaces of center field in the Polo Grounds and could throw no-bounce strikes to any base from any distance.

This World Series also represented a racial landmark for baseball. There would be three black starting players on the field; none of them were with the Yankees. Besides Irvin and Mays in the outfield, Henry Thompson, acquired from the St. Louis Browns, was supposed to hold down third base for the Giants. But, when Don Mueller was injured in the playoffs, Durocher didn't hesitate to stick his finger in the eye of baseball's white traditionalists by sending out an all-black outfield. He brought Bobby Thomson in to play third and sent Hank Thompson to join Irvin and Mays. In 1951, five years after the signing of Jackie Robinson to a professional contract, integration was limited to four of the sixteen teams in major league baseball. The Boston Braves had speedster Sam Jethroe in the Opening Day lineup on April 18, 1950. Bill Veeck, the only American League owner committed to integration, brought Larry Doby to Cleveland on the heels of Robinson in 1947 and added Satchel Paige in 1948.[16]

The Giants performed the Miracle of Coogan's Bluff on October 3; the World Series started on October 4, at Yankee Stadium. For the Giants, Durocher had to look outside his three aces for a starter. His choice was Dave Koslo, an off-speed left-handed veteran of ten seasons who had completed only five games all season while going 10–9, but had the virtue of being the only Giant who had not appeared in the three-game playoff. It proved to be more than just an act of necessity. Durocher knew what he was doing. Stengel set his pitching for the first three games. After Reynolds, he would want Lopat to pitch in spacious Yankee Stadium, and then hand the ball to Raschi to open in the Polo Grounds.

With two out in the bottom of the first inning in Game One, Allie walked Hank Thompson. Monte Irvin singled and Whitey Lockman doubled home the first run for the Giants. Then, under the astonished eyes of 65,673 fans, Irvin gave them a taste of exciting Negro league baseball: he stole home.

Up in his special box, George Weiss was outwardly seething. Two black ballplayers had scored two runs, and one of them did it on the most spectacular play in all of baseball. But the rational part of his brain also was telling him that times were changing when a 6'1", 195 pound slugging outfielder who had led the league in runs batted in could steal home at the age of thirty-three. Jackie Robinson had done it already a half-dozen times, but now Weiss saw it with his own eyes.

Of all the time for his bone chips to lock in his right elbow, it had to be today, thought Allie. He knew it five minutes after he started warming up that this was not his day. Jim Turner, who watched Allie loosen up for every start he ever made during their time together, could tell, also. But no one else would know, not out in the distant visitors' bullpen, where he threw. His closest pitching comrades would have known just by looking at him. He didn't have velocity or location. When the game ended, the Giants had won, 5–1. Allie had walked an unprecedented seven batters, and when he managed to get the ball over the plate, the Giants belted him for eight hits in six innings. Monte Irvin had three singles and a monstrous 450-foot triple to go with his steal of home. On defense, he made a spectacular catch to rob Bauer of a home run. The Yankees looked at Dave Koslo and finally understood why Eddie Lopat drove American League batters crazy. On that day he was so much like the Yankee left-hander, even to the point of being a Polish-American whose real name was Koslowski! Koslo threw a tidy seven-hit complete game and throttled the American League champs with off-speed pitches. It was the high point of a journeyman's career.

Allie, sitting in the clubhouse after the game with his friends and his right arm in a bucket of ice water, contemplated his first World Series loss. Reynolds had learned how to take it. He had come to realize over the years of giving his absolute best in every outing that he could not be tyrannized by events he could not control. He knew he was fallible, would fail from time to time, and would come back to triumph. Vic felt worse for him that he did for himself. "Don't worry. Eddie will get them tomorrow." They picked each other up; they cared for each other as much as they did for themselves. Eddie will get them tomorrow. And he did.

The Giants were riding a wave of extraordinary energy. With no pause between the supercharged playoff and the start of the World Series, beating Allie Reynolds in the opening game at Yankee Stadium accelerated their confidence into another gear. The pitcher they considered their *real* ace, twenty-three-game winner Larry Jansen, was on the mound. This had been his second twenty-win season in five years.

Lopat, demonstrating his usual loquaciousness that hid the churning in his stomach, walked through the clubhouse before the game bell rang. He stopped in front of Mickey Mantle, the kid from Oklahoma who the day before had played in his first World Series game. "You want to give Allie a present today? Let's win this one for him." He knew that Mantle worshiped Reynolds, who had taken the time to make his young fellow Oklahoman feel at ease in the Yankee clubhouse. Allie knew how lonely it was for this small-town kid who had never seen a crowd larger than 500 people until he arrived in New York. When Mantle had been sent back to the minors, Allie told him to relax: he would be back soon. When Mickey returned, the first person to greet him was Reynolds. Now, Eddie was asking for a special effort. He rubbed the teenager's blond crew cut and went over to his favorite shortstop. "Scooter, let's do it!"

Lopat set the Giants down in the top of the first. Mantle led off for the Yankees. He took a curveball strike, and in what the veteran Giants assumed was rookie eagerness and inexperience, did not step out of the box but glanced toward the right side of the infield. Jansen had been told that Mantle struck out because he could not handle a fastball up around the letters, which is exactly what the Giant pitcher now threw. He didn't want to give Mantle time to set or step out. He would dispatch this teenager quickly. Koslo had no trouble with him, he thought; neither will I.

In a split second, Mantle, hitting left-handed against Jansen, deftly dropped the bat off his shoulder, slid his left hand down on the barrel, loosened his grip on the bat knob, and started running before the ball even reached him. The bat made a soft contact with the ball and Mickey dragged it with him for a step, until he exploded toward first base while the ball rolled past the outstretched hand of the pitcher and dribbled toward Eddie Stanky, who picked it up while charging in from second base, in time to see Mantle streak across the bag at first. There was not even a play. The Giants on their bench looked at each other. No one can run that fast, thought Durocher, slapping his hands together in order to break the spell. The Yankee bench, almost as one, jumped up to the first step to cheer the kid who with a beautifully executed drag bunt had caught the Giants back on their heels.

As Phil Rizzuto, hitting second, walked to the plate, he was thinking, "How do I make them feel even worse? They looked so dumb out there on Mickey's bunt. Lockman looks shaky." Whitey Lockman, playing first, was pawing the ground near where Mantle stood on first base. Phil wasted no time. Jansen, working from the stretch and looking over at Mantle, did not want to start Rizzuto off with a curve, so he threw his fastball. To everyone's astonishment, Rizzuto dropped *another* perfect bunt in almost the identical spot where Mantle's went. Lockman fielded it this time and tried to make a flip toss to his pitcher covering first and stumbled. He threw it away. Mantle never broke stride and coasted into third base on the error. With the count 2–1 on Gil McDougald, the Yankee infielder spanked a single to center, giving Mantle his first World Series run scored. The Yankees had drawn first blood, which is exactly what they had hoped for. In the second inning, first baseman Joe Collins lined a Jansen curveball into the short right field porch, and the Yankees led, 2–0.

Through six innings, Lopat gave up one harmless single and walked no one. He kept his concentration even when Mantle, running down a fly ball in right center field, stopped suddenly when he caught his spikes in a water drain and tore up his knee. Eddie watched the youngster being carried off the field; now he had someone else to win for. In the top of the seventh, Irvin and Lockman had leadoff singles. Lopat got the next out, but Bill Rigney hit a sacrifice fly that scored Irvin, cutting the Yankee lead in half, 2–1. In the bottom of the eighth inning, Bobby Brown singled, and Stengel sent Billy Martin in to run for his nonpareil hitter. Martin managed to move into scoring position with two out, with Lopat scheduled to hit. Durocher had pinch-hit for Jansen earlier and now George Spencer was working for the Giants. He looked to the Yankee dugout to see who was selecting a bat. Adding to his peace of mind, he saw Lopat walking out to the batter's box, hitting for himself. Spencer relaxed. He shouldn't have.

Allie, Vic and Eddie used to bet nickels on base hits. Besides the hearts card games, the only other competition they took delight in among themselves concerned who was the better hitter. Each one took pride in being a pitcher who was not an automatic out and who could help himself with the bat. Each was a superb athlete with eye and hand coordination that provided them with the ability to make contact.[17] In this situation, with a man in scoring position and two out, Eddie stood in the batter's box with a hitter's resolve. He was also trying to get into Spencer's head. "He'll throw me a breaking ball on the first pitch, just to set me up. He'll go for the outside corner." The crafty Lopat feigned a pitcher's indifference in stepping in to hit. He knew he was not going to waste any time. If he saw a good first pitch, he would go for it. Spencer looked at Martin, rocked into his motion, and through a not-very-sharp curveball that started on the outside of the plate and would break in a way that gave Lopat a very good look at a pitch he now was anticipating. The old first baseman's instincts sharpened, he shot his bat out, turned his hips only slightly, and rapped a line drive over shortstop, driving in the third Yankee run. Reynolds and Raschi leaped out of the dugout, along with Jim Turner. The Yankees and Lopat tied the World Series with Eddie getting a complete game five-hitter, 3–1. That night, three couples celebrated over dinner.[18]

Weiss could not get Monte Irvin out of his mind. In Game Two he added three more hits to the four of the previous day. The black outfielder had banged out seven consecutive hits against Yankee pitching and ran the bases with brilliant abandon. Although he was concentrating completely on the game, in the recesses of his mind, the bigoted Yankee general manager knew that he would have to do something. Mantle had astonishing talent, but this year had been a hard test for the young rookie. Could he deliver? Weiss believed that Mantle's extraordinary talent would match up against any of the black athletes he had seen so far; but Mays and Irvin on the Giants and Robinson, Campanella, and Newcombe in Brooklyn made it clear that one superbly talented white ballplayer on the Yankees would not carry the day in the long run. He would have to instruct his scouts: look for black talent, but make certain they are "the right kind."[19]

There was to be no break in the action without any travel time. The competition now moved to the Polo Grounds for Game Three, Vic Raschi against Jim Hearn. The 53,035 fans represented the largest crowd ever to see a World Series game in a National League park. They would not see Mickey Mantle, who was in Lenox Hill Hospital, following surgery on his damaged knee. The other hopeful rookie, Willie Mays, drove in his first World Series run with a single in the bottom of the second. It stayed 1–0 until the bottom of the fifth, when the roof collapsed on Vic. Two errors by Rizzuto and Berra let in five unearned runs and Raschi was knocked from the box, the earliest he had ever been lifted in World Series competition. The Giants went on to win, 7–2, and took a 2–1 lead going into a game the next day when the Yankees could only throw rookie Tom Morgan. Suddenly, the odds from Las Vegas made the Giants favorites. This was it. Finally, the Yankees, like DiMaggio, were wearing down.

It rained the next day. Turner went to Stengel. "We are down by one game, we are playing the next two games in the Polo Grounds. Give the ball to the Indian. He is madder than hell. We have to win the next game." Allie was indeed seething. He had seen only his friend Eddie Lopat win so far; Raschi and Reynolds, two of the Yankee stalwarts, had been driven off the mound. Something had to get straightened out. In this state of mind, Turner knew that he would get 150 percent out of his pitcher. Reynolds got the start.

At the end of the first inning of Game Four, the Giants were on top, 1–0, but the Yankees tied it in the second on Bobby Brown's long sacrifice fly. Allie brought his friends to the top of the dugout in the fourth inning by singling in a run off Giant starter Sal Maglie. Then, Joe DiMaggio, who had been pitiful at the plate, got hold of a Maglie fastball and smacked a two-run homer into the left-field stands, his last in a World Series.[20] Reynolds went into the ninth inning with a 6–1 lead, but he had been in trouble for the whole game, nearly a dozen times going to full counts. In the last inning, the Giants started in, again. They scored, and with two on and one in, Willie Mays came to bat. For all the trouble that Allie had had with the Giants that day, he had Mays' number. The rookie, first-ball swinging, had killed two rallies with inning-ending double plays. Now, he had a chance to redeem himself. Reynolds had reached back each time with Mays and had thrown him one of his patented up-and-in fastballs. Mays, straining to get the fat part of the bat on the ball, with his unbelievable reflects got *on top* and drove it twice sharply into the ground. It was no small feat to double up Mays, who, like Mantle, exploded out of the batter's box. But, these two ground balls had been hit hard to the left side of the infield and ended up as 6–4–3 twin killings.

Casey was worried about his warrior on the mound. He called time and went out to speak to Reynolds. The conversation lasted ten seconds. Stengel seemed to ask two questions, which Allie answered with one word. The manager turned to walk back to the dugout, swung around again for a parting thought, and then walked again. As Stengel reached the dugout, Reynolds was going into his stretch, with Mays coiled at home plate. The pitch came in. An observer would have noted, in less time than the thought could shoot through the mind, that Mays was off balance when he swung, reaching over the outside of the plate to attempt what for most right-handed hitters is a fruitless gesture: trying to pull a low-and-outside curveball. Mays got wood on the ball, but drilled it on two hops to Rizzuto, who started the third double play that poor Willie Mays had hit into that day, this time ending the game in a 6–2 Yankee World Series victory.

The conversation with Casey? It went like this: "Did you throw him fastballs the first two times?" "Yes." "Have you thrown him a curve?" "No." "Well, try one." Then, as he was walking back to the dugout, Stengel turned to remind his pitcher: "Keep it down." Which is exactly what Allie did.

Game Five was the last to be played in the Giants' home park, and it was a reprise of Game Two, Lopat versus Jansen. The Series was tied at 2–2, and each team had a chance. Eddie had never started twice in a World Series, and he was thrilled. On a cold, raw day, the Giants jumped off to a 1–0 lead in the first — and that was the end of their offense for the day. The Yankees scored five runs in the third, four coming across on Gil McDougald's grand slam, the first by a rookie in World Series history. The Yankee onslaught went on all day, until Eddie Lopat walked off the hill with his second complete game five-hitter of the World Series, a 13–1 crushing of the Giants. But, Eddie had paid a price. Relaxing in the clubhouse after the game and answering reporters' questions, he stayed in uniform, because he knew that he would not be able to raise his arm in order to take off his sweatshirt. After the crowd had left, he admitted to Turner, Vic and Allie that he had popped something in his shoulder.

Now, the Yankees were in control, with a 3–2 lead in games and a chance to close out the World Series in Yankee Stadium in Game Six. Allie had redeemed himself; now it was Vic's turn. Dave Koslo was back for the Giants. Game Six was a 1–1 tie going into the bottom of the sixth, when Hank Bauer tripled with the bases loaded to give the Yankees a 4–1 lead. When the Giants led off the bottom of the seventh with two singles, Casey went to the mound and took out his big right-hander. Vic, exhausted, let Johnny Sain have the next two innings. (DiMaggio doubled in the bottom of eighth, his last major league hit.) In the ninth, still leading 4–1, Sain faltered. The Giants loaded the bases on three singles with none out. Monte Irvin was the hitter, and Bobby Thomson of home run fame, was on deck. The Giants could rally.

Here, Stengel showed one of those characteristic acts of managing that left observers stunned and in awe. He had two powerful right-handed hitters coming up, in a ballpark with notoriously inviting stands not even 300 feet from home plate. His pitcher Sain had not been hit hard, even in this bases-loaded inning. He was an experienced relief pitcher who had been in tight World Series spots before. Stengel consulted Jim Turner, but it was Casey's move: he called for Bob Kuzava, a left-hander, the mid-year acquisition from the Washington Senators, with no World Series experience. He was calling him to a game before 61,711 people in the ninth inning with the bases loaded and none out to face two of the most formidable right-handed hitters in the National League.

A left-hander to face Irvin and Thomson? The reporters in the press section looked at each other and thought Stengel had finally lost his marbles. Irvin batting; he drilled a long, high fly ball to deep left center, taken by Woodling. A run scored, the runners tagged up and advanced, score, 4–2. Thomson next, hit another long, high fly ball to deep left center, again taken by Woodling. The second run of the inning scored, the lone runner left advanced to third, score, 4–3. Durocher now called on back-up catcher Sal Yvars to hit for left-handed hitting Hank Thompson, and Yvars drilled a low line drive to right field, where Bauer made the catch six inches off the ground, sliding on the seat of his pants. Game over, Kuzava a savior, Stengel a genius. Yankees win, 4–3, and win their third consecutive World Series. It was October 10, 1951, and Joe DiMaggio had played his last game in a New York Yankee uniform.

Eddie Lopat had won two complete games and had a glittering 0.50 ERA. His buddies had struggled somewhat, but each had won a game; over the three World Series from 1949 to 1951, Eddie, Vic and Allie had been responsible for 10 of the 12 victories. In this World Series, they were on the mound for forty-four of the fifty-three innings pitched and all four of the victories. The two right-handers delighted in the new public recognition of their friend

It was a happy, but solemn clubhouse after the victory. DiMaggio had told the reporters that he had played his last game, although he had come alive in the last few games and banged out six hits. Comparing his performance to that of Willie Mays, who hit a pathetic 4-for-22 with a .182 batting average without an extra-base hit, the Yankee star didn't look too bad, but he knew that he was through. Some of his teammates were crowding around, hugging him. When the crowd broke up, DiMaggio, with a cigarette dangling from his lips and a half-cup of coffee in his hand, pulled himself up from his stool and walked over to a corner of the clubhouse, to where the three pitchers were sitting. "You thanked me before. Let me thank you. Over these last few years we weren't the best ball club in the league, and I couldn't always play the way I wanted to. But we had the three best pitchers in the world." He shook hands with Eddie, Vic, and Allie and walked away from baseball.

That night at the Biltmore, there was another Topping-Webb victory celebration that lasted late into the night. The Reynolds would leave early, because Earlene wanted to pack up so she could get back to the kids in Oklahoma. Sally and Vic wouldn't wait much longer, either, to get back to Conesus in upstate New York. None of them drank much. Libby always kept an eye on Eddie's sensitive stomach. Yogi and Carmen came over to the table where the six friends were sitting. The Berras had bought a house in New Jersey, near the Lopats and Rizzutos, and were going to spend their first winter off-season away from St. Louis.

A few weeks later, Yogi got a phone call. He had been voted the Most Valuable Player in the American League. "How could you do this?" he said. He had hit only .294 and knocked in only eighty-eight runs. "What about Allie?" he asked. "Seven shutouts, two no-hitters?" He was championing his pitcher, but it didn't make a difference. Reynolds came in third in the MVP voting. No other pitcher was in the top ten.

Allie would, nonetheless, get his share of recognition. The New York chapter of the Baseball Writers Association of America picked him as Player of the Year. The *Los Angeles Times*, at its National Sports Award dinner, also named Reynolds its Player of the Year.

The most remarkable award that Allie received that winter was the Ray Hickok Award as Professional Athlete of the Year, only the second year of the award's existence. Reynolds was presented with a diamond-studded jeweled belt that had nearly three pounds of gold in it and was encrusted with diamonds, rubies and sapphires.

All three of them would be busy the coming winter with promotions and advertisements. Their names and faces appeared in ads for cigarettes, hot dogs, ice cream (Eddie's favorite), oatmeal and many other products. Weiss also reminded them of this profitable activity when it came to salary negotiations.

They would keep in touch, but as usual, the families were ready to go home. Allie would probably be back in New York City at some time in the winter since he had taken over from Tommy Henrich as player representative for the Yankees. His teammates had elected him. He was the senior statesman on the team, prepared to be outspoken, if necessary, in his dealings with management.

His teammates knew that George Weiss respected him, and that he would stick up for the players' rights. Most important, he didn't have to worry about negotiating with the general manager. Everyone knew that Allie, like Casey, had interests in oil and was independent when it came to having to negotiate salary.

As they said goodbye at the end of the season, there was an added nostalgia among the three friends and their spouses, a little chill of winter at the passing of time. DiMaggio, at age thirty-six, was gone, representing the end of an era. It was not lost on them that Allie was about the same age as Joe, and that Eddie and Vic were not far behind. Bobby Doerr had told the Red Sox that he was finished, his back miseries forcing him into retirement at age thirty-three. The years were moving along. How much more time did they have together, making magic? They had put up numbers during this regular season that represented their best years ever. The older they got, the more efficient was their performance. Lopat's ERA, 2.91, the second best in the league, 209 hits in 235 innings; Raschi's 3.28 ERA, 233 hits in 258 innings, leading the league in strikeouts with 164; Reynolds, with an ERA of 3.05, a meager 171 hits in 221 innings, seven shutouts. Even Weiss, grudgingly, acknowledged their value to the team by giving them salaries that reflected their accomplishments. Although he preferred to add in the World Series shares — an additional six or seven thousand dollars each year — the three pitchers wanted those dollars kept out of the negotiations. They were making as much as $30,000 a year, which was more than outstanding position players were earning. Yogi had made $30,000 for the 1951 season. Robin Roberts, the outstanding Phillies pitcher, made $25,000. Roy Campanella, the great Dodger catcher, received $19,000. Monte Irvin, who hit nearly .600 in the World Series, got $12,000 for the year. The rookie Mickey Mantle earned $7,500.

For three years the three Yankee hurlers had accomplished feats that had been attained by only a handful of pitchers in major league history. Now, they were beginning to see the cost of their efforts. Allie's bone chips might require surgery; Vic's knees were giving out; and Eddie's arm was feeling arthritic. It had been a great run; perhaps it was coming to the end. Some of their friends were retiring from the game. There were more rookies, more young kids like Mantle, Billy Martin and Eddie Ford. They seemed a little different, less experienced, even maybe less responsible, without the concerns of children and families. Henrich and Keller were gone; now DiMaggio, too. The three were now clearly the veterans, the senior Yankees, the enforcers, along with Bauer and Woodling. It was not a role that came easily for Rizzuto and Berra. The Yankee intangibles would depend on the three pitchers more than ever. Could they maintain their skills and still lead by example?

Weiss was also being reflective about age, but not his own. He noticed

Raschi's occasional limp and had spoken to the team physician about torn ten-
dons and cartilage damage. He was concerned about Reynolds' bone chips, and
he also knew how old Allie actually was. Lopat, who didn't throw as hard as
the other two, really never had a smooth motion, could easily — and quickly —
break down. Weiss was not interested in friendship, loyalty, or even team chemistry, that intangible quality that is found rarely in a clubhouse, a quality that
can bind a team together to accomplish feats that individual statistics could
not produce. If he had a problem with a player, he either traded him or hired
a private detective to follow him. He was an ingenious evaluator of talent; he
knew little about human nature, and cared less. His mind working, the general manager in the off-season began his quest for the next generation who
would eventually take the place of his three aces. He even had his own order:
Raschi first, then Lopat, finally Reynolds; but, wait a while, not long. It was
time to start thinking.

On November 23, the Yankees traded one of their surplus catchers, Clint
Courtney, to the St. Louis Browns for twenty-four-year-old right-handed
pitcher Jim McDonald, who during the 1951 season had only four wins, but had
beaten the Yankees twice, and his other two victories were against Cleveland
and Boston. Weiss was planning for the future.

That winter, Weiss and Allie met to talk contract. With his two no-hitters, Reynolds was looking for a reasonable salary increase; Weiss was not.
"Well, Allie, it's good to see you. You didn't finish too many games for us, but
we are not going to cut your contract." "Well," said Reynolds, "I'm going to
cut you, right below the belt. I had much better than a fair year." After a hard
negotiation, Allie got what he thought he deserved. Nothing was easy with
Weiss, and nothing was pleasant.

7

Rickey's Dodgers

Great baseball minds come in generations. The first decade of the twentieth century produced John McGraw, Connie Mack, and Clark Griffith, each with a genius for identifying talent and nurturing it, each with a philosophy of the game uncommon to the times, each with a legacy whose influence could be felt well into the 1930s. All three produced a mini-dynasty of excellence: McGraw with the New York Giants, Mack with the Philadelphia Athletics, and Griffith with the Washington Senators. All three are enshrined in baseball's Hall of Fame.

McGraw and Mack attained an eminence as managers that made their names famous and secured their reputations for all time. Clark Griffith, who started out like McGraw and Mack as a player, also became a manager, but he made his lasting impact as an owner by daring to pick managers for his teams in Washington that no other owner would risk. In 1924, he made his twenty-seven-year-old second baseman Bucky Harris his player-manager, and in 1924 and 1925 stopped the Babe Ruth-led New York Yankees dead in their tracks while taking two consecutive American League pennants and a World Series title. In 1933, he repeated his daring move of the previous decade by handing the team over to his twenty-six-year-old shortstop, Joe Cronin, who also happened to be his son-in-law, and again took the pennant away from New York. From then on, the Washington Senators became a model of futility and mediocrity. But, Harris and Cronin, Griffith's two bold choices, went on to careers that lasted decades as managers, general managers, and in Cronin's case, president of the American League, from 1959 to 1973. Harris managed until 1956, nearly 4,500 games. Casey Stengel played for McGraw, learned from him and built his own managerial philosophy on McGraw's ideas.

There was only one figure in twentieth century baseball history who became a generation unto himself. Branch Rickey was unique and inimitable, a true transformer of the game. He spanned two centuries. Born in 1881, educated in a strict Methodist tradition at Ohio Wesleyan and later at the University of Michigan Law School, Rickey was an authentic God-inspired visionary, showman and confidence man who found in baseball administration the perfect instrument for his unique talents and mission. He had been a player, coach, teacher and manager, but it was as the general manager of the St. Louis Cardinals in the early 1920s when Rickey's talent for organization and ideas first transformed baseball. He believed that the Cardinals could not compete with the likes of Yankees owner Jacob Ruppert, who was willing to spend limitless amounts of money to procure talent from other teams. Rickey had an idea that intrigued his owner Sam Breadon: buy lots of cheap, young talent before anyone noticed how good some of these players were, stock them on minor league teams that the Cardinals also controlled, and then, as the players matured, skim off the best and bring them to the major league team. The less gifted could be sold at a profit to other teams. Rickey, with his usual rhetorical flourishes and evangelical passion, announced that he would plant his talent, watch it grow, then harvest the riches: he had created the farm system. As long as the reserve clause protected the owners from outside competition, Rickey could control these youngsters, who simply had no other options. In the 1920s and 1930s, Rickey turned the St. Louis Cardinals into an efficient baseball machine that produced quality players, particularly for the Cardinals, but for other teams as well. He also had an exceptional eye for talent.

Branch Rickey, ca. 1949: Perhaps the most important baseball executive of the 20th century (National Baseball Hall of Fame Library, Cooperstown, N.Y.).

After the 1942 season, Rickey left St. Louis to become general manager and then part owner and president of the Brooklyn Dodgers. He arrived in Flatbush at the age of sixty-one; in the next seven years he built the foundation for one of the greatest baseball dynasties in history, and in doing so, changed baseball forever. He also forged the link that tied two names together for all of baseball eternity: Robinson and Rickey. It was Branch Rickey's uniquely American evangelical fervor that viewed the integration of black ballplayers into Organized Baseball as both morally right and potentially enormously profitable. He had judged himself to be the best possible instrument of social justice and capitalism. In Brooklyn, he integrated baseball and went beyond what he had built in St. Louis. Starting in 1943, Rickey gained complete control over those Brooklyn Dodger farm teams with whom there had been only working agreements. He took charge of their baseball operations, instructional methods, coaching, everything. Every player signed by Brooklyn was to be taught the proper skills of baseball the way it would be played by the Dodgers. Rickey was totally dedicated to the centralized instruction of the talent he wanted to develop. In 1947, the Navy announced that it was abandoning a naval air station at Vero Beach, Florida. Rickey immediately bought up this government surplus facility. He soon transformed it into a baseball camp that has become the model for every major league franchise, right into the twenty-first century. At Vero Beach the Dodgers brought together all the minor league players, coaches, managers, and personnel from top to bottom, for a shared experience. It was from Rickey's Vero Beach incubator that Casey Stengel hatched the idea of the Yankee instructional school.

By 1949, the results for Brooklyn were clear to everyone in baseball. The Dodger team whom the Yankees beat in the World Series had been together for only one year. No position player was over thirty, the ages of Robinson and shortstop Pee Wee Reese. Gil Hodges was twenty-five, Carl Furillo twenty-seven, Duke Snider twenty-two, Roy Campanella twenty-seven, Don Newcombe twenty-three, Carl Erskine twenty-two, Ralph Branca twenty-three. All but Campanella and Newcombe came out of the Dodger farm system and had spent time at Vero Beach; all were personally scouted by Rickey before they were signed. Campanella and Newcombe were products of the Negro leagues, where Rickey and his special scout Clyde Sukeforth had spotted them. Only third baseman Billy Cox and pitcher Preacher Roe were acquired by trade, in a shrewd Rickey deal with the Pittsburgh Pirates that got rid of the irreconcilable southerners — Kirby Higbe, Dixie Walker and others — who would not play with a black man.

Rickey was gone by the end of the 1950 season, beaten out of owner-partnership by the shrewd maneuvers of another owner-partner, Walter O'Malley, who eventually gained complete control of the franchise and put himself in a position to reap the harvest of Rickey's efforts. They seemed to have everything in place, even the chemistry and off-field camaraderie that marked the unique intimacy of the Yankee teams of this era. Many of these Dodgers lived together in Brooklyn neighborhoods, ate in local restaurants, were in every way part of the community. They liked each other, and they had in Pee Wee Reese a leader around whom everyone could join. Reese almost single-handedly settled any racial issues that might exist between Robinson and his teammates. Once this Kentuckian put his arm around Jackie's shoulder in the middle of the diamond near second base during warm-ups between innings, the team was completely unified. Reese was the only Dodger who could look the often prickly Robinson in the eye and say, "Jack, some of those guys hate you because you're black. Others don't like you because you can be a real pain in the ass."

Yet, as these homegrown Dodgers ripened as a superb team, they still somehow managed to lose the National League pennant in 1950 to the Whiz Kids and in 1951 in the disaster to the Giants, ironically, because of flaws in the personalities of these two otherwise smart but incompatible operators, Rickey and O'Malley.

One of the characteristics of the entrepreneur — which Branch Rickey clearly was — requires that he alone stand at the center stage, pronouncing and generally holding forth. Rickey saw himself as the Grand Old Man, *the* authority on all things pertaining to the Brooklyn Dodgers; the press dubbed him "the Mahatma." In Rickey's case, he also believed that he was the best judge of how the team should be run. He inherited the charismatic Leo Durocher, who in 1941 had led the Dodgers to their first pennant in twenty-one years and was a shrewd baseball strategist, but Rickey hated Durocher's morals, filthy mouth, and ability to hog the limelight. When Durocher got himself suspended for the 1947 season, Rickey turned to a low-profile, reticent baseball veteran who didn't even like to wear a uniform in the dugout (and did not for his entire tenure as Brooklyn manager). Burt Shotton was sixty-two years old and any flare that he possessed had died out years earlier. He was no one Rickey would have to share the stage with. He also was a minimalist manager and took little advantage of the enormous talent he had on those teams. Shotton managed in the suspension year of 1947, then Rickey brought him back again when Durocher jumped to the Giants in 1948, when the Boston Braves beat out both the Dodgers and the Giants. Shotton under-managed Rickey's young Dodgers to a squeaker pennant victory over St. Louis on the last day of the season in 1949 and the last-day loss to the Phillies in 1950. In both years the Dodgers were clearly the best team in the National League.

With Rickey gone and O'Malley now completely in charge, he looked around for someone who knew the game and how it should be played. Clearly O'Malley did not. He was a lawyer, a businessman, and was interested primarily in making money. In 1957, the people of the borough of Brooklyn discovered that he wasn't even interested in *them*.[1]

O'Malley turned 180 degrees from Rickey and selected Charlie Dressen, the ultimate "over-manager" who was later famous for having said to his Brooklyn team during a tight game, "Keep 'em close, fellas, until I can think of something." Dressen, whom the Yankee pitchers and catchers universally hated when he coached for Bucky Harris, was considered an uncontrollable meddler, particularly with pitchers. Now, he had as his instrument one of the premier squads in major league baseball. Dressen had managed in the big leagues in the 1930s and had flopped. He had been a coach under Durocher and Harris and had managed in the high minor leagues. It was Dressen, with his Dodgers thirteen games ahead, who pronounced to the press in August of 1951, "The Giants is dead!" As the Giants closed the gap, Dressen panicked and overworked his starting pitchers, leading to the tragic fate of Ralph Branca and Bobby Thomson's home run. O'Malley, instead of blaming his manager, fired the third base coach, and Dressen was re-hired.

As preparations for the 1952 season began, the Brooklyn Dodgers appeared ready to fulfill all their promise and to blot out the memory of the previous two years. Finally, the Dodger dynasty had arrived.

"How's the arm, Allie?" Vic asked over the telephone, calling from Conesus, New York.

"Not good, and my back is aching. You, Vic?"

"I'm not walking well. Both knees are swollen. I threw yesterday for the first time this winter, and I could feel the mechanics were off. Jim called. I could tell he was worried. Eddie told me his arm still aches. We're all creaking. See you in a couple of weeks. Hey, we're all signed!"

True, they all would be in St. Petersburg for the opening of camp. Weiss, uncharacteristically, had made salary offers that all three pitchers could accept in what was normally the first round of a tough negotiation. For the first time, Vic, who always seemed to have the biggest problem with the general manager, signed his contract without first sending it back. Weiss, with DiMaggio's $100,000 salary gone, could be a little more flexible.

This was not a promising exchange between old friends before the start of spring training in 1952. They would arrive at spring training, not merely with the usual need to get loose and to shake off the winter's stiffness. They were coming to St. Pete to work with the trainer and team physician. No one wanted surgery.[2] But, something had to be done. The three Yankee aces were in no shape to start the season.

There were other troubles, as well. With the Korean War still raging, Ford was gone; Bobby Brown and Tom Morgan had been told that they would be called up shortly. Also, Jerry Coleman, a veteran pilot in World War II, received word that he would soon begin jet training when his reserve status would be activated for duty in Korea.

Many of the married players were bringing families. Casey and Edna, who never had any children, let the team out early the first couple of days so the players could take their kids to the beach. There would be plenty of time for hard work. The press got on Stengel for running a "country club," but Casey told them, "You say I'm running a country club because I let them bring their families to Florida. But for some reason I never have to worry about my ballplayers at night. I know where they are. The best protection in the world is their wives and kids."

As usual, the three pitchers had rentals near each other, along with Yogi and Carmen; the Colemans, too. Jerry was very much the family man and gravitated to the world that the Raschis, Reynolds and Lopats had shared, along with Gil and Lucille McDougald and Gene and Betty Woodling. Eddie Lopat was the godfather of little Timmy Berra. Phil Rizzuto was godfather to Larry, Jr. It was not unusual, after a double-session workout at Miller Huggins or Al Lang Field, to see ten or twelve Yankees going out for a beer or going home to what looked like an enormous team barbecue put together by the wives, with *everyone* invited. There were no cliques. The enforcers would not permit it.

As Yankee spring training got under way, the New York and national press were in evidence everywhere, ironically, because of someone who was *not* in camp. The Yankee Clipper, Joe DiMaggio, after thirteen years in pinstripes, was gone. The media kept up a constant drumbeat: the Yankees could not win without DiMaggio. Within a month, the drums turned into a full orchestra. Mantle was still hobbled from the knee injury and surgery (he would run for the rest of his career with a limp). Berra pulled ligaments in his foot and then sprained his wrist swinging. The doctors told Stengel that Berra might miss the first month of the season. Billy Martin, while demonstrating his sliding technique, broke his ankle; and the three pitchers were not sound. Raschi, Lopat and Reynolds had not pitched more than three innings at a stretch for the first month of spring training. With these injuries and the Yankee losses to the draft, the overwhelming consensus to win the American League pennant was Cleveland. Hank Greenberg, now general manager of the Indians, confidently told a gathering of reporters that this Yankee team could expect a second-division finish. The Yankee performance in the Grapefruit League was in deep contrast to the fantastic pitching of Feller, Lemon, Garcia and Wynn, who were cutting down Cleveland's pre-season opposition day after day in exhibition games. It didn't seem to matter that they had no left-handed starter and hadn't had one since 1949. So what if the Yankees had some formidable left-handed hitters in Berra, Woodling, Mize, Collins, and the kid switch-hitter Mantle? Even if right-handers would pitch 90 percent of their innings, the Indians were too tough; they also had the bats. Luke Easter, Ray Boone, Al Rosen and Larry Doby would provide plenty of power. There was no doubt in the minds of the press: There was no one to replace DiMaggio, and the three Yankees aces were finished. It was Cleveland's year. Writer Robert Creamer remembers, "The sportswriters agreed that this was Casey's worst team with the Yankees."[3] The Bible of baseball,

The Sporting News, picked Cleveland. Greenberg beamed in newspaper photos.

Stengel was worried. He didn't care so much about his infield problems. He had McDougald, who could play third, shortstop and second and be an all-star at all of them. In the outfield, he had Mantle, who would heal; Jackie Jensen, another golden boy who was almost as fast as Mantle and hit with power (he was also white); and promising rookie Bob Cerv. One of them would start between Woodling and Bauer, who would finally play full-time. Even Berra would be back soon enough. As for the pitching, Stengel knew that without his three aces, he was doomed. He talked to Turner every day about prospects, training regimens, who looked good, who looked bad. Finally, he had to ask the tough question and went to Turner. "Jim, how are my old men doing? Will the Indian come through? What about the Dago's knees? And Lopat's arm? Are they done for? If so, I gotta talk to Weiss." Turner had grown as wary of the general manager as had his pitchers, and did not want to expose any weakness. He also knew that the three of them were pacing themselves very carefully. They were in superb condition, even though Vic could not run as hard as he normally did. He made it up by running longer and slower. Jim had kept them on a very limited pitch count all during spring training. "When the gun goes off, they will be ready. We may have some trouble with the lefthander. It's in the shoulder, not like the other two. Allie says Eddie only needs some WD 40, but it's more serious. Sain is going to have to start and relieve; and Allie will, too. Don't worry."

That's all that Stengel needed to hear. His coach and wisest of the wise when it came to the care and nurturing of his pitching staff had told him: don't worry. Casey knew that these three men were closer to their pitching coach than they were to any other person on earth, with the *possible* exception of their wives. They not only pitched for the team; they pitched for each other, and above all for *Turner*, for his approbation. If anyone knew what the capacity of these three arms would be during the season, it was Jim Turner. There were no secrets. This was a relationship that no one else shared. Casey stopped worrying, or at least worried less.

With the sun shining down on Al Lang Field, four men stood in the outfield, watching batting practice. Jim Turner was speaking. "We have more young kids this year. DiMaggio, Coleman and Brown are gone. You three are going to have to step up even more. You know that Yogi and Phil can't do it. Watch Mantle and Martin when they are together. You need to scare the shit out of them." It had become clear to most of the older players that Mantle and Martin were capable of getting into a special kind of trouble. They hustled and played very hard, but once the game was over, you could see them disappear into the nightlife of St. Petersburg, such as it was, even though young Mantle

Mickey Mantle: The kid from Oklahoma, age 17 in 1951 (National Baseball Hall of Fame Library, Cooperstown, N.Y.).

had gotten married over the winter. "Chief, you are the player representative. You can give 'em hell whenever you want. Vic, you just look at 'em. Eddie, Mickey is already scared of you." It was true. In Mantle's rookie year, he was brooding out in right field after striking out in the previous inning. With Lopat on the mound, he got a slow jump on a fly ball that cost a run. When they came into the dugout, Eddie tore into the rookie: "Do you want to play ball or not? If you don't then get the hell out of here!" That day, Allie played "the good cop," went up to the humiliated teenager and spoke to him. "How about two Oklahomans having dinner in this big city? My treat." Allie, who made it a point of making rookies feel comfortable, knew that Mantle needed some fatherly advice that day, and not Billy Martin's brand of liquid consolation. From that time on, Reynolds made a point of spending as much time as he could with Mantle, driving to Yankee Stadium together when they were both staying in a hotel, and even in the off-season, always attending events back home when Mickey was being honored. On May 6, 1952, Mickey's father, who had been the pivotal force in making him a ballplayer and keeping him at it, succumbed to cancer. The twenty-year-old was devastated by the loss. Allie consoled him, talked to him, helped him grieve. Mantle never forgot this.

Now, the three war horses were preparing themselves for the team effort and sacrifice that would be required for the Yankees to win a fourth pennant and World Series. They had John Sain, who like Allie could start and relieve. No one thought it was possible, except the four of them. They trusted their coach to shepherd and protect them, not to overuse, particularly not to strain Allie if he had to start and relieve. Turner would always look out for his pitchers. Casey deferred. When it came to who was conducting business on the mound, the boss was Jim Turner. He would make certain that there was enough left in the tanks come September.

The Season of 1952

During September, when the pennant was up for grabs, Raschi, Reynolds and Lopat were unbeatable. They just wouldn't lose. — Yogi Berra

Things started off very badly. Lopat's shoulder just would not come around. Raschi's knees could not support him for a complete game. Only Reynolds exploded out of the gate, but it was not enough. He tossed five complete games in his first five starts and got a total of seven runs in support. In the first twenty-seven innings of Reynolds pitching, the Yankees scored two runs. He had a 2–3 record and an ERA under two! Lopat was 1–3, didn't have a complete game, and was in pain. As the end of May approached, the Yankees were 15–17 and stuck in fifth place, while Cleveland had gotten off to a terrific start. The sportswriters clucked and shook their heads. They had been right: DiMaggio was irreplaceable. Jackie Jensen was hitting .118, rookie Bob Cerv couldn't get over .240, and the kid from Oklahoma was still limping in right field. The end had finally come. Articles started appearing, describing the twilight of the gods, the aging of the Yankees, particularly the three veteran pitchers, who were being carried now by Allie Reynolds, the oldest of the gang. It was only a matter of time before he, too, would break down. The writers saw signs of early front office panic. Jensen, who started the season in center field, fell to an anemic .105, and Stengel gave up on him. On May 3, two weeks into the season, the Yankees traded their starting center fielder along with Bucky Harris-holdover Spec Shea to the Washington Senators for veteran outfielder-first baseman Irv Noren. But, what Casey really wanted was Mantle permanently in the lineup. He also wanted him in center field, as DiMaggio's replacement. When Mickey finally got there, on May 20, he stayed for the next fifteen years.

When Lopat could lift his left arm and pitch, he was effective enough. He did not get much run support, but still managed to post a 5–5 record with an

ERA around three when he finally gave up before the All-Star break and went on the disabled list for the first time in his major league career. He would not pitch for six weeks. The team physician diagnosed his ailment as tendonitis and inflammation. Eddie's arm needed rest. His buddies would take up the slack. Vic, doing daily strength exercises for the torn cartilage in his knees, put together three complete games. Meanwhile, Johnny Sain jumped into the starting rotation.

But Reynolds was relentless. By June 19 he had twelve consecutive complete games and three shutouts. His record was 8–4, and he also had three saves in three relief appearances! The Yankees weren't scoring many runs, but Allie wasn't giving up many, either. Hank Bauer led the team with just six home runs. Mantle and Berra, going into June, had three home runs each.

Stengel was also at his improvisational best. Every day was an adventure in lineup creation. One day McDougald would lead off, next day he would hit fifth and Woodling or Bauer would hit in the first spot. That year McDougald would hit in *eight* different places in the batting order. The same pattern worked for everyone, depending on the day's needs. Berra hit anywhere from second to seventh in the order, as did Noren. Casey would use Mickey anywhere from leadoff to the fifth spot.

Then, in June, with Eddie on the shelf and Sain in the rotation, Vic and Allie put it all together, and the Yankees also started hitting. The Cleveland Indians and their confident general manager Hank Greenberg began looking over their shoulders as their lead vanished. Reynolds, Raschi and Sain went 25–9 up to the All-Star break. Berra hit ten home runs in June. Mantle, playing regularly in center field for the first time in his life, was leading the league in outfield errors and was on a course to lead the league in strikeouts, but he was hitting over .300 and had notched some stupendous home runs, both left-handed and right-handed. Woodling and Bauer, as usual, were hitting around .300 and driving in runs. Stengel, when Billy Martin's leg healed, put him at second base and moved McDougald to third. Martin's bat got hot, and so did his fists. Twice during the season he met opposing players under the stands and knocked them both cold. No matter what they thought of Martin's nocturnal exploits with Mantle, the pitchers were glad to have him in the lineup. He was a spark plug. By July 4, the Yankees were, to the shock of the denizens of the press box, in first place; not by a lot (at times as small a lead as one-half game), but in first place. Four teams were within three games of each other, and everyone expected the Cleveland Indians to make a charge and push the Yankees back where they belonged. But, the All-Star game told the rest of the league that when it came to stepping up, the Yankees were in no way dead: Raschi, Reynolds, Berra, Rizzuto, Bauer and Mantle were named to the American League squad.

Into August, the Yankees doggedly held on. The Indians gave every indication that they were ready to charge ahead, even taking first place — for one day — when New York lost three in a row to the White Sox and one to the Indians. They felt confident. Lopat was not around.

Weiss was desperate. He looked at the waiver lists for any pitching help. He had taken note of the September schedule. The Yankees had eighteen of their last twenty-one games on the road. Cleveland played twenty of its final twenty-two at home. Weiss knew he could not rely on Reynolds, Raschi, and Sain for three months, especially with Reynolds and Sain carrying the bulk of the relieving chores as well as starting. He needed to deal. On August 1, Weiss purchased veteran left-hander Johnny Schmitz from Brooklyn; on August 22, he picked up right-hander Ray Scarborough from the Red Sox. Schmitz started two games and was ineffective. On August 28, Weiss traded Schmitz and three minor league players to Cincinnati for five-time All-Star Ewell Blackwell. Scarborough and Blackwell helped, even though both had arm problems and were years past their peak. They won six games between them and saved one more. The only development that kept the Yankees a nose ahead of the Indians was Bob Feller's continued collapse during the last two months of the season. While his three pitching mates were on their way to twenty-win seasons, Feller would finish at 9–13 for his first sub-par year since arriving in the big leagues as a seventeen-year-old Iowa farm boy in 1936.

Then came the shot of adrenaline for the Yankees. Eddie Lopat had been in uniform all the while he was disabled and not pitching. He traveled with the team, cheered them on, sat with his pitching buddies, shared a road trip hotel room with Allie Reynolds as usual, and waited. In the middle of August, he came to Yankee Stadium early and looked for Charlie Silvera, Berra's back-up catcher. "Let's toss," he said, and began lobbing a baseball, waiting for the twinge of pain in his shoulder. It didn't come. He threw harder fastballs, then some curves, then a screwball. No pain. He told Turner that he was ready. The pitching coach took out his six-week schedule and circled a date: Sunday, September 14, at Cleveland. The Indian Killer would be ready.

As the season came to its climax, Early Wynn, Bob Lemon, and Mike Garcia were at the top of their form. The Yankees used fourteen different pitchers as starters, desperately trying to maintain momentum. But, when Eddie walked out to the bullpen to warm up for his first start in six weeks, against the St. Louis Browns, his teammates — and especially his two closest friends — were smiling. Things were back to normal.

Turner used Lopat very carefully, pitching him only once a week. In his first start, Eddie went five innings and got the win. He was now 6–5. Berra was thrilled. He always loved catching Lopat, because for the last two years he never gave any signals. They would just play catch, and Yogi could adjust to whatever Eddie threw: sneaky fastball, curve, screwball, knuckler, change of pace off the change of pace, overhand, three-quarters, sidearm. The hitters were confounded, but for his catcher it was a lark, and his catcher loved it.

Berra had evolved into a superlative psychologist for his three aces. He knew them intimately, understood their personalities and character. He was, in 1952, their equal, their peer, no longer a "project." When Berra thought that Vic was losing concentration, he would goad him into throwing harder, walking halfway out to the mound and calling, "Hey, Onionhead, is that as hard as you can throw?" which would infuriate Raschi. "Get down behind the plate, you sawed-off Dago ape, or I'll kill you!" raged Vic, and then he would throw harder. After the game, it was all forgotten. With Reynolds, Berra didn't need to stoke him; the Chief was ready at all times. The supreme compliment came when Allie told him to call the pitches during the game. Reynolds would shake him off if he wanted something else, but he gave his catcher the captain's chair. Berra had gotten into the heads of the three veterans so thoroughly that he was rarely shaken off. He knew what they wanted to throw, sometimes before they knew it.

When September 13 arrived, the Yankees had a razor-thin one-half game lead over Cleveland, who had won nine straight at home. Easter, Doby and Rosen had been beating up on pitching staffs throughout the league. Easter particularly had been swinging a lethal bat. The only American League team ahead in the season series was New York, 11–10. For the Indians' finale against Boston, Eddie caught a plane to spend the night resting in Cleveland. He would also catch the game in Municipal Stadium. He was worried about Vic, who was going against the White Sox in Chicago. His knees were acting up again. But, Cleveland was mostly on Eddie's mind. He spent the afternoon watching a baseball game.

Cleveland, riding on a nine-game winning streak, lost to the Red Sox in ten innings, 4–3. That night, Eddie picked up a late evening newspaper and read about the Yankee 6–5 victory over the Chicago White Sox. Vic Raschi pitched only into the sixth inning, but he was relieved by Johnny Sain with a 4–3 lead. Sain held off the Chisox in the seventh and eighth innings, but when the first two batters in the bottom of the ninth singled for Chicago, Stengel turned to his bullpen and brought in what *New York Times* veteran reporter John Drebinger called "Casey's unanswerable trump." Three ground balls later, Allie had his sixth save in six tries and preserved Vic's sixteenth and final victory of the season. This would not be a fourth consecutive twenty-win season for his friend. As he absorbed the details of the newspaper story, he thought that Vic was done for the season. Eddie read with tight lips that pitcher Vic Raschi, while covering first base in the fourth inning, had crashed and fallen hard. He only hoped that Vic could recover for the World Series—if the Yankees won the pennant.

Cleveland had blown a big game and had given the Yankees a game-and-a-half cushion. Now it was Sunday, for a one-game series, a make-up of a rainout.

But what might have been a routine game early in the season was now, with a handful of games remaining, of monumental importance. The Indians could close to within a half-game, a virtual tie, with a win. A loss—too terrible to contemplate—would put them two-and-a-half behind. *Cleveland had to win this one.*

On the date Jim Turner had circled a month before on his schedule, September 14, the biggest crowd of the year at any major league baseball game poured into Cleveland's Municipal Stadium: 73,609. Manager Al Lopez had his hottest pitcher ready to go. Mike Garcia had nineteen wins and a current streak of twenty-eight scoreless innings. He was 4–0 so far in the season against the Yankees. Lopez knew who would pitch for New York. He had known weeks ago, when Lopat came off the disabled list. It became inevitable when he read that the sly left-hander had started pitching and had not lost in his last three decisions. But the dead certainty came the day before, when the Indians took the field for the game against the Red Sox. Lopez was in his dugout watching his players loosening up when he heard a familiar voice from just behind him in the stands. "Hiya, Al. Give 'em hell today." Lopez turned around, and his blood ran cold. There smiling at him, out of uniform and just a spectator, was the Angel of Death: that goddam Polack Lopat! The manager felt cursed.

The next day, the previously unhittable Garcia gave up four runs in the third inning and was gone by the sixth. The Cleveland hitters, salivating as usual while they waited to hit against Lopat, peppered eight singles in the first five innings, but showed only one meager run for their efforts. In the top of the sixth inning, while taking his warm-ups, Eddie made a pre-arranged signal to Jim Turner: get someone ready, I'm tiring. He had a 4–1 lead.

Out in the visitors' bullpen there was movement. Lopez felt comfortable. It couldn't be *him*. He relieved yesterday and has been in the regular rotation without missing a start. No. It couldn't be *the Indian*. The deeply recessed Cleveland visitors' bullpen was just out of sight. Lopez could see the crouched Yankee catcher, but not the pitcher warming up. He noticed the popping sound as the warm-up pitches hit Charlie Silvera's mitt.

With two runners on base and one out, Eddie walked off the mound, rubbing the ball. He was finished, exhausted, and stalling. *He* knew who was coming in, because they had worked it out with Turner before the game started. After Lopat's seductive wizardry, bring in the smoke. Stengel went to the mound and waved his right hand. The Cleveland bench watched in stony silence as Allie Reynolds came striding in to relieve his friend and roommate and to protect his 4–1 lead.

It didn't take long. Reynolds, coming to the rescue for the second consecutive day, ended the inning quickly. He gave up one single over the next three innings of relief to save the win for his buddy in a 7–1 decision, and the Yankees

Steady Eddie at work (1951): Lopat was the quintessential off-speed left-hander (National Baseball Hall of Fame Library, Cooperstown, N.Y.).

continued to hammer Garcia's relievers. Eddie was now 35–9 lifetime against the frustrated Cleveland Indians. The hottest hitter in the Cleveland lineup, Luke Easter, struck out twice, hit into a double play, and stranded seven runners. The Yankees had won the season series, 12–10, and were two-and-a-half games in front.

To the relief of Lopat, Reynolds, Turner, Stengel, and the rest of the Yankees, Raschi's collision in the game against the White Sox did no permanent damage, although his knees could barely bend. He pitched the first half of a doubleheader against Boston nearly two weeks after his crash and threw seven shutout innings, with Sain getting the win in ten innings. He would have sixteen wins and get no more.

The season was coming down to the wire. For the Yankee hitters, it was ending just as it had begun: with complete futility. It didn't matter. In a Friday-Saturday-Sunday three-game series against the Philadelphia A's—the only games played at home in the past two weeks by the Yankees—New York's batters accounted for a *total of four runs*. In the first game little Bobby Shantz, on his way to an astonishing twenty-four wins for the fourth-place Athletics, shut out the Yankees, 2–0, on four hits. On Saturday, Lopat reciprocated with a 2–0 blanking of the A's, giving up four singles, also. Reynolds pitched on Sunday, going for his nineteenth victory. He threw a three-hitter, winning 1–0. It was his sixth shutout of the season. Drebinger could not let go of his bridge imagery: "Casey Stengel still seems to be holding trump and yesterday he played the most powerful card in his hand, the redoubtable Allie Reynolds."

The Yankee offense was anemic, and they still won two out of three games. The Yankee pitchers gave up a total of two runs in three games. In the two contests they won, Lopat and Reynolds gave up no runs. In a tribute to the total lack of political correctness of the time, the sub-headline describing Reynolds' shutout proclaimed, "Wahoo Leads League in Strikeouts."

Cleveland played exceptional baseball down the stretch, taking advantage of the home field and going 19–5. The Yankees, playing almost all of their games on the road, also went 19–5. Time ran out for the Indians. Allie was the pitcher of record for the second consecutive year in the game that clinched the pennant, in the 151st game of the season, with three remaining. Although he did it with a no-hitter the year before, this time was just as sweet, as he beat the Red Sox on September 25 in Fenway, 3–2, for the first twenty-win season in his career. Added to that, Allie drove in the winning run with a single in the ninth inning, bringing Vic, Eddie and Jim out of the dugout with cheers. His eight strikeouts nailed down the league lead. As a final punctuation to another remarkable season for Reynolds, he led the league with an ERA of 2.07 on a record of 20–6. His six saves put him in fourth place among closers.

The next day, the Yankees won their fourth consecutive pennant, beating

Philadelphia, 5–2, in eleven innings. Eddie went into the ninth inning tied at 2–2, was relieved by Sain, who got the win. Stengel had won the pennant in his first four seasons with the Yankees. He had done it, as columnist Arthur Daley proclaimed the next day in the *New York Times*, with the worst team he had had in the four years. In the clubhouse celebration after the clincher, it was not lost on Jim Turner that the manager called over to the photographers and yelled, "Take a picture with these guys. They gave me these pennants." He was pointing with a bony finger to a corner in the clubhouse.

For the first time since 1949, the opposition in the World Series would be the Brooklyn Dodgers, the club that had been heralded in New York City as the new dynasty. Looking at the Dodger lineup from top to bottom, the working press could only see a team that should exercise total domination over all opposition. Most sports writers considered the previous two seasons aberrations: freakish in 1950 when the once-in-a-lifetime Whiz Kids inexplicably won the pennant on the last day of the season; and existential in 1951, when undoubtedly the gods intervened to curse Charlie Dressen's big mouth by placing a lightening bolt in Bobby Thomson's bat. (Did Bernard Malamud take a measure of his inspiration from "The Shot Heard 'Round the World" for his 1952 novel *The Natural?*)

The Giants started the 1952 season where they had left off the previous year, by winning sixteen of their first eighteen games. But the loss of Monte Irvin to injury and Willie Mays to the draft cut the heart out of the offense, then Maglie and Jensen came down with back miseries. Even the loss of Newcombe to the military could not deter Brooklyn. By the All-Star break the Dodgers, playing .700 baseball, were pulling ahead of the only other contender, the Giants. For the rest of the season, they coasted and finished leading both major leagues in home runs with 153, runs batted in with 725, and stolen bases with 90, again demonstrating that unique combination of power and speed that characterized Robinson's (and Rickey's) Dodgers.

Only in starting pitching was there general agreement among the press box experts that the Yankees had an edge, and that was in experience more than anything else. With the loss of Newcombe, Dressen found three first-year players who moved into the rotation with Carl Erskine, the slender right-hander with the drop-dead curveball, and Preacher Roe, now thirty-seven and a once-a-week pitcher. Rookies Billy Loes and Ben Wade started forty-five games between them.

What saved Dressen's team was his discovery of a twenty-eight-year-old rookie who was not even on the spring training roster. Joe Black had graduated from Morgan State College, a historically black public institution in Baltimore County, Maryland. Even with a college education, Black's best hope was the Negro baseball leagues, where he labored until spotted by a Dodger scout, who signed him at the age of twenty-seven. After one sub-.500 season in the minors, Black got to Vero Beach and impressed Dressen. He turned out to be Brooklyn's answer to whatever savior Joe Page had been for the Yankees in 1947 and 1949: the durable and totally reliable relief pitcher, which the Yankees no longer had except in the person of Allie Reynolds, who was also now their most reliable starter. Black pitched in fifty-six games, won fifteen in relief, saved fifteen more, and even started twice. He clinched the pennant for Brooklyn with a complete game three-hitter on September 21.[4]

The World Series of 1952

"They aren't the same Yankees I used to pay to see. There is nothing in that lineup to be scared of."— Joe Black, looking over the Yankee roster.

It had been a tough year for Eddie and Vic. Physically, they had broken down. Although Vic had refused to go on the disabled list and had not missed his turn in the starting rotation, he had completed only thirteen of his thirty-one starts. His knees were failing him. After three consecutive twenty-one-win seasons, he knew this was a falling off, in spite of an eminently respectable 16–6 record and a 2.78 ERA, 223 innings and only 174 hits. Regardless of the fewer games won, he felt very good about the performance of the pitching staff and the team. That's all that counted for him and for his teammates. He let no one down. Individual statistics meant little to him, and especially to the Yankee pitchers. Winning as a team was all that mattered. The fact that Allie won twenty games for the first time in his career was significant and they celebrated this accomplishment. As for the rest, he appreciated his own value to the common effort, and he knew that his friends, coach, manager, and teammates did, also. He would worry about the general manager later. He was willing to argue his value. He was prepared to tell Weiss that sacrificing oneself for the team was important; and Vic had almost made himself a cripple. If his teammates knew, even Weiss could understand that.

Eddie felt pretty good coming into the World Series. The pain in his shoulder, while not completely gone, was manageable; and the final month of the season showed that he had enough velocity and more than enough cunning to keep winning in the big leagues. He finished the season at 10–5 with an ERA of just 2.54, with 127 hits allowed in 149 innings. Hardly a full season, but good enough to get them into the World Series. Casey and Jim would trust him with the ball.

The two of them reveled in Allie's success. This was not merely a 20–6 record, a *major* league-leading 2.06 ERA, league-leading six shutouts and 160 strikeouts. Allie threw 244 innings, his most ever as a Yankee, completed twenty-four of his twenty-nine starts for an .828 won-lost percentage (another major league tops), and surrendered only 194 hits to go with his 97 walks, his fewest in a full major league season. Allie Reynolds, at age thirty-seven, starting and relieving, was at the top of his game. For Stengel, he had been certainly the most valuable pitcher in the American League; Casey would tell anyone in earshot that Allie was the most valuable *player*.[5]

In spite of Brooklyn's vaunted offense, the mere presence of Allie Reynolds on the mound made the difference for the bookmakers. The headline in the *New York Daily Mirror* on October 1 screamed at the very top of the page in oversized black letters what the bookmakers had decided for the game that day: **ALLIE 5–6½ OVER BLACK.** Dressen, convinced that Joe Black could improve on what Jim Konstanty had done in 1950, announced that the star relief pitcher would start the opening game. The newspaper was not saying whom the odds makers in the World Series favored; it stated only that, when Reynolds started any game, he was the favorite.

Still, there were writers who were hinting that age was going to catch up with the Yankees. Rizzuto, now thirty-six years old, had clearly slowed down a step. His arm was never a genuine gun. Two-thirds of the core rotation was obviously diminished, and their best pitcher started *and* relieved at age thirty-seven.

With an enormous coast-to-coast national television audience looking on with the record-setting 34,861 fans at Ebbets Field, the pundits who were skeptical about another Yankee World Series victory made satisfied noises when Joe Black beat Allie Reynolds and the Yankees, 4–2, on a six-hitter. Allie gave up only five hits and three runs in seven innings, but home runs by Snider and Robinson put him behind. Reese homered off Ray Scarborough in the eighth, the first Brooklyn Dodger ever to hit two home runs in World Series competition (his first came in 1949). For the second consecutive year, Reynolds had lost the first game in the World Series, and he raged internally. As usual, everyone was staying in the city for the duration, and after the game Earlene saw how bothered Allie was, and also knew that he felt that he had let down his team. He was civil, but she knew him; he was seething, barely able to wait for his next start against the Dodgers. He particularly hated losing to a team managed by Charlie Dressen, whom he and the other pitchers had learned to dislike intensely. The sight of a smirking Dressen particularly enraged Vic, who remembered Dressen's role in sending him back to the minor leagues during spring training in 1947. He told his wife Sally that he wanted to turn in early; he had some thinking to do. This time, Vic did not wait until game day to put on his game face. He began that night. He knew he had a score to settle as well as a friend to defend.

The Las Vegas odds had shifted in Brooklyn's favor. If they can beat Reynolds, they can beat anyone, it was now generally thought. This was not the overmatched New York Giants of a year earlier; the Yankees' opponents were one of the most formidable offensive teams in baseball history, now with a one-game lead and having beaten the Yankees' best pitcher.

In Game Two, the next day again in Ebbets Field before another standing-room-only crowd of 33,792, the pitchers were Carl Erskine and Vic Raschi. Sally was late getting to her seat because of parking difficulties around Bedford Avenue, but got there before the first pitch. Earlene and Libby were waiting. "It's going to be a wonderful game!" she told her friends. Erskine, who at 14–6 had thrown a no-hitter earlier in the season, was Brooklyn's most reliable starter. To have him going in Game Two, with his extraordinary curveball and deceptive change-up, was a huge plus for Dressen.

But not this day. With knees throbbing, Vic had set himself a task, and he would not be denied. The Yankees in his time had never lost two consecutive World Series games. It would not happen now. To be sure, this was not the same Vic Raschi. The *Herald Tribune's* Harold Rosenthal had interviewed Dodger Pee Wee Reese after the game: "He used to have the big fastball and the good curve. Now it's different, change-ups and a good slider." Without the power driving off his legs and the knees that supported them, Vic could no longer throw the heavy yet rising fastball that was his trademark. "Not the same pitcher at all," the Dodger captain had said, "but still a very good one."

On October 2, he was still a very good one. Erskine lasted into the sixth inning, when Billy Martin hit a three-run homer off reliever Billy Loes and New York scored five runs to break open a tight game. The Yankees won, 7–1, with Vic tossing a complete game three-hitter, striking out nine. He evened the Series for the Yankees and his friend Allie. The Yankees had pounded out ten hits. Three were by the youngster in center field from Commerce, Oklahoma. Mantle had two singles in Game One and now added a hard double and two sharp singles: five hits in two games.

That evening the three couples dined together. Allie wanted to ask Mickey and his wife, Merlyn, to join them, but Mickey had already gone off into the night with the other celebratory, his buddy Billy Martin, who was now a constant companion.

Next day, Friday, October 3, without interruption, the Series moved to Yankee Stadium. This proved to be a nightmare game for Yogi Berra, one he never forgot. Although he had pitched barely half a season, Eddie Lopat was Stengel's choice. It was a cold, raw day, and Lopat struggled against the seven powerful right-handed hitters in the Dodger lineup, but he persevered. Pitching into the ninth inning, the left-hander gave up ten hits and an uncharacteristic four walks, but only three runs. When Reese and Robinson led off the top of the ninth with singles, the Yankees were trailing, 3–2. Stengel and Turner knew that the gritty Lopat was spent, and rookie Tom Gorman came into relieve. With two strikes on Andy Pafko, Reese and Robinson pulled a double steal. The ball broke sharply down and bounced off Berra's glove. Yogi turned, yet couldn't find the ball that had bounced away near the dugout. Reese and Robinson never broke stride. They both scored on a passed ball, giving the Dodgers a 5–2 cushion. Mize's home run in the bottom of the ninth made the final score 5–3. The Dodgers were ahead again in the World Series, 2–1, with Black against Reynolds again.

In the clubhouse after the game, the first person to come up to Berra was Vic. "Don't think anything about it, Yog. We'll get them tomorrow. The Chief will get them." Next day, Reynolds warmed up with back-up catcher Charlie Silvera. He was silent, unapproachable, and seething. Silvera knew why. Commissioner Ford Frick had come into the clubhouse of both teams before the first game and warned them about "headhunting" and knockdowns. He told the players that this was a nationally televised event, and he did not want any racially charged incidents to take place. Larry Doby's warning to Jackie Robinson that Reynolds threw at black hitters had gotten around; Robinson had spoken up in television interviews and said that the Yankees were a bigoted organization. Reynolds had been touched up in the first game against Brooklyn. Did he keep the ball too far away from the black ballplayers, not close in enough? Maybe he should have thrown tighter to Robinson to prevent the home run? This time, Allie would make sure, no matter what Frick had warned. Was it on Allie's mind? Silvera knew it was, because the only phrase he uttered when he finished his warm-ups was, "Fuck the commissioner."

Five years after baseball's integration, race was still very much an unselfconscious preoccupation of the game, as much as it was with the nation. In 1952, only a handful of teams had a black player in the major league lineup; the Dodgers were clearly the leaders, with Robinson, Campanella, Newcombe, and now Black all playing an important role. They had a prospect in the minors, Jim Gilliam, ready to move up. They had already given a Cuban black outfielder, Sandy Amoros, a brief visit to the majors, and he would be back. That did not necessarily mean that the Dodger clubhouse was a model of integration and racial harmony. There were Dodgers who were not particularly happy to play with black ballplayers, but they kept their mouths shut. No one was eager to complain when the white players went by bus to the elegant Chase Hotel in St. Louis, while their black teammates went to the blacks-only Hotel Adams on the other side of town.[6] Billy Cox, the sure-gloved Brooklyn third baseman who lost his job in 1953 when Gilliam went to second base and Robinson shifted to third, asked Roger Kahn, "How would you like a nigger to take your job?" With Newcombe's imminent discharge from the army, the Dodgers could have six black ballplayers in critical roles.

When it came to getting on the other team, Robinson's Dodgers were as vicious as the next team. If the Yankees didn't have a black ballplayer, they had the next best target: an Indian. Jackie Robinson knew how to dish it out.

A crowd of 71,787 paid its way into Yankee Stadium. In the top of the first, Reynolds was in trouble with runners at first and third with one out. It could be a short outing, with Brooklyn's mighty four and five hitters coming up, Robinson and Campanella. The howls from the Dodger dugout came rising up: "Hey, Big Chief, you're gonna get scalped today! Hey, Wahoo, where's the fast-ball?"

Robinson took a 100 mile-an-hour fastball under his chin. The yelling continued. Then Robinson took three strikes without taking the bat off his shoulder. He went back to the dugout and starting yelling at Reynolds. "Try throwing that shit again, Wahoo! I dare you!" Campanella dug in. No sooner was he settled in the batter's box than he found himself going in three different directions, with a Reynolds' fastball coming straight for his head. Bat, hat, and feet went flying. In his box seat, commissioner Frick moved uncomfortably. Campanella got up, stood in, and struck out. End of inning. In the fourth forty-year-old Johnny Mize drove a fastball into the right field stands for a 1–0 Yankee lead. It stayed that way until the eighth inning, when, with John Rutherford relieving Black, Mantle tripled and scored on a relay gone astray. The Yankees were ahead, 2–0, which is how it ended.

The Dodgers did everything they could to rattle Allie, led by Jackie Robinson, whose high-pitched voice could be heard yelling war chants even by the press corps. If they could get him throwing hard enough, maybe he would throw himself out. As Roger Kahn reported it, "The Dodger tactic of goading Reynolds to throw harder did half of what was intended. Reynolds did indeed throw harder, ever harder. He struck out ten Dodgers, including Robinson three times and Campanella twice. But, he did not throw his arm out." The three Robinson strikeouts were all looking. Later, after the game, Robinson shouted, "You can't hit what you can't see." Stengel, not gracious in victory, told reporters, "Before that black son of a bitch accuses us of being prejudiced, he better learn how to hit an Indian!" Allie simply got better and better. Over the last four innings he faced one hitter over the minimum number. Black gave up three hits in seven innings and pitched well enough to win. Reynolds surrendered four hits in the complete game and was simply dominating. The Series was tied again, two games each.

In the clubhouse in front of reporters, some of the Yankees were shooting off about Robinson's bench jockeying and his strikeouts, calling him "a loudmouth." Allie silenced them: "The man is a good hitter. He just had a bad day. We all have them." His teammates changed the subject.

For the finale at Yankee Stadium, Turner and Stengel gambled on Ewell

Blackwell and lost. It was only the second time in twenty World Series confrontations since 1949 that at least one of the three aces had not appeared in a game for the Yankees, and they lost both of them. They watched Carl Erskine throw one of the most courageous games in World Series history. Thanks to Snider's three-run homer, the Dodgers had a 4–0 lead when Erskine was hammered for four hits and five runs in the fifth inning, the big blow being Mize's three-run homer. But Dressen, now fearful of using his bullpen, stayed with the tough little right-hander and Erskine shut down the Yankees completely. Brooklyn tied the score in the seventh and won it in the eleventh inning, getting a run off Johnny Sain to win it, 6–5. Erskine gave up four hits in one inning, and then surrendered *one* in the other ten. He pitched nine no-hit innings.

With the World Series now shifting back to Ebbets Field, where the Dodgers should have been nearly invincible, it looked like curtains finally for the Yankees.[7] With a 3–2 lead in games, they needed one more victory at home, and Brooklyn would have its first World Series title in history.

Casey and his pitching coach knew what they needed. Sain had pitched five innings in Game Five and was finished. It would come down to his three veterans, and maybe Gorman or Morgan out in the bullpen, if needed. There was no break in the schedule between the two ballparks: from October 1, they played a game every day. The weather held; no rainouts, no additional rest for his beleaguered pitchers. Stengel took the risk on Blackwell to give Vic an added day's rest, and now Raschi had to do the job for his teammates. This was it. As he sat in front of his locker, alone, he was preparing himself for perhaps the biggest game of his career. There was no losing this one. He had pitched many times on three days rest earlier in his career, but this year had been the hardest for him. His fastball was diminished, he had noticed that the upper thigh of his right leg was not quite as large as it had been; he was atrophying, as the muscles of his leg reacted to the torn cartilage in the knees. It compromised his mechanics and his strength, his capacity to push off the rubber with the force that had characterized his best fastballs. But, today there could be no excuses.

Then, he saw a shadow cross his folded hands. "Who the hell ..." It was Allie, the only one who would dare come near him as he prepared himself for this game. "Vic, don't look for me on the bench. I'm going down to the pen. Go as long as you can. I'll be ready."

Twenty-two-year-old Billy Loes was on the mound for Brooklyn to wrap up the Series. He had pitched two innings against Raschi in Game Two and was rested. Both pitchers sat down all the hitters through the first three innings. In the fourth Vic struck out the side and gave up his first hit. It was still scoreless into the bottom of the sixth when Duke Snider blasted a leadoff home run, putting the Dodgers ahead, 1–0. If the lead held up, the World Series would be over. Allie moved around restlessly in the visitors' bullpen. Far in the back of his mind, Turner had a fleeting thought: the only pitcher who could really challenge Snider when he was hot would throw hard stuff, fastballs up and in, and sharp breaking curves, down and away, a kind of left-handed Reynolds. There was someone like that in the Yankee bullpen, but this was not the time.

Berra led off the seventh with a home run that tied the game. Vic's legs were tiring, so he was glad went Woodling followed with a single. He could sit a little longer on the bench. Then, one of those strangely memorable events occurred that is burned into the historical memory of the game of baseball. Woodling took his lead off first base. Billy Loes, looking in for the signal from Campanella, with his foot on the rubber, began his motion to go into his stretch — and dropped the ball. The Yankee bench erupted at the same split second that home plate umpire Art Passarella waved his hands and leapt out from behind Campanella to give the balk signal, waving Woodling to second base. Vic knew all about balks. He set the major league record in May 1950 by committing four in one inning! The umpires that year had instituted a mandatory one-second delay for the pitcher when coming to a stretch with men on base. Raschi's motion had always been fluid and uninterrupted. He brought his hands down into the stretch and when he did not intend to look over at the base runner, he made no effort at holding for a one-second delay. On May 3, according to the new rule, Vic was in violation four times in the one inning. But, his friend would come to the rescue. Next day, with Reynolds on the mound and a runner on first, Allie went into his stretch — and refused to throw the ball. After warning Reynolds, a furious umpire went out to the mound and yelled at Allie to throw the damn ball! Reynolds replied in a calm and calculated manner: "I don't want to take a chance on having a balk called on me. You can't make me throw if I think I am at risk." Two weeks later, the new rule was rescinded.

Loes shook off the embarrassment of a dropped ball balk and went to work. He retired Noren and Martin, and the pitcher was coming up, probably a pinch-hitter for Raschi. Instead, Vic came lumbering out with a bat in his hand. He would hit for himself. Billy thought that he would make short work of the tiring Yankee pitcher with the bad knees; first, a good fastball inside, to let him know that Loes meant business.

Vic was thinking the whole time he was walking slowly out to the batter's box. The kid pitcher will want to get ahead of me, he'll want to throw a strike, probably buzz me a little. It's getting dark; he'll throw some heat. Vic slowly stood in, in spite of his size appearing lethargic and not particularly interested in hitting. Loes stretched, looked back at Woodling at second, and threw his fastball off the inside corner of the plate, around belt high. A good, intimidating pitch.

As soon as Loes started his kick to throw, Vic coiled and crouched slightly, with his eyes fixed on the pitcher's hand. He picked up the ball quickly, and as it left Loes' hand, in an instant, without thinking, Raschi knew that he had guessed right: fastball, inside. Instinctively he fell away from the plate as he brought the fat part of the bat around to make contact. He thought he saw a look of surprise on Loes' face as the bat uncoiled and made contact, sharply. The ball was drilled on the ground up the middle, heading for the pitcher, it smashed off Loes' leg and ricocheted wildly between first and second as Gil Hodges tried to change directions and catch up with it, but he couldn't. As the ball went into right field, Woodling carried the second Yankee run across home plate. Yankees lead, 2–1.

Raschi set down the Dodgers in the bottom of the seventh. In the top of the eighth, Mickey Mantle uncoiled from his left-handed stance and hit a 420-foot bullet into the center field stands, putting the Yankees ahead, 3–1. When Vic got up to take off his warm-up jacket and go out to the mound in the bottom of the eighth inning, he turned to Jim Turner and said, "Get Allie up." He walked to the mound.

He got Pee Wee Reese on a grounder for the first out. He wanted to be very careful with his walks. So far, Raschi had surrendered only one free pass to the Dodger hitters. He knew that he was throwing well, but he was not wasting many pitches, not making the hitters swing at bad balls. Duke Snider, striding to the plate, had seen more good pitches in the strike zone from Raschi than he had ever seen before. He had already hit one home run off Vic that day. He settled in, and waited for the fastball he knew would be coming sooner or later. When it came, Snider hit it over the right field fence for his second home run of the game off Raschi and his fourth of this World Series, making the score 3–2. Vic's control was too good; his pitches were all within reach of the menacing Dodger bats. But, he was still able to handle the right-handed-hitting Dodgers. Robinson made the second out on a fly ball to the outfield, but George Shuba, along with Snider the only left-handed hitters in the Dodger lineup, ripped a double to left center. Vic knew that his time had come when he saw Casey walking out to the mound. He had given up eight hits; one more would be too many. Phil Rizzuto, standing out by second base, felt a warm comfort come over him as he saw the big Indian striding resolutely in from the bullpen. Vic waited for his friend, to hand him the ball. "Think you are up to it, Chief?" Raschi bantered. "Let's find out," answered Reynolds.

With Sandy Amoros running for Shuba and the tying run on second base, Allie struck out Campanella. In the bottom of the ninth, still trailing 3–2, Dressen sent up Rocky Nelson to pinch-hit for the humiliated Gil Hodges, who had batted seventeen times in this World Series without getting a hit. Raschi had struck out nine in his 7⅓ innings; and three times Hodges had been the victim. Reynolds threw three fastballs past the hapless pinch-hitter; Nelson never had a chance. Furillo walked, Pafko popped up, and Cox grounded to third to end the game. In relief of his friend, Allie had thrown 1⅔ innings of hitless ball for the save. The instant McDougald's throw nestled into Joe Collin's glove at first base, the Yankees exploded out of the dugout and mobbed Allie. The first one out was Vic Raschi.

The Series was tied, 3–3. The Yankee clubhouse, mobbed with reporters, was noisier than anyone could remember. Their teammates were all over Vic and Allie, and the reporters were all over Stengel: "Who goes tomorrow, Casey?" "Don't ask me now, I don't know, I gotta think about this. Ask me tomorrow, before the game, which is the last one." He looked at Jim Turner, who never seemed to have reporters around him, but his pitching coach made no sign. "Will it be Gorman or Morgan, Case?" shouted one reporter. Tom Gorman, twenty-seven, and Tom Morgan, twenty-two, had started occasionally during the season and were rested. But, for a World Series seventh game? "I'll see you in the morning. I gotta sleep on this." He also had to speak to Turner. After things quieted down and the clubhouse had emptied out, Jim had stayed behind, still in his uniform, because he knew that Casey wanted to talk. "I wanted to use the Indian if there was a seventh game. Now I can't." Turner, pulling off his baseball socks, spoke to the manager. "Yes you can. He'll be ready. *They'll* be ready; all three of them. Start with the lefthander. Yeah, I know, it's Ebbets Field, but he can go at least once through the batting order without getting hurt. After seeing the two right-handers, it will take them time to catch up with Eddie. Allie and Vic will be in the bullpen. They are both wiped out, but if we ask them, they will come on, and just the sight of them could give us a couple of innings. After that, who knows, let's see where we are. Remember how it ended last year, with the other lefty?" Stengel thought for the first time in a week of Bob Kuzava, who the next day would be described by Red Smith in his *Herald Tribune* column: "Kuzava is a Polish name that sounds like some kind of melon."

Next morning, Stengel told the gathering journalists in the clubhouse: "It'll be Lopat, then we'll see."

Eddie, who had lost Game Three when two runs scored on Berra's passed ball, was ready. He knew that Casey preferred that he pitch in spacious Yankee Stadium, but there was no choice. When he sat down to dress for the game, he was cool. That's why they called him Steady Eddie. He didn't need a game face. He would try to bedazzle the right-handed Dodger sluggers, who had seen nothing but smoke and heat the day before. Now they would see something else. He had already talked over the Brooklyn lineup with Turner. They had worked out the strategy. If you are going to get hurt with the long ball, make sure there are no runners on base. No walks. Nibble, throw strikes, but keep the ball moving around. Never two pitches in the same place. Give them the singles; try to keep them off the bases. Watch out for Snider, he is hitting everything. Snider already had four home runs in the Series and nine hits.

Reynolds and Raschi, whom Roger Kahn had described as "twin cobras," sat on either side of him, protecting him from the writers. He didn't mind making small talk; Eddie liked the image of coolness that he had developed over the years. But, one look at Reynolds and Raschi kept everyone away as they dressed. "Eddie, we'll be out in the bullpen," Allie said, as they got up to answer the game bell, which had just gone off.

Dressen gave Joe Black his third start in seven days. Only Christy Mathewson and Dizzy Dean had started three games in seven days, but Black wanted the ball, and the talk up in the press box leaned to a seven-game win for the Dodgers. Lopat, pitching against this right-handed power in a bandbox ballpark, would be lucky to get past the first inning. Also, the weather was downright frosty, and Lopat hated the cold. He always started slowly at the beginning of the season; it took him a while to crank up his creaky arm on a day like this. The conventional conversation dealt with what the buffet in the Dodger victory celebration would be like, since the Yankees always had put out a very good table. Now the Brooklyn management would have to step up to the plate.

In the top of the first, with 33,195 screaming Brooklyn fans on hand, Black looked strong. McDougald, Rizzuto and Mantle went in order, Mickey by strikeout. In the bottom of the first, the Yankees looked unsettled, all except Lopat. He struck out Cox to lead off, but Yogi uncharacteristically couldn't handle Lopat's stuff and had to chase Cox down the line to tag him out. After the debacle of Game Three, Berra had to settle down. Eddie put his arm around the upset catcher and told him to relax. Reese then grounded to McDougald at third, and the mostly immobile Johnny Mize could not handle the throw; this was the first of McDougald's two errors. The Yankees would commit *four* in this decisive seventh game, their worst defensive performance of the Series. But, Lopat was as steady as he could be. He struck out Snider and got Robinson on a fly ball to Noren in right field.

It stayed tight for three innings, with Black and Lopat putting up zeroes. Black looked like he could go on forever. Then, unexpectedly, he started getting hit. In the top of the fourth Rizzuto drilled a double down the left field line and scored on a single by Mize, right after he had hit a blast over everything in right field that just went foul. All of a sudden Black looked vulnerable, maybe even tired. Only Berra's hitting into a double play prevented a bigger inning. It was 1–0, going into the bottom of the fourth.

Turner had been right. After a diet of Raschi and Reynolds fastballs, the Dodger power hitters were over-swinging on Lopat's soft stuff. He had already struck out three and had walked none. The Dodgers had gotten only one hit so far, a shot up the middle by Shuba. He had walked no one and had kept the Dodgers off the bases.

But, Turner also knew that the second time through the batting order, it could be very different. The Dodgers were too good a hitting team not to adjust. They had also seen good off-speed left-handers in the National League: Dave Koslo with the Giants, Al Brazle and Harry Brecheen of the Cardinals, the Cincinnati Reds' Kenny Raffensberger, and Howie Pollet, now pitching for Pittsburgh after a long career with St. Louis. Their own Preacher Roe was a taller, thinner version of Lopat: a junkman from Arkansas. When Eddie came into the dugout for the top of the fourth inning, Turner was waiting for him. "I'm going to get Allie up, just in case." Lopat, who was always very much in touch with his energy level as well as the condition of his arm, said, "Good idea." The raw weather was taking its toll.

Turner, with an almost mystical presence, proved to be right, although Lopat ironically did not fall victim to any great onslaught. Snider, who Eddie handled the first time around, lined a hit to right field. Robinson, who was having a terrible time at the plate, picked out one of Lopat's soft serves and beat out a bunt down the third base line. Campanella, who was also having a dismal time with the bat, surprised everyone by dropping another bunt in almost the identical spot, catching McDougald back on his heels, and the lumbering catcher beat it out. Bases loaded; none out. This is what Stengel feared: a situation where one swing could make the difference and end the World Series. He did not want that mistake to be made on a soft pitch that got too close to the plate. If the Yankees were going to get beat by a big hit, let it come against a challenge. Casey had seen how Reynolds had simply tyrannized Robinson and Campanella in Game Four, striking them out five times. No matter how much he had left in his arm, Allie was the one Stengel wanted out there now. When he called time and walked to the mound, he threw a glance at the visitors' bullpen; Allie had already grabbed his warm-up jacket and was on his way. Lopat waited for his roommate, chatting with Stengel. He hadn't given Casey the ball; he would hand it to Allie himself. He flipped Reynolds the ball and quipped, "OK, Chief. What's left in the tank?" Reynolds rubbed it once. "Enough to get the job done," he said and watched Lopat and Stengel walk back to the dugout. This was his third appearance in seven days. Hodges, still hitless, got his first and only run batted in when he lined to Woodling in left, and Snider scored the tying run. Robinson advanced to third on the throw; runners at the corners, one out. Reynolds bore down. He struck out Shuba, and Furillo grounded out.

Allie always had a warm spot in his heart for Gene Woodling. The two families had spent time together at Wilkes-Barre in what seemed a lifetime ago, but Betty and Earlene remembered those lean times and how the two families relied on one another. In Reynolds' two 1951 no-hitters, Woodling had hit important home runs, one producing the only run of the game, when Allie beat Feller, 1–0. Gene never forgot how Allie had praised him to the press. He always called him "Chief" with deep affection. Now, in the top of the fifth, Woodling, with his peculiar left-handed crouch and feet together, looking like a stubby version of Stan Musial, was hunting for one of Joe Black's inside fastballs and got it. He whacked it on a line over the right field fence for a 2–1 Yankee lead.

But, Allie was pitching with only vapors in his tank. His thirty-seven-year-old arm was dead. In the bottom of the fifth, after Black struck out, Cox doubled and Reese singled to drive him in, score tied again at 2–2. Reese took second on Woodling's throw, so the lead and potential winning run was in scoring position, with the number three and four hitters coming up. Reynolds dug deep inside, and got Robinson and Snider to end the threat.

They were now entering the last third of the last game of the World Series. Standing out at shortstop, veteran Phil Rizzuto felt his chest constricting, but he didn't want to let anyone on the Brooklyn bench see him taking deep breaths. When Allie got Snider to end the fifth, Phil raced into the Yankee dugout, sat down, and took in a lungful of air as he relaxed. But, he was leading off the sixth and had to get a bat. He stood in against Joe Black, large and formidable as ever. The first pitch was a curve, down and away, and it didn't move. Leading off the inning, Phil wanted to take at least one strike, so he had no intention of swinging at the next pitch. When it came, Rizzuto tied a knot in the handkerchief in his mind, to remind him to tell Mickey on deck: Black is losing it. The curve isn't biting, and the fastball has lost a couple of feet. Rizzuto settled in and saw another fastball that looked like a melon. This time he drilled it hard, but Rizzuto didn't have time to leave the batter's box before he saw his opposite number at shortstop, Pee Wee Reese, grab the hot line drive without moving an inch. As he ran back to the dugout past Mantle, Phil sputtered, "He's lost it, Mickey." Mantle settled into his left-handed stance. He knew how they liked to pitch him: up and in, although in this series he had been slamming the Dodger pitching. Mantle knew he was most vulnerable when he was crowded with a fastball and could not get around fast enough, if the ball was in tight. He thought to himself, "Let me give Black a reason to throw me a fastball inside. I'll get closer to the plate. He'll see the chance to jam me."

The twenty-year-old Mantle had matured enormously in his second season. The Dodgers had seen it. He was battering them. But, they didn't know that his mind had also grown agile. He stepped in, crowded the plate, and Black saw his opportunity. He didn't want to start Mantle off with a fastball, so he dropped a curveball over the outside corner, strike one. "Now I'll bust one in on his hands, and maybe get a pop up," Black thought. Black rocked back and forth, reached over his head and then back with his right arm, the left leg went up, and he pushed off with all the force he had in his tiring right leg. The fast-ball was going just where he wanted it, in tight where this kid couldn't handle it. But just as Black had released the ball, Mantle started falling back, bringing his huge shoulders and arms around with the thirty-six-ounce Louisville Slugger in his hands. He made contact.

Even before his mature career unfolded, the kid from Commerce hit some awe-inspiring home runs that left pitchers embarrassed and opposing teams struck dumb. Mantle's home runs could actually leave a psychological scar on a victim. This was one of those times. Mantle crushed Black's fastball, and it left the ballpark on a trajectory and with a velocity that took the air out of lungs. The ball disappeared in a second over the thirty-foot fence in right field and even beyond the confines of Bedford Avenue, the thoroughfare adjacent to Ebbets Field. It looked like it would never stop rising and would never come down to earth. Mantle was always embarrassed when he performed such feats, and starting running as quickly as he could around the bases, with his head down. He had electrified his teammates and stunned the opposition, as well as the thirty thousand Dodger fans who were now frozen in their seats. The Yankees were ahead again, 3–2. When Mize singled, Dressen had seen enough. He brought in Preacher Roe, and the valiant Joe Black was through. The Yankees loaded the bases on Roe, but he got out of danger without any more damage.

Reynolds shut down the Dodgers in the bottom of the sixth. Before going out, Allie told Turner that he was finished, but that he would keep pitching. Jim came to the top of the dugout and got Silvera's attention in the bullpen. He waved his right arm, and Vic Raschi got up. When Allie came in at the end of the sixth, he sat down heavily on the bench. He had pitched more than twenty innings in this Series. When it was time for Reynolds to bat in the top of the seventh, Houk hit for him and grounded out. Then McDougald singled, Rizzuto sacrificed him to second, and Mantle, now hitting right-handed, ripped a single to left, scoring McDougald and giving the Yankees a 4–2 lead. When Mize fouled out to Furillo, Vic started slowly walking to the mound. He had pitched nearly eight innings just twenty-four hours earlier and had not relieved at all during the entire season.

For the first time in their history together, the three friends were appearing in the same game. Bringing Raschi in was a gamble greater than any taken by Stengel and Turner during the 154 games played before the World Series and now in these last six-plus games. He was physically beaten up, relatively immobile coming off the mound. Any bunt to the right side, if Mize were playing first, was almost a guaranteed hit, so Casey brought in Joe Collins for defensive help. Vic also did not have the arm required of a reliever. He took a long time to warm up and did not get loose easily. But Casey insisted that they give Vic the ball. For Stengel, no one had greater courage than Raschi. He was a big-game pitcher and choosing between him and the two other young right-handers available, Gorman and Morgan, was for Stengel an easy decision: he went with experience, courage, and heart. That added up to Vic Raschi.

And Vic reached back and threw hard. He ignored the pain in his knees and back. He found, somewhere in the sinew and muscle of his right arm, the strength to throw as fast as he ever had in the past five years.

Vic, however, could not find the plate. He walked Furillo, got pinch-hitter Rocky Nelson on a pop up, then fell behind on Cox and had to come in, and Billy got a seeing eye hit through the left side. When Vic walked Reese to load the bases, Turner turned to Stengel: "Don't let him pitch to Snider. Bring in the lefty." Few had noticed when Raschi had begun his walk in that someone else had gotten up in the Yankee bullpen. One of the reporters in the press box put his binoculars on the movement and focused in on the back of a gray visitingYankee uniform, a figure pawing the ground in front of the bullpen rubber, with a baseball glove on his right hand: number 21. It was Bob Kuzava, again, not seen in a game since the end of the regular season, with no appearances yet in this World Series.

Stengel's bowlegs sprung out of the dugout as he yelled "Time!" to the home umpire and jogged out to his exhausted pitcher. Raschi didn't argue with his manager when Casey took the ball from him. Raschi walked off the hill, and the Yankee manager waited for his left-hander, who first would face the hottest hitter on the Dodger lineup, Duke Snider, cheered on by a ballpark filled with hopeful fans.

Kuzava and Snider went back to 1948, when the one pitched for Baltimore and the other played center field for Montreal in the International League. Now, Snider was tapping his spikes, deep in thought. He didn't feast on Kuzava's stuff.

With the bases loaded, the count went to 3–2, with no place to put anyone. A big hit here — and Snider had already smashed four home runs in this series— and it could be all over. Kuzava took a deep breath and fired a good fastball that looked like it could paint the outside corner of the plate. Snider lunged and popped the ball high in the air to third base, where McDougald grabbed it for the second out. When Robinson moved into place with two out, every inhabitant of the press box would have bet his typewriter that Stengel would go with the percentages and bring in one of the right-handers warming up. Instead, he confounded everyone and stayed with Kuzava, who came right at Robinson, up and in, with fastballs. Jackie, totally confounded by Yankee pitching and having been unable to adjust that day to Lopat's soft stuff, then the right-handed fastballs of Reynolds and Raschi, and now the hard left-handed offerings of Kuzava, kept holding his bat higher and higher in an effort to get good wood on one of these tight fastballs. He swung again, but Kuzava had spun off a high curveball, not a good pitch, yet all that Robinson could produce was a high popup around the pitching mound. Now came the play that installed Billy Martin in the Yankee pantheon for all time.

Immediately, Kuzava's defensive pitcher's instincts took over: his play to call, and he yelled for Collins to take the ball. He could not have known that Collins, looking into the late afternoon Brooklyn sun, was blinded and never saw the ball. Kuzava blocked off McDougald and Rizzuto from making a move from the left side of the infield. That left Martin at second base, who in an instant saw what was happening. With the ball moving away from his second base position with backspin and breeze, he sprinted. He knew all three base runners were on the move. His hat flew off, and he made the catch at full gallop with his glove somewhere between his ankles and his knees. It was that picture that made national headlines the next day.

Brooklyn never threatened again. Kuzava stayed in the ballgame, allowing no hits in 2⅔ innings of superb relief pitching and enjoyed his second moment of immortality as a Yankee, saving the win for Allie Reynolds and closing the door for the second consecutive year on a threat to a Yankee World Series victory. The final score was 4–2 in this epic seven-game struggle.

The New York Yankees, under Casey Stengel, had now won four consecutive World Series, equaling the record of Joe McCarthy's 1936–1939 Bronx Bombers, the teams of Gehrig, DiMaggio, Dickey, Lazzeri, Gomez, Ruffing: all early-vote Hall of Famers; and Joe Gordon, Tommy Henrich, Charlie Keller, Spud Chandler: all Yankees eternally seated on Mount Olympus. Those Yankees dominated their league totally during the season, and dominated again in the World Series, losing two games only once, one game twice, and no games once. During the season they won the league title by margins of nineteen, thirteen, ten, and seventeen games. In all four years between 1936 and 1939, the Yankees led the major leagues in home runs and runs batted in, and individual players won a host of batting titles. Joe DiMaggio put together what many contend were the best four consecutive offensive years in the history of baseball. This was an offensive dynamo, with enough quality pitching in two regular twenty-game winners, Lefty Gomez and Red Ruffing. In World Series competition, Gomez won five games and lost none; Ruffing won four and lost one. Neither had a save.

Stengel's Yankees were a very different ball club. As the great baseball journalist, Leonard Koppett, described the comparison, it was "four straight world championships for Stengel the Clown and his platoons, matching the push-button perfection of McCarthy and his Aristocrats." The 1952 team, as had been the case over previous three years, were not the favorites to win, and inevitably squeaked to victory only in the last week of the season, if not the last *day.* If McCarthy needed only to push a button, Stengel was forced to perform a juggling act of rare dexterity. In 1952 he had settled on Bauer and McDougald as full-time players; before that, he used only Rizzuto and Berra every day in the starting lineup. In only one of those four years—1950—did the Yankees have *anyone* who batted in one hundred runs or more.

What made the difference for these Yankees over the four years were three pitchers who performed feats of consistency on the mound and leadership in the clubhouse that compensated for and complemented whatever patchwork lineup Stengel could put on the field. Framed by the fading DiMaggio and the uncertain Mantle, Casey knew how these Yankees could flourish, in spite of obvious shortcomings clearly seen every year by the professional writers. He had a catcher whom the three pitchers had groomed for stardom, a shortstop who could provide substance in the middle of the infield, and three matchless pitchers.

The manager with nine who had been with him for the first five years. From left to right: Lopat, Berra, Woodling, Silvera, Reynolds, Stengel, Rizzuto, Bauer, Raschi, Mize. Photo taken in 1953 (National Baseball Hall of Fame Library, Cooperstown, N.Y. / AP).

This was the series where Stengel's Yankees should have hit the wall. These were still Rickey's Dodgers, even without his physical presence, and it was the best team in baseball, except in one critical area where Rickey failed consistently: he could not match the Yankee pitching. During his spectacular life in baseball, Rickey had a remarkable analytical and intuitive eye for talent. His ability to find material for the St. Louis Cardinal farm system was unique among general managers. The Cardinal teams from 1920 to 1942 were a tribute to his instincts to select the jewels among the hundreds of ballplayers who played in the Cardinal farm system. He would find them, nurture them, and develop them into durable stars like Stan Musial, Enos Slaughter, and Marty Marion.

But, in more than twenty-five years Rickey produced only one Hall of Fame pitcher, only one whose career went on long enough as a Cardinal to gain admission to Cooperstown, and Jesse Haines was really the kind of pitcher you could not tamper with too much, because he threw a knuckleball. Rickey, the consummate tinkerer, left behind him in St. Louis a host of promising pitchers who somehow came down with a series of career-limiting sore arms. Dizzy Dean's problems may not have been caused by Rickey's insistence that the curveball should be thrown directly overhand, but this instruction certainly did not help his brother Paul or the other great pitching prospects that Rickey tried to mentor, such as Paul Derringer and Mort Cooper, only to have their best years end prematurely or develop elsewhere under less demanding tutors. If the Cardinals' young stars of their 1942 World Series winners had stayed healthy, St. Louis might have challenged for a dynasty role, but Ernie White, Johnny Beazley, Howie Pollet, and Murry Dickson had a few great years and then faded into permanent injury or ordinary accomplishments.

Rickey personally signed every pitcher for the Dodgers during his reign. He believed that he had a special "calling" to build a great pitching staff. In fact, he took a host of talented hurlers and saw them end their careers in bitter disappointment or premature sore arms. Rex Barney threw a fastball described by Joe DiMaggio as the liveliest he had ever seen. He was seventeen when he came under Rickey's tutelage, and out of baseball, after seeing a psychiatrist to help him find the strike zone, by age thirty. Ralph Branca was a twenty-game winner before he was twenty-two years old. Rickey and later Charlie Dressen turned him into a tentative worrier who gave up without nearly reaching his potential. His best Brooklyn products were Carl Erskine and Don Newcombe, both of whom were forced to quit early because of sore arms. As Roger Kahn wrote, "A model Rickey pitching staff writhed with aching arms and nervous stomachs."

Branch Rickey, among others, looked at the results of the 1952 World Series and could only applaud in bitter admiration. Three veteran pitchers, who should have been in the twilight of their careers, had taken the heart out of this powerful

Brooklyn Dodger team. Only Duke Snider and Pee Wee Reese held up the offense. Snider's four home runs accounted for 80 percent of all Dodger round-trippers. Campanella hit .214, with six singles and one RBI; Robinson, hitting cleanup, batted .174, with two runs batted in. The four and five hitters drove in a combined three runs. Poor Gil Hodges set an all-time record for futility in a World Series, going hitless in twenty-one plate appearances. Furillo hit .174, Pafko .190. The Brooklyn team batting average was .215.

This Yankee pitching effort belonged this time to the two right-handers. Reynolds pitched more than twenty innings over four games, gave up twelve hits, struck out eighteen, won two, lost one, and had one save. His ERA was 1.77. Raschi pitched in three games for a total of seventeen innings, allowed twelve hits, also struck out eighteen, and won two games while losing none. His ERA was 1.59. Eddie Lopat, the star of the 1951 World Series and twice conqueror of the New York Giants, happily took a back seat to his friends. They would all celebrate together. No one cared who got the "W" as long as it was a Yankee.

For the fourth year in a row, it was Yankee World Series pitching that sustained an otherwise ordinary gathering of talent. New York hitting was, at a team average of .216, a point better than Brooklyn's in the series. But, the Yankees had banged out ten home runs, and for the first time in his career, Mickey Mantle emerged as a star. His ten hits tied him with Snider at .345, and two home runs put him just behind Johnny Mize's three.

Again, for the fourth consecutive October, the six friends gathered at the team celebration. Casey was sitting with Edna and the Weisses, Hazel and George. He was talking with animation, and every once in a while he cast a glance over at the table where the Reynolds, Raschis, and Lopats were sitting. They knew what he was saying.

Mickey walked over to thank Allie for being around for the time that Mantle's father had died early in season. Allie said, "I'll see you this winter back home. You'll have a lot of celebrating to do."

They talked about Eddie's plans to barnstorm, Allie's business, and the Raschis home up in Conesus, where Vic was already getting involved with the local high school and college. But, most of all they talked about resting up. Vic had a difficult time getting out of his chair. Libby had to help Eddie with his overcoat. Before the party had begun, Earlene had laid Allie down in the hotel bed where she had improvised a stretching and traction device so he would be able to sit and even do a little dancing. They looked around and saw Mickey and Merlyn, Yogi and Carmen, and a few of the other younger Yankees. This was the future.

Next day, the *New York Daily Mirror* carried a front-page picture of Allie carrying his luggage out of Yankee Stadium, with a caption and text that ran

"INDIAN SIGN-OFF. Big Chief Allie Reynolds, whom the Dodgers wish they'd never met, waves farewell from favorite stamping ground — the Stadium."

The friends said goodbye, said they'd call from time to time, but the families were growing and the children were growing up. As Allie was leaving his summer home in New Jersey, near the Lopats and Raschis, Vic shook his hand. "I wonder what George Weiss will send me this time?" He could do the arithmetic: sixteen wins were five less than twenty-one, his total for each of the previous three years. Allie was insistent. "Don't let him screw you, Vic. You know what you are worth to this team. *I* know what you are worth to this team. Let me hear what's going on." Somehow, Eddie was not worried. He was more philosophical about Weiss. He could take him or leave him, but he also knew that Weiss would help him stay in baseball when the time came. For now, it was goodbye to his friends. The Lopats would settle into their New Jersey home until Eddie got going with his barnstorming plans.

When Mickey and Merlyn got back to Commerce, the mayor, who told Mickey to get ready for the biggest party he had ever seen, met him. Sure enough, the next day the mayor proclaimed a school holiday; a football game scheduled to be played in Miami between Oklahoma A&M and Eastern Oklahoma A&M was moved to Commerce, sixteen bands from local communities came to march up and down the seven blocks of Commerce's Main Street, which were festooned with flags and decorations of every sort. Mickey and Merlyn were put in the rear of a Cadillac convertible and paraded in front of a crowd that was three times the 2,500 population of Commerce, Oklahoma. Mickey's mother and brothers were in another Cadillac. When the caravan stopped in front of the town hall, the mayor announced that the governor of the state of Oklahoma had made Mickey an honorary colonel! One of the many signs in front of the town hall read, "All Commerce is proud of Mickey Mantle. A country boy who made good in the big city."

That night, at the banquet, Mickey was handling the accolades pretty well until he looked toward a crowd gathering near the entrance. Then he saw Allie Reynolds walking toward the podium. He had driven over from Oklahoma City. Allie took the microphone and paid tribute to the young Yankee star. When he finished, he went over to Mantle. "I told you I'd be seeing you soon. Congratulations. You deserve all of this. Your father would have been proud." For the first time all day, Mickey wanted to cry.

8

Seeing the Finish Line:
The Return of Whitey

"Whitey Ford was gifted, but by the time he arrived Allie, Vic and Eddie were looking at the finish line."—Sally Raschi

"Allie Reynolds, Vic Raschi, Eddie Lopat and Whitey Ford are the best balanced pitching staff in the history of baseball."—Branch Rickey

By way of his off-season activities, Reynolds was, of the three friends, the one most likely to keep attention focused on him when he wasn't throwing a baseball. Vic was by nature a reserved man, quiet except when he was with his family, preferring their company to all others. Eddie was a baseball man twelve months of the year, consulting with George Weiss from time to time in New York City, organizing instructional camps for kids, adults, and umpires, planning barnstorming trips around the country, and thinking about a Japan junket. His life, his business, his vocation was the game.

Baseball players did not enjoy a reputation as good businessmen, and Allie's success in the oil industry was becoming notable. He brought in a gusher, and he was rapidly becoming an Oklahoma tycoon, in demand inside and outside his native state. Besides his own oil holdings, Allie went into the oil-field service business that winter and was on his way to making a fortune. He also didn't mind exploiting his heritage for the good of his fellow Native Americans and would appear at charity events everywhere. He was articulate, educated, and comfortable talking to people. Reynolds dealt with George Weiss as an equal, and casually accepted early in the winter the $38,000 salary offered him. He was making much more from his oil interests. Earlene preferred staying home with the children. When he was home, their greatest pleasure came from competing in husband-and-wife match play golf tournaments. Allie was one of the best golfers in baseball; Earlene was one of the best women golfers in Oklahoma. They were a formidable team and both great athletes. That winter, before the training camps opened in Florida, Allie won the annual National Baseball Players golf championship in Miami.

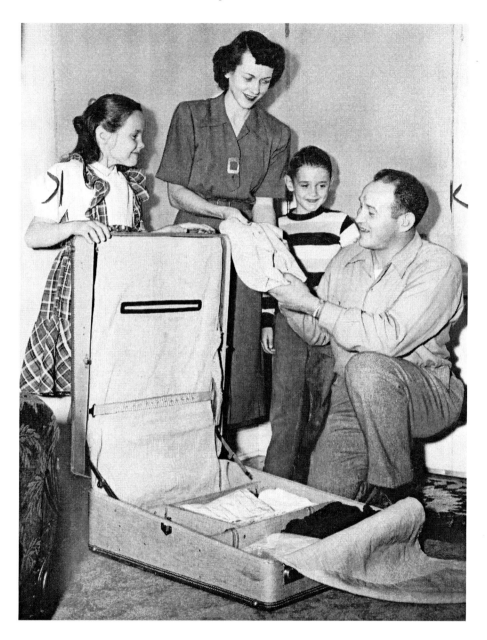

Allie packing up for spring training in 1949. Earlene and the children would stay in Oklahoma whenever possible (Copyright 1949, The Oklahoma Publishing Company).

He was a celebrity. He was also preparing himself and Earlene mentally for the finish line. He had told friends that, after the seventh game of the World Series, he could not raise his hand to comb his hair. The bone chips and spurs in his elbow were not getting any better, and Reynolds simply decided that he would not have surgery. He was thirty-eight years old, no time to go under the knife, and ready to settle down. He told Earlene: get ready to have me around a lot more, and soon. She was delighted.

Then, something else associated with baseball unpredictably entered his life and took advantage of Allie's negotiating skills and near-celebrity status.

For the past two years, since the retirement of Tommy Henrich, Reynolds had been selected by his teammates to be the Yankee player representative. His responsibility was to serve as a spokesman for the Yankee ballplayers in what was a fledgling organization that still terrified the owners. It didn't even have an official name. But, Congress had started looking into the extraordinarily regressive business practices historically associated with baseball, and the owners began worrying. After all, they had succeeded in legitimizing indentured servitude with the reserve clause. They also could cut salaries without any limits, and give a player no more than a ten-day notice that he would be released and out of work. Management received a shock in 1946 when a labor lawyer named Robert Murphy, on his own, started meeting with baseball players in an effort to get them organized. He proposed the American Baseball Guild as a first step, a brotherhood of players that could lead to a genuine labor union. His first proposal was for some modest pay for spring training: the players got no salary and only a most nominal stipend, not enough to subsist and certainly not enough for families. Some players got excited about Murphy's efforts, but baseball players were notoriously conservative and voted against forming a union. The owners discovered Murphy's efforts, and in an effort to throw a bone to the players, they began making stipends of $25 a day for spring training expenses. Today, although most players have no idea about the origins, old-timers still refer to any spring training stipend as "Murphy Money."

Each league had designated one player to represent all of the teams in any discussions with the owners. The other seven player representatives in the American League had selected Red Sox Dominic DiMaggio, perhaps because he looked so scholarly. But, Dom's back miseries forced him out of baseball at the end of the 1952 season. Perhaps as a token of gratitude for the players having told Congress that the reserve clause was good for the game and because there were eight anti-trust suits against baseball moving forward in the courts, the owners in 1950 had expanded a modest pension plan with receipts taken from the All-Star game. At meetings of the team representatives just before the end of the 1952 season, Allie had spoken up in favor of a higher minimum wage (currently $5000), a limit on the size of salary cuts, and larger contributions to the pension plan. He had been home for only a few weeks when a call came from Dominic DiMaggio: the other player reps wanted Allie to take DiMaggio's place in dealings with the owners. The National League representative was perennial home run king Ralph Kiner, who also had shown a willingness to stand up to management.

Reynolds did not have to be asked twice. He called Kiner, and they arranged to attend the baseball winter meetings in Atlanta, where they would meet with the executive committee chaired by the Dodgers' Walter O'Malley. Allie and Ralph had no mandate, no instructions, no advisors, and paid their own way. When they walked in, facing a battery of lawyers, O'Malley started playing hardball about the future of the pension plan and other issues. Reynolds and Kiner didn't blink. Instead, they told the committee that they wanted legal counsel. The owners said no. Allie and Ralph walked out. The owners had taken on the wrong pair.

When they walked back into the room the next day, they had New York lawyer J. Norman Lewis with them. Allie had gotten in touch with him. O'Malley at first refused to allow the two player representatives to have legal counsel present, but Reynolds and Kiner put their knuckles on the table, and even Walter O'Malley had to yield. When negotiations were finished a week later, the endangered pension plan had been strengthened, salaries were guaranteed for spring training, and a maximum salary cut of 25 percent was agreed to. Allie remembered seeing Weiss at the breakup dinner talking to Stengel and looking over at Vic. He thought of Raschi's sixteen wins and Lopat's ten and wondered what cuts the Yankee general manager would propose for his friends. He called Vic and told him about the maximum cut being limited to 25 percent. "Thanks, Allie, I just sent back my contract unsigned. Weiss wants me to come back for the same. I told him no. Let's see where this goes." As it turned out, Raschi went to spring training in 1953 unsigned. He told Casey that sixteen wins deserved a raise. Stengel, always sticking up for his players, agreed and worked on Weiss. Finally, as the players were gathering in St. Petersburg, Raschi and Weiss had one more session, and an angry George Weiss gave in, and Vic got his modest raise to nearly $40,000. As he was leaving the office, Weiss got off one more shot: "Don't you *ever* have a bad year, Raschi!" Vic knew that he meant it.

Years later, Allie told a reporter, "The best thing I ever did in baseball was to make the game better for the players." What he and Kiner did in the winter of 1953 would set the stage for revolution. In 1954, Allie took the lead with his old friend Bob Feller to create the Major League Baseball Players Association (MLBPA), with Feller as its first president. Twelve years later, in 1966, the MLBPA hired its first executive director. His name was Marvin Miller, and baseball would never be the same.

But, the owners, historically never able to see past their immediate issues, were focused only on the newest devil in their lives: television. In 1952 Yankee attendance had led major league baseball with 1,600,000 fans pouring into Yankee Stadium. Topping and Webb, however, saw a 300,000 drop from the previous year. Television revenue, as promising as it looked, did not make up for the short fall. Other owners looked at the Yankee horde of money with disbelief and envy. A desperate Lou Perini of the Boston Braves was thinking "out of the box," contemplating moving the franchise, an idea that had not been part of ownership discussions for fifty years. Boston was becoming a one-team baseball town, with the Red Sox, disappointing as they may have been, still the object of attention for the ever-hopeful fans. The Braves, who won a pennant in 1948, just could not sustain sufficient fan interest. On March 18, in the middle of spring training, Perini dropped the bomb: the Boston Braves would open the season in Milwaukee, the first franchise move since the major leagues signed the basic agreement in 1903.

Allie showed his trophy from the baseball players' golf tournament to Vic and Eddie. Yogi came over. "I'll win that someday," he said. Allie laughed. "First you have to beat Earlene." The summer before, the Berras and Reynolds had gone golfing, and Earlene just about beat everyone in Yogi's country club.

Everyone was finally in camp. Vic had had his final acrimonious confrontation with George Weiss and received what he wanted. Weiss was unusually easy on Lopat. Eddie was convinced that Weiss and he would be somehow involved with one another when Lopat's playing career was over. Casey had even hinted at this. Anyone could see that Eddie was the natural teacher, especially after he sharpened Whitey.

It was Vic that Weiss had it in for, although it was the Springfield, Massachusetts, native whom he had known the longest, more than fifteen years, going back to before his William & Mary college days. Weiss's run as general manager after 1947, coinciding with Vic's emergence as the most consistent Yankee pitcher, was in some ways a great tribute to Weiss's career as director of minor league personnel. Vic Raschi had emerged from the Yankee farm system and become the steadiest pitcher on the staff, someone who won twenty-one games three years in a row. Yet, Weiss expected constant gratitude, and Vic was a man of principle and private determination. He was also educated and would take none of Weiss's arched condescension. He believed that the Yankees had received payment in full for any investment they ever made in him. Weiss held that the players never really gave back in full measure what he as general manager had paid them. For Weiss's part, he felt that Raschi owed the New York Yankee organization everything: his college degree, his career, and an uncomplaining vassalage. Of all the Yankees who negotiated contracts, Vic was the one who infuriated Weiss the most. He was an annual holdout, never signing the first contract sent to him. Raschi was also a formidable opponent when roused; he forced the general manager to admit his value to the team, even when he won fewer games. Weiss did not like meeting with Vic; he did not look him in the eye during negotiations.

Now the families were back for yet another lovely late winter vacation in St. Petersburg. It was getting a little more difficult as the children reached school age, but Earlene, Libby and Sally could manage; being together was more important than anything else.

Their Final Spring Together

"When we got together for the first time in spring training in 1953, we all looked around at each other and said, 'One more time, huh?'"—Eddie Lopat

Whitey was excused for the first day that pitchers and catchers showed up before the position players, and Jim Turner was glad. He wanted a chance to sit with his three oldest students and their catcher. The February Florida sun was once again shining down on the Yankee spring training facility. The coach was standing nearby while the pitchers and catchers were finishing the morning wind sprints, with Raschi trailing behind, still hobbling. Jim had watched Vic dress that morning and noticed that his right leg had visibly atrophied. He called Yogi; Vic, Allie, and Eddie jogged over. "This will be the toughest year for you guys. Vic will not be in the same shape he has been because his legs won't carry him. His conditioning has to be less demanding. He'll tire. Eddie is coming off his tendonitis and will pitch once a week, no more. Allie, they want you to start and relieve again, but with Sain still around and Whitey, you may not have to start as much. But, you'll still have to pace yourself. Let Yogi know when you are losing it, when you are tiring. We've got some arms in the bullpen. Yogi, give them a breather, walk out there, talk to them about anything. Vic won't get mad. He knows he needs the time. OK?" The three older men nodded. It was OK. This year would be one of getting the most out of a diminishing resource of ability, while the will, intensity, and perseverance were still there, the desire to help each other and to perform for their coach. They went out every day because of loyalty to each other, to the team, and to their coach, to whom they each felt a personal debt.

Later Turner spoke alone to Berra. "When Whitey is out there, you call the game. You know the hitters better than he does. It's not like the other three. With Ford, you are in charge. Eddie will work with him, too." Turner also knew that Ford and Berra had become true baseball buddies, friends who went out together with their wives, young enough to look up with respect to the older pitchers, but seeking friendship with each other. He also saw that Ford, who

UNIFORM PLAYER'S CONTRACT

American League of Professional Baseball Clubs

Parties	Between _____ New York Yankees, Inc. _____
	herein called the Club, and _____ Victor Raschi _____
	of _____, herein called the Player.
Recital	The Club is a member of the American League of Professional Baseball Clubs, a voluntary association of eight member clubs which has subscribed to the Major League Rules with the National League of Professional Baseball Clubs and its constituent clubs and to the Major-Minor League Rules with that League and the National Association of Baseball Leagues. The purpose of those rules is to insure the public wholesome and high-class professional baseball by defining the relations between Club and Player, between club and club, between league and league, and by vesting in a designated Commissioner broad powers of control and discipline, and of decision in case of disputes.
Agreement	In consideration of the facts above recited and of the promises of each to the other, the parties agree as follows:
Employment	1. The Club hereby employs the Player to render, and the Player agrees to render, skilled services as a baseball player during the year _____ 19__ including the Club's training season, the Club's exhibition games, the Club's playing season, and the World Series (or any other official series in which the Club may participate and in any receipts of which the player may be entitled to share).
Payment	2. For performance of the Player's services and promises hereunder the Club will pay the Player the sum of $ _____25,000.00 _____, as follows:

In semi-monthly installments after the commencement of the playing season covered by this contract, unless the Player is "abroad" with the Club for the purpose of playing games, in which event the amount then due shall be paid on the first week-day after the return "home" of the Club, the terms "home" and "abroad" meaning respectively at and away from the city in which the Club has its baseball field.

If a monthly rate of payment is stipulated above, it shall begin with the commencement of the Club's playing season (or such subsequent date as the Player's services may commence) and end with the termination of the Club's scheduled playing season, and shall be payable in semi-monthly installments as above provided.

If the player is in the service of the Club for part of the playing season only, he shall receive such proportion of the sum above mentioned, as the number of days of his actual employment in the Club's playing season bears to the number of days in said season.

If the rate of payment stipulated above is less than $5,000 per year, the player, nevertheless, shall be paid at the rate of $5,000 per year for each day of his service as a player on a Major League team.

Loyalty	3. (a) The Player agrees to perform his services hereunder diligently and faithfully, to keep himself in first class physical condition and to obey the Club's training rules, and pledges himself to the American public and to the Club to conform to high standards of personal conduct, fair play and good sportsmanship.
Baseball Promotion	(b) In addition to his services in connection with the actual playing of baseball, the Player agrees to cooperate with the Club and participate in any and all promotional activities of the Club and its League, which, in the opinion of the Club, will promote the welfare of the Club or professional baseball, and to observe and comply with all requirements of the Club respecting conduct and service of its teams and its players, at all times whether on or off the field.
Pictures and Public Appearances	(c) The Player agrees that his picture may be taken for still photographs, motion pictures or television at such times as the Club may designate and agrees that all rights in such pictures shall belong to the Club and may be used by the Club for publicity purposes in any manner it desires. The Player further agrees that during the playing season he will not make public appearances, participate in radio or television programs or permit his picture to be taken or write or sponsor newspaper or magazine articles or sponsor commercial products without the written consent of the Club, which shall not be withheld except in the reasonable interests of the Club or professional baseball.
Player Representations	4. (a) The Player represents and agrees that he has exceptional and unique skill and ability as a baseball player; that his services to be rendered hereunder are of a special, unusual and extraordinary character which gives them peculiar value which cannot be reasonably or adequately compensated for in damages at law, and that the Player's breach of this contract will cause the Club great and irreparable injury and damage. The Player agrees that, in addition to other remedies, the Club shall be entitled to injunctive and other
Ability	equitable relief to prevent a breach of this contract by the Player, including, among others, the right to enjoin the Player from playing baseball for any other person or organization during the term of this contract.
Condition	(b) The Player represents that he has no physical or mental defects, known to him, which would prevent or impair performance of his services.
Interest in Club	(c) The Player represents that he does not, directly or indirectly, own stock or have any financial interest in the ownership or earnings of any Major League club, except as hereinafter expressly set forth, and covenants that he will not hereafter, while connected with any Major League club, acquire or hold any such stock or interest except in accordance with Major League Rule 20 (e).
Service	5. (a) The Player agrees that, while under contract, and prior to expiration of the Club's right to renew this contract, he will not play baseball otherwise than for the Club, except that the Player may participate in post-season games under the conditions prescribed in the Major League Rules. Major League Rule 18 (b) is set forth on page 4 hereof.

Raschi baseball contract pages 1 and 2. Sol Gittleman received this contract from Don Leypoldt who stated, "Truthfully, it's been so long since I received the contract that I'm not exactly sure. I put out an APB for Raschi memorabilia in *Sports Collector's Digest* back in 1994; a collector mailed me a copy of the contract to try and get me to purchase it."

(3) If this contract is so claimed, the Club shall, promptly and before any assignment, notify the Player that it had requested waivers for the purpose of terminating this contract and that the contract had been claimed.

(4) Within 5 days after receipt of notice of such claim, the Player shall be entitled, by written notice to the Club, to terminate this contract on the date of his notice of termination. If the Player fails so to notify the Club, this contract shall be assigned to the claiming club.

(5) If the contract is not claimed, the Club shall promptly deliver written notice of termination to the Player at the expiration of the waiver period.

(g) Upon any termination of this contract by the Player, all obligations of both parties hereunder shall cease on the date of termination, except the obligation of the Club to pay the Player's compensation to said date.

Regulations

8. The Player accepts as part of this contract the Regulations printed on the fourth page hereof.

Rules

9. (a) The Club and the Player agree to accept, abide by and comply with all provisions of the Major and Major-Minor League Rules which concern player conduct and player-club relationships and with all decisions of the Commissioner and the President of the Club's League, pursuant thereto.

Disputes

(b) In case of dispute between the Player and the Club, the same shall be referred to the Commissioner as an arbitrator, and his decision shall be accepted by all parties as final; and the Club and the Player agree that any such dispute, or any claim or complaint by either party against the other, shall be presented to the Commissioner within one year from the date it arose.

Publication

(c) The Club, the League President and the Commissioner, or any of them, may make public the findings, decision and record of any inquiry, investigation or hearing held or conducted, including in such record all evidence or information, given, received or obtained in connection therewith.

Renewal

10. (a) On or before February 1st (or if a Sunday, then the next preceding business day) of the year next following the last playing season covered by this contract, the Club may tender to the Player a contract for the term of that year by mailing the same to the Player at his address following his signature hereto, or if none be given, then at his last address of record with the Club. If prior to the March 1 next succeeding said February 1, the Player and the Club have not agreed upon the terms of such contract, then on or before 10 days after said March 1, the Club shall have the right by written notice to the Player at said address to renew this contract for the period of one year on the same terms, except that the amount payable to the Player shall be such as the Club shall fix in said notice; provided, however, that said amount, if fixed by a Major League Club, shall be an amount payable at a rate not less than 75% of the rate stipulated for the preceding year.

(b) The Club's right to renew this contract, as provided in subparagraph (a) of this paragraph 10, and the promise of the Player not to play otherwise than with the Club have been taken into consideration in determining the amount payable under paragraph 2 hereof.

Commissioner

11. The term "Commissioner" wherever used in this contract shall be deemed to mean the Commissioner designated under the Major League Agreement, or in the case of a vacancy in the office of Commissioner, the Executive Council or such other body or person or persons as shall be designated in the Major League Agreement to exercise the powers and duties of the Commissioner during such vacancy.

Supplemental Agreements

12. The Club and the Player covenant that this contract fully sets forth all understandings and agreements between them, and agree that no other understandings or agreements, whether heretofore or hereafter made, shall be valid, recognizable, or of any effect whatsoever, unless expressly set forth in a new or supplemental contract executed by the Player and the Club (acting by its president, or such other officer as shall have been thereunto duly authorized by the president or Board of Directors, as evidenced by a certificate filed of record with the League President and Commissioner) and complying with the Major and Major-Minor League Rules.

Special Covenants

Said player to receive an additional sum of Two Thousand Five Hundred ($2500.00) Dollars at the end of the 1950 season if Manager Stengel so approves.

Approval

This contract or any supplement hereto shall not be valid or effective unless and until approved by the League President.

Signed in duplicate this .... day of .... March ...., A. D. 195 0

.... (Player)

New York Yankees, Inc.
.... (Club)

.... (Home address of Player)

By .... (President)

Social Security No. 019-10-9400

Approved MAR 16 1950 .... 195....

....
President, American League of Professional Baseball Clubs

had a wild streak in him and was drawn to the other two young stallions on the team, had a wife who controlled him better. He also possessed an internal mechanism that warned him when he was getting close to crossing a dangerous line. Of the three close friends for life, it would be Ford who avoided the marital crises and family failures that marked the lives of Martin and Mantle. He was more disciplined than "the Dead-End Kid" who was Billy Martin, and his fellow night owl delinquent, Mickey Mantle. Besides, Lopat was all over Whitey, never letting him out of his sight, always being tough on "the fun lovers," as he called Whitey and his friends. Ford worshipped the older left-hander, his mentor and guardian. Martin, to the astonishment of many of the veterans, had been married in 1950 and was already divorced. Mickey was also married, but he was quickly losing his country boy innocence and leaning more in the direction of Martin as a role model than Ford. This would be a project for Allie, dealing with his fellow Oklahoman, and Turner spoke to him. Allie would take care of it.[1] Vic and Eddie would handle the other two, as well.

As Casey Stengel sat with his bowlegs crossed in the dugout of Al Lang Field, watching his veteran athletes loosen up, he was alone for one of the rare times when reporters were not hovering, looking for another printable quotation. He saw clusters of ballplayers, stretching, running, doing drills, and occasionally relaxing. One group was comprised of his marvelous pitchers, his three sturdy pillars and their coach. He noticed that when there was a moment's respite, Bauer and Woodling would walk over for some easy conversation or to challenge Reynolds—pushing forty and still one of the fastest men in camp—to race from home to first base. Then Casey's eyes would wander to another side of the field, where he saw his twenty-one-year-old phenom from Oklahoma clowning around with his best buddy, Billy Martin, another Stengel favorite. Casey was now looking for his white-haired left-hander. Occasionally, he would be part of the pitchers' group, talking, but also listening to Lopat or Turner. But, just as often he was with his preferred gang, with Mickey and Billy, clowning, wrestling, and, Stengel knew, plotting the night's revelries. He thought of Vic, Allie, Eddie and their wives, their stability over these past four years, of the role they all played in bringing a disciplined and selfless sense of sacrifice to the team, an aura that permeated the clubhouse. And he wondered: "When they're gone, who will lead?" The intangible ability to bring character to a baseball team is not something that a manager could create, Casey knew. McGraw could not have done it with Mathewson. It had to come from the chemistry that shapes a team's personality, its will. Stengel knew that he had it for the past four years, that there were innumerable times that he could walk away from his responsibilities because someone else would do the job for him. The veterans policed the team, chewing out someone for not running out a ground ball or popup, getting on Mantle when he went into a rage after striking out or on

Martin for being hung over or breaking curfew. They created a mood in the clubhouse of mature responsibility, respect, or even terror: don't mess with those three.

The source of this immeasurable quality was one day going to be gone. As he looked to his younger players, romping around, Stengel knew that they had enormous talent. Berra, Mantle and Ford could be among the best ever. But, the intangibles? The ability to *command*, to show the way it had to be done. As he looked at his three veteran pitchers, he wondered: Who could do what they do? Who would *want to?* Not the sweet-natured catcher, not the slick kid pitcher, nor the good-time boy in center field who liked to drink too much with the wise-guy second baseman. It was a thought that haunted him for years to come as the Yankee manager, when the magic had gone.[2]

The Season of 1953

> *"Our pitchers were getting old — Reynolds was thirty-eight, Lopat thirty-five and Raschi thirty-four. But, everybody seemed to help everybody else at just the right time."* — Yogi Berra

This time, the journalists were not taking any chances. Having gotten it wrong four years running, they were not going to be fooled again: all ten reporters covering the Yankee spring training camp picked the Yankees to win the American League pennant. Ironically, they chose to ignore what they saw. Eddie Lopat did not throw a ball in a Grapefruit League game; Reynolds and Raschi were shelled regularly, and there was a clear diminution of Vic's velocity. He could not push off his damaged knee and shrunken leg. Berra was injured or ill much of the time. But, no one cared, because Mickey Mantle was hitting gigantic home runs over everything in Florida. No ballpark could contain him. That, plus the return of Whitey Ford from his two-year military service to the Yankee rotation, focused the press's attention on him, and not on the aging core of Stengel's pitching staff. Often in the newspapers they were still referred to as "the Big Three," and after so many years of consistent excellence, Reynolds, Raschi and Lopat arrived at a taken-for-granted immortality that suggested to the New York City working press that they would go on forever. The journalists did not notice that forever was coming to an end.

Ironically, they got it right this time. In 1953, the Yankees exploded out of the starting gate and held first place in the American League for 158 of the season's 167 days, from May 11 to the end. On May 28, they cemented their grip on first place by beginning an eighteen-game winning streak — the final fourteen on the road — that destroyed the rest of the contenders, namely Cleveland and Chicago. They took on the Indians during this road trip and in four games swept Wynn, Feller, Lemon and Garcia, the great Cleveland rotation. These four games represented a microcosm of the entire season. A Cleveland sweep would have reduced the Yankee lead to 2½ games. Instead, the Yankees left Cleveland's Municipal Stadium and 74,708 shocked fans after a Sunday doubleheader on June 14 with the Indians 10½ games behind. The winning Yankee pitchers were Ford, Lopat, Sain and Raschi; Reynolds saved two games for Ford and Sain, pitching five innings of shutout relief. As Louis Effrat reported in the *New York Times,* Stengel "called for Reynolds, and that was that." Allie, now the Yankee stopper as well as a starter, had not lost in relief since August 22, 1951. Ford and Lopat, after their victories against Cleveland, were a combined 14–0, each with seven victories and no defeats. Allie had seven saves so far in the season in seven opportunities and had not been scored on in his last eleven relief appearances. By the end of June, he was being used exclusively out of the bullpen. Casey had spoken with Topping and Webb. He wanted it made clear that if Reynolds went to the bullpen, he would still get a salary appropriate for a successful starting pitcher. The owners agreed.

Only Vic was showing signs of severe wear. This complete game 3–0 shutout of Cleveland brought his record to 4–3, far from the level of the previous Yankee years. Still, he was on the mound for every turn, doggedly pitching for his friends, his coach and his team. As long as his arm allowed, he would not quit, even as his body failed him. This shutout revealed a different pitcher. He gave up three hits, but struck out only two. He was throwing to spots, increasingly using his slider and curve, changing speeds and location. Allie, during the years rooming with Lopat and endless conversations about pitching, had learned Lopat's craft: the art of pitching, the cunning that even a power pitcher could use. He didn't have to bear down on every pitch. Instead, he used the whole field, and took advantage of the hitter's false enthusiasm and misguided belief that he could hit a lesser pitch thrown in the perfect place. Reynolds had learned guile from Lopat. Vic was a profoundly focused man, deeply wedded to what he considered the ethics of his pitching philosophy: give it all you have on every pitch. Stengel used to marvel at Raschi's single-minded intensity, throwing as hard as he could for as long as he could, never letting up. In his autobiography, Casey wrote: "Raschi was the greatest pitcher I ever had to be sure to win. And he would never give in any time that he pitched, even when his stuff was ordinary.... He wasn't a graceful pitcher — he just put so much on it."

Now the vaunted Raschi fastball was a weapon of the past. Only the concentration and ferocity of competition was still driving him. The heart that beat, the one that Stengel, Turner and his two comrades knew so well, was as true as ever. Turner, whom Vic trusted as an older brother, spoke quietly to him. Eddie and Allie would sit with Vic, then walk to the mound and try things out. It was time to use the other weapons, they told him; he learned well.

After this explosion, the Yankees teased the opposition by losing nine straight, including three to the Indians in Yankee Stadium, but by then the gap never closed sufficiently to give Stengel any worries. On June 28, the second-place Cleveland Indians were 39–26, a respectable .600 pace. But, they were seven games behind New York, who, with an incredible 46–19 record, had a .708 won-lost percentage. The White Sox went on a tear, winning seven straight — and made up only one-half game. On July 5, they were in second place, ahead of the Indians, at 44–29. The Yankees had "slumped" to .694 with a 50–22 record. For the rest of the season, the Yankees coasted. But, there was still high drama, and much of it involved Allie.

On the night of July 7, the Yankee bus was heading for the train station in Philadelphia after a game with the A's. As the speeding bus came within sight of the station, the Yankee players started out of their seats to get ready to disembark. The driver took a wrong turn into a taxi lane and slammed into a low bridge overhead pass at considerable speed. The players were thrown in every direction. The bus driver went through the window and lay unconscious. Reynolds smashed into the seat railing behind him, wrenching his back. Of all the injuries suffered in this accident, Allie's would prove to be the most serious. It virtually ended his career.[3]

For the rest of the season, Reynolds was not the same pitcher. He had his usual velocity for three or four innings, then the back spasms would come along, and he would lose location. He could not control his fastball. The trainer would freeze up his back with a spray during games, just so he could keep going. Reynolds was basically finished as a starter for the rest of the season.

The other career-threatening event involved the fragile young Mantle, who already had damaged his knee in the first game of the 1951 World Series. Now, in an early August game against the White Sox, cutting sharply in the outfield, he came down hard on the same right knee, and it buckled under him. Mantle had torn more ligaments and damaged the cartilage. Mickey would miss almost thirty games in the 1953 season, and he had to play with what at that time was a bulky and awkward knee brace that hampered his running. Yet Mantle was not a quitter, and it was this characteristic that later endeared him to his teammates and made life-long cheerleaders and genuinely loyal friends out of older veterans like Woodling and Bauer, friends who were willing to look the other way when Mickey showed up hung over before a game. They would see him bandage his legs with yards of tape, put on a brace, play with extraordinary pain, and never complain. He never lacked courage. But, Mickey was no natural leader and refused to play that role; nor did his other buddy with the potential star status, Whitey Ford.

George Weiss just could not believe it. What made this team so much better than the previous four, when the Yankees barely won the American League pennants by 1, 3, 5 and 2 games? His friend Casey *must* be a genius. He always knew that Stengel had one of the best baseball brains in the business. It was Stengel who told Weiss in mid-season: get me a backup shortstop, someone who could play defense for four or five innings, in case I have to hit for the little Dago. Rizzuto was going on thirty-six, an advanced age for a premier short-stop, especially one with a weak arm to start with. Stengel had a strong corps of pinch hitters and was increasingly inclined to use them early. On June 12, New York purchased the contract of a slick-fielding, weak-hitting shortstop from the ever-accommodating St. Louis Browns. Willie Miranda was exactly what Casey was looking for, and as soon as Miranda arrived, Rizzuto was vul-nerable to be lifted, if the situation warranted it, even before his first at-bat. Rizzuto, never an admirer of Casey, resented being hit for early in the game and was embarrassed. But, when he saw Reynolds heading down to the bullpen every day, he understood what sacrifices had to be made to win.

The tight-jawed Weiss kept watching all season from his seat in Yankee Stadium. No matter what happens, he thought, there will be changes. Individ-uals are not performing and they will still want to get paid. No. There will be changes.

As the season moved to its end, Yogi Berra could praise himself for his best year of generalship. He had gotten the most out of his aging veterans, who looked with great satisfaction on the product of their attention. Berra was now, with Roy Campanella, the premiere catcher in the major leagues. Yogi was more durable, less injury-prone than Campy. He was agile behind the plate, a lethal clutch hitter, and recognized by everyone as one of the most valuable players in baseball. He became a three-time MVP, and during the great Yankee run from 1949 to 1953, was always in the top five voting. In this season, he also proved to be a subtle and intuitive master of his position. He could sense how much Vic, Allie or Eddie had left once the game got underway. Berra had lived inside their minds, at first hesitantly, for five years. He had attained a level of com-fort and understanding that gave them complete confidence in his judgment. It could only have happened if the three pitchers had permitted it; and indeed, they did. They invited Berra into their thoughts, allowed him to study how they pitched, their strategies, their cunning and authority. He grew to understand the fear that Reynolds could engender in a hitter when one of his 100 mile-per-hour fastballs shook the spikes loose from the batter's box. When the batter stepped back in, he was a changed, often frightened man. Berra, who brought his own affable and warm personality to his position, loved to keep up a friendly chatter behind the plate. "Boy, am I glad I don't have to hit against the Chief today," he would say, even to the lordly Ted Williams, who would turn around and yell, "Yogi, shut the fuck up!" But Berra just kept chattering.

By the 1953 season, it was as if there was only one mind involved, regardless of who was pitching. The rapport between Berra and his pitchers was complete. Befitting their relationship and experience, Ford deferred to Berra in the calling of the game. Whitey admitted it with his usual matter-of-fact candor: Yogi knew the hitters, knew the situation. Whatever Yogi called for, Whitey would throw.

The great challenge for Yogi this year was to understand what limitations their bodies now put on his three older mentors. After the bus accident, Allie's arsenal of weapons was significantly diminished; he lost his consistency, even when he maintained his velocity. He and Vic both pitched in pain. This year, Yogi no longer taunted his fellow Italian-American, whom he would playfully insult just to get his attention and to add a little more steam to his fastball. For Vic, it had been critical to have the extra yard, because Yogi knew that, unlike Allie, he really would not throw at a hitter. If a batter started crowding in on Raschi, looking for a fastball over the plate, Berra would mutter, loud enough to be heard, "Jeez, don't get hit by one of this Dago's fastballs. It could kill you!" But, this year, it was different. Vic could not reach back for the little extra; it wasn't there. When Raschi's record was a miserable 3–3 in June, Yogi sat first with Turner, then with Vic to talk strategy. He became part of the friendly conspiracy that encircled their wounded and vulnerable comrade. "We can change speeds better, move the ball around, get them to hit balls out of the strike zone. Eddie's been living that way all his life!" Vic now trusted Berra as much as he trusted Eddie, Allie, Jim or even his wife Sally; this was the special relationship of a pitcher to a catcher whom had learned to trust with one another's life, like a marriage.

At this stage of his career, with time drawing short, Vic listened and became a different pitcher. He turned the season around, finishing the year with a respectable 13–6 record, a winning percentage of .684, yielding only 150 hits in the 181 innings pitched, the fewest he had thrown since becoming the most reliable starter in post-war Yankee history. His statistics reveal the extent of the metamorphosis that he willed for himself and that his teammates and coach urged on him. He completely remade himself as a pitcher. For the first time in five years, Vic was not in the top ten in strikeouts, innings pitched, and games started or completed. He took the ball as a starter twenty-six times, and was still holding it at the end in only seven games. No longer the power pitcher that he had been for his entire career, Raschi's control improved. He had the second best record of hits and walks allowed per game, surpassed only by teammate Eddie Lopat. He had four shutouts, his highest total for a season over this five-year stretch. His record was a tribute to his character and to Berra's intelligence.

As a catcher, Berra always had a special relationship with Eddie Lopat. By

1951, the synergy had been completed: Yogi could anticipate Eddie's pitches so well, had gotten inside his head so completely, that they stopped having signals between them. For Berra, there was no danger that a ferocious fastball would smash into his facemask; it was like playing catch with a pal. He always had time to react to Eddie's variety of pitches and arm directions. It proved to be for Lopat, Berra, and the Yankees an unbelievable year. Mostly starting once a week because of what was now chronic tendinitis, Eddie produced a spectacular 16–4 record. He only completed nine games, and Berra was a master of the moment for both Vic and Eddie. They both now were perfectly willing to tell their catcher if they were tiring. What a change from their first year, when they were prepared to murder their catcher if he gave any signal to Stengel or Turner! Lopat threw fewer innings than Raschi, 178, but had a league-leading ERA of a miserly 2.43. He had the best won-lost percentage in baseball at a gaudy .800, led the majors in fewest walks per nine innings of pitching, and for good measure threw three shutouts, as usual dominating the Cleveland Indians.

Whitey Ford was the only Yankee pitcher who had thirty starts. Yet, he, too, did not take the ball into the clubhouse at game's end very often: he completed only eleven. He threw a staff-high 207 innings, a far cry from previous years when the Big Three each would have more than 200 innings. His 18–6 record placed the twenty-four-year-old Ford now at the top of the pitching chain. He had an ERA exactly at 3.00. But, he did not kid himself. He knew who made this all possible: the Chief in the bullpen.

There may not have been a comparable year for any pitcher in recent baseball history similar to the one that Allie Reynolds had in 1953. He appeared in forty-one games—the most on the Yankee staff—won thirteen (13–7, 3.41 ERA, .650 won-lost percentage), started fifteen, completed five, and, had a shutout. He relieved in twenty-six, won seven, saved thirteen more (third in the league), and finished twenty-three. Vic, Eddie and Whitey knew who made it happen for them that year: it was Allie coming in from the bullpen, even after the terrible injury in July. No matter how deep the spasms or how much pain he felt, he somehow would reach back and find the old flame for two or three innings. Yogi was the timekeeper for the starters, and he kept Vic, Eddie and Whitey going for as long as they could go, pacing and resting them inning by inning. Johnny Sain, a lower case version of Reynolds who could also start and relieve, had been a big help in sparing Allie, but in the big games, Stengel would turn to his Chief. He couldn't break old habits. Reynolds pitched only 145 innings, struck out just eighty-six batters, but in his manager's mind, when he saw his Indian put a leg over the bullpen railing, he knew in his heart that batters still grew faint.

In a two-game series against Cleveland on September 13 and 14 in Yankee Stadium, Stengel ended the misery for the Indians. Two days earlier he had begun preparing for the World Series by bringing Allie Reynolds back into the starting rotation. Allie, who had not thrown a complete game since June 30, went ten innings against Detroit, gave up seven hits, struck out five and walked one. It was only the fourth time he had gone the distance. Although losing 3–2, everyone was satisfied. Allie had controlled the back spasms, and was ready for October. His offerings would be needed to stop the powerful right-handed bats in the lineup of the mighty Brooklyn Dodgers, who had clinched the pennant in record time on September 11.

The Yankees needed a win in the first game of the series to clinch the tie. With Reynolds not available, Casey went to his other valiant big-game winner. Vic Raschi was not the same force he had been, but Stengel often found his hunches validated in his heart. Vic did not let him down. In front of 48,492 cheering Sunday fans, Raschi clinched the fifth pennant for Casey, beating Cleveland's Mike Garcia, 6–3, with yet another cagey six-hitter for his thirteenth win of the season. He walked three and struck out three: again, not the overpowering Vic Raschi, but a winner nonetheless.[4]

Next day, Casey wanted to give the new big kid on the block a chance to pitch the game that made history, the fifth consecutive pennant clincher, and handed the ball to Whitey Ford. Ford got shelled in the third inning and left the game trailing 5–0. But, this was a team destined to make history, and they wanted to do it against the closest competition. The Yankee bats exploded against Cleveland ace Early Wynn, and Casey had his fifth in a row with an 8–5 comeback victory. Johnny Sain got the win in relief. Cleveland left New York City trailing by 13 games. There were nearly three weeks left in the season with little to do. The Yankees coasted to an 8½-game final lead, finishing with a 99–52 record, the best of their five straight pennant-winning seasons. Casey had surpassed his mentor, John McGraw, and the earlier Yankee legend, Joe McCarthy. The Yankees had made baseball history.

The World Series of 1953

> *"The Dodger team of 1953 won 105 games, the most in its history, and may have been the best club Brooklyn ever fielded."*— Historian John P. Rossi

The Dodgers had run away with the National League pennant. Their offense was genuinely frightening. They led the league in runs (955, nearly 200 more than any other team), hits (1,529), home runs (208), with Campanella and Snider hitting more than 40 each and eight players in double numbers, RBIs (887), bases on balls received (655), stolen bases (90), team batting average (.285) and slugging average (.474). They had in Carl Furillo the National League batting champion (.344) and the RBI champ in Roy Campanella (142). Snider and Hodges had driven in more than 120 runs apiece. They had five .300-plus hitters in the starting lineup. The pitching, traditionally the Achilles' heel for Brooklyn, boasted five hurlers in double figures, anchored by twenty-six-year-old Carl Erskine, who put together a brilliant 20–6 season with a league-leading .769 winning percentage. No Dodger pitcher had a losing record. The only downside of the season was the sophomore jinx that hit Joe Black, whose ERA ballooned to 5.30. He was ineffective as a starter and had lost the stopper role to Clem Labine. An observer could forgive the combined Brooklyn ERA of 4.10 by accepting the fact that National League hitting had exploded in the early 1950s, and the balance of power was literally shifting away from the American League. This time, the Dodgers looked unstoppable. After the All-Star break Brooklyn played at a 41–9 clip and buried the opposition. They entered the World Series energized, confident, and at the peak of their performance.

The Yankees could not match the firepower of the Dodgers. Berra was the sole regular with more than 100 runs batted in; Mantle, after hitting .340 for most of the season, slumped badly after his injury, finishing under .300 with twenty-one home runs. Berra led the team with twenty-seven. The Yankees had seven regulars in home run double figures, but three of them had just ten. They led the American League in team batting average with .273, twelve points less than the Dodgers.

What had sustained this team of platooners over the previous four years, when there was no one New York Yankee leading in any American League offensive category, was the extraordinary performances of the three pitchers. Now, they were among the oldest starters in a regular rotation in the century! Only twenty-four-year-old Whitey Ford prevented the Yankees from setting an all-time record for age among a starting staff. Lopat and Sain were thirty-five, Raschi was thirty-four, and Reynolds thirty-eight. They were also infirm, each pitching with pain. For the first time in these five years the Yankees had no twenty-game winner, no power pitcher who could blow it by the opposition for nine innings. Their ace was a young, blond-haired trickster who completed only eleven games in thirty starts. The two giant cobras, Raschi and Reynolds, who gave Campanella "jelly legs" in 1949, seemed like ghosts of their former selves. It looked like an overmatch. As the season ended, the Yankees lost three in a row to Boston left-handers, who held them to two runs in twenty-seven innings.

Then, Stengel startled the baseball insiders by naming Reynolds his starting pitcher in Game One. Allie, who had been ineffective as a starter since his bus injury, had relieved twenty-six times in the season. What was Stengel thinking? He was opening with his courageous but ailing right-hander in Yankee Stadium, which meant he would have to use one of his two southpaw starters in tiny Ebbets Field. Casey always said he preferred using Lopat in big parks, and

Ford had been likewise successful when he had open spaces for his outfielders to chase down long fly balls.

Stengel was a superb tactician of baseball, but he was also a man who would occasionally think with his heart. In the five World Series between 1949 and 1953, Allie started four of those first games, and in the fifth series, against Philadelphia, Raschi started Game One because Eddie Sawyer used Jim Konstanty, and Stengel was determined that Allie would pitch against the Phillies' ace, Robin Roberts. For Casey, his first-game pitcher was his Indian, and he would have no other against Brooklyn, no matter what his condition or record for the year. Turner assured the manager that Reynolds would go as far as he could, that he could be counted on for a maximum effort, even though he was not the same domineering force he had been. What's more of all his pitchers, Allie would be ready for relief no matter how long he would go in Game One. Reynolds' opponent would be Carl Erskine, the Dodger twenty-game-winning ace, who after July 1 had a 15–2 record. He also had proven the year before that he could beat the Yankees.

So whom did the bookmakers install as the favorite? It must have been the magic of Allie. The Yankees were 6–5 favorites to win the first game and to take the Series.

After two innings of Game One, in front of Yankee Stadium crowd of 69,374, the gamblers looked like geniuses. Erskine was rocked for four runs in the second inning when he walked three and gave up two triples, the second with the bases loaded to Billy Martin. But this was a game destined to go its own way. Casey had put Reynolds back in the starting rotation during the last three weeks of the season, trying to get him ready. He won twice against the A's and the Browns, but Allie was no longer physically able to handle the strain of nine innings. He started to weaken in the fifth, when he gave up a solo home run to rookie Jim Gilliam. In the sixth, he came unglued. Hodges and George Shuba sandwiched homers around a single by Billy Cox, and the Yankee lead was reduced to one run. Casey went out to the mound and took the ball from Reynolds. Johnny Sain came in, got out of the inning, and later gave up the tying run before the Yankees exploded on Erskine's relief pitchers for a 9–5 victory.

The Dodgers had tied the score 5–5 in the seventh, and threatened to blow the game open. There were none out, runners on first and second. Cox dropped a sacrifice bunt just down the third base line, but not far enough away from Berra, who pounced on it and forced Hodges at third. Then pitcher Clem Labine surprised everyone by dropping a bunt in *exactly the same spot*. Berra sprung out of his crouch, jumped on the ball and gunned down Furillo at third. To seal the inning, Berra handled Gilliam's popup behind home plate. Yogi had made two spectacular defensive plays and had broken the back of the Dodger rally. Sain got his second World Series win, the first since 1948 when he beat Bob Feller, 1–0, for the Boston Braves. Yankee Stadium gave up five home runs; the Dodgers had three of them, but the Yankees were ahead in the series, 1–0.

In the clubhouse, Allie was on the trainer's table, with ice on his back, shoulder, and elbow. He looked gray. He slowly got off the table and tried to walk; he couldn't. "How's it feeling, Chief?" Jim Turner asked him. "I'll be ready if you need me." Reynolds the warrior was always ready when they needed him.

Game Two, again Yankee Stadium, in front of 66,786 fans. Stengel hesitated. He was not yet ready to abandon those arms that had gotten him his five pennants and four World Series victories. His ace of the staff was clearly Whitey Ford, who had already won a World Series game in 1950, but not yet, not now. Stengel turned to his veterans. The Dodgers had beaten *eighteen consecutive left-handers* during the season. Even the dominant Warren Spahn, 23–7 with a 2.10 ERA, stayed far away from the Dodger right-handed power. Now, Casey wanted Steady Eddie.

Casey loved overpowering right-handers, but nothing gave him more satisfaction than watching the off-speed pitchers who could infuriate free-swinging sluggers and send them back to the dugout talking to themselves. He knew that in Ford he had the potential for one of the greats of that species, but in the second game against Brooklyn, he wanted the master, and he loved Eddie Lopat. He also admired Preacher Roe, and seeing them together in a game brought out the contrarian in him. "To pay all that money to great big fellas with a lot of muscles who go up there and start swinging. And those two give 'em a little of this and a little of that and swindle 'em." He remembered well Roe's 1–0 shutout of the Yankees in the second game of the 1949 World Series and Lopat's two complete game wins over the Giants in 1951.

Turner spoke to his pitchers before Game Two. Allie might come back as a starter, depending on what happened. But, the coach and manager had come to a decision: they wanted Reynolds to close, to finish off, to be there for the last out. They knew he couldn't throw the terrifying fastball in the right spots for any length of time now, but they wanted it for the most crucial moments in the Series. Whitey would wait for Game Four, in Ebbets Field. It would be Eddie today, then Vic tomorrow in the Ebbets Field opener. Ford understood. In spite of having the most wins and innings, on this team he was still the kid on the block; he accepted it. He would watch Raschi work the small park and learn from him. Whitey sat with the three veterans and his coach, surrounded by mentors; he knew his place. Today, he would see the two masters at work.

Sitting on the bench in the first inning, Ford was watching with intensity. With one out, Pee Wee Reese hit a Lopat-patented long fly ball into the deepest part of right center field, an easy out for Hank Bauer — who fell down. Reese wound up on third base with a triple. He would have scored, except Mantle, learning his position better each day, raced over to back up and held Reese at third. Now, Eddie had to work on the heart of the Dodger order, with a runner in scoring position and one out. The third and fourth hitters were coming to the plate. Whitey's lips moved quietly as he played out, along with Lopat, the sequence of pitches. In a few minutes, he got up, smiling, and moved to the water fountain. Snider had popped up to Berra, and Robinson had flied out to Mantle. No damage.

Roe, who feigned a laconic Arkansas hillbilly pose to reporters even though he was a college graduate and math teacher, looked rattled as the bottom of the first got underway. He walked Woodling and Collins. Woodling took third on Bauer's fly to deep right. Berra also hit to deep right, and Woodling scored, with Collins taking second on the throw home. Then, it looked as if Preacher were coming unhinged as he walked Mantle and hit McDougald to load the bases with two outs. Charlie Dressen was going crazy in the Dodger dugout, but Billy Martin flied out to short center, leaving Brooklyn trailing, 1–0. It stayed that way until the Dodger fourth, when, with two outs, three right-handed bats got to Lopat. Hodges and Furillo singled, and Cox doubled them both home to give the Dodgers a 2–1 lead.

The game stayed that way for six innings, with Roe settling down and giving up nothing. Eddie was pitching his typical game: a few walks, a bunch of hits, an occasional strikeout, and no runs. Dodgers reached everywhere except home plate. Eventually, they would strand ten runners.

In the bottom of the seventh inning, Billy Martin hit a 2–2 pitch into the first row of seats in left field to tie the game. Martin, a .257 hitter during the season, was turning into the Brooklyn nemesis. But, in the bottom of the eighth, the deathblow came from a more predictable source. With Hank Bauer on first with a single, Mickey Mantle drilled a long home run deep into the left field stands, just inside the foul pole.

Turner spoke to Lopat before he went out to pitch the top of the ninth. "I got no Indian today, he can't lift his arm yet, but Sain will be loose. Let me know." Eddie nodded his head, but as he walked to the mound there was no way he was going to give up the ball. For weeks reporters had been telling him that left-handers couldn't beat the Dodgers, and they sure as hell couldn't go the distance. Lopat delighted in proving them wrong, and he was determined today to show them.

In the top of the ninth, matters became a little tense. Lopat had two out and two on, via a single and a walk. Coming to the plate was the only left-handed hitter in the Dodger lineup: Duke Snider, the forty-two home run Snider. The crowd was on its feet screaming when Casey came out of the dugout and called time. Eddie took a quick look out toward the Yankee bullpen, but Sain was looking back at him. With a left-handed hitter coming up, no one thought that Stengel would pull his pitcher. But, Casey needed to talk. He waved a hand toward Berra to join them. "How ya feeling?" he asked his pitcher. "Feelin' fine," said the cool Lopat. Casey put his craggy face right up to Eddie's. "You sure? How about it, Yogs?" The wrong word from Berra might have caused some mischief, but Yogi had seen enough: Eddie was in control. Stengel turned back to Lopat and got into his face again. "You ain't lyin' to me, are you?" Eddie looked his manager right in the eye. "How long have I been pitching for you? Six or seven years? Have I ever lied to you? No. You think I'm going to start now?" Casey looked his veteran pitcher in the eye for a long second — and left the mound.

Snider, on a slow screwball that he misread, grounded feebly to second base for the final out of the game. The Yankees won, 4–2, were two games up, and Eddie Lopat had thrown a tidy nine-hitter. The Yankees got five hits off Preacher Roe. Well into his seventies, Duke Snider could not forget making the last out. "You hate to make the last out in any game, from recess to sandlot to spring training. But, in the World Series, when you feel you should be able to hit Lopat's slow stuff, it really stays with you."

With the action shifting to Ebbets Field, Dressen made a strategic decision that reminded some reporters of his pitching management during the fateful 1951 chase when the Giants caught up with the Dodgers. In August and September of that year Dressen burned out his starting pitchers, using them in relief as well. Now, with two days rest, he came back with Carl Erskine, who was shelled in the Game One loss. He bypassed his fifteen-game winner Russ Meyer, whom the Dodgers had acquired from the Phillies. Meyer had been pivotal during the run for the pennant, because he dominated the Milwaukee Braves, who were the strongest contender. He was 5–0 against them. Meyer was one of the legion of pitchers whose bitterness toward Dressen continued into their retirement from the game. Years later, historian Peter Golenbock still found that reservoir of anger when he interviewed Meyer. "There was one word Charlie really loved, and that was 'I.' Make that two words: 'I' and 'me'.... We get to the World Series, and I'm not good enough to start. To this day I'll never understand that. You ask if Charlie knew anything about pitching!"

But, on this day, Dressen looked like a genius. When Erskine was on, he had an overhand curveball that was as lethal as any in baseball lore.[5] He started striking out Yankees in the first inning and did not cease until he had racked up *fourteen* for a new World Series record. Mantle and Collins, helpless in the face of this devastating pitch, went down four times each. The Yankees could scratch out only two runs on six hits.

As planned, Casey called on his brave warrior, Vic Raschi. Some Dodgers remembered the overpowering Raschi of 1949, whose fastball and stare could freeze a hitter in his tracks. Jackie remembered Vic from 1947, and he knew that once he got on base, he could drive Raschi to distraction. Vic lost the 1–0 game in 1949 because of Robinson's baserunning.

The Dodgers encountered a different Vic Raschi now. When Reese came back to the dugout he confirmed what the scouting reports had told the Dodgers: He keeps the fastball low. If he tries to throw the high, hard one, it just doesn't look the same. He'll use the curve low and away much more, and the slider as well. Raschi can still throw hard occasionally, but his arm speed is clearly diminished. Also, look for the telltale limp. His knees are gone. Pee Wee went past Campanella and stopped. "If he gets a fastball up, kill it, Roy."

Vic kept pace with the staggering performance of Erskine, run for run. The Yankees had tied the game at 2–2 in the top of the eighth. Like Lopat the day before, Raschi was giving up hits—nine in all—but valiantly kept Brooklyn from reaching home plate. As the Yankees were getting ready to go out in the bottom of the eighth, Casey took Vic aside. "Campanella likes that first one. He's leading off this inning. Don't give him anything to hit. Remember, watch the first pitch."

Campanella came back to the Dodger dugout and started taking off his shin guards and chest protector. He was the first hitter. Reese came by, put his arm around his enormous shoulder. "Campy, he started me off with a fastball three times so far. He likes to get ahead. Look for it."

As Campanella started walking to the batter's box to lead off the bottom of the eighth, Casey came to the top of the dugout and yelled through cupped hands to his pitcher, "Don't forget!" Vic had not forgotten. He would not let Campanella hit the first pitch. Raschi decided he would throw the fastball as a waste pitch, but not completely. He wanted to throw it down in the strike zone, but over the plate, maybe get rid of this dangerous hitter on a ground ball, since Campy liked the first pitch.

As soon as the ball left his hand, Raschi knew that he had made a mistake. It was his best fastball—as hard as he could throw it. As he pushed off the rubber, his right damaged knee gave him a surge of pain that shot through him, affecting the arc of his arm and the direction of the pitch. The ball was going over the plate—but waist high. The thoughts raced through Vic Raschi's brain faster than they could be processed: a bad pitch, an error, maybe Campanella won't see it, won't make me pay, won't get it all.

Campanella's bat came around, whipped with his short, stubby arms and fantastic bat speed. He had one of those squat bodies—at 5'9" and 200 pounds very much like his Yankee counterpart Yogi Berra, who was an inch shorter—made for contact hitters: a quick, powerful, compact swing with no wasted motion. The forty-ounce bat, which looked like a twig as Campanella waved it waiting in the batter's box, came around with a deadly ferocity and made perfect contact with Raschi's pitch. The ball exploded off the bat on a line and reached the left-field stands in bandbox Ebbets Field in what seemed a heartbeat of time. The Dodgers were ahead, 3–2. Vic stood on the mound, unable to look into the dugout where his manager stood, combustible. In the Yankee owners' box, George Weiss wrote a note to himself. In the top of the ninth, the Yankees went quietly, and Erskine had his win, 3–2. There were only a few people in the ballpark that day who suspected that Vic Raschi had pitched his last inning in a Yankee uniform.

Next day, Ford got his chance against another New York City street kid, Billy Loes, whom the Yankees had tested the year before. Ebbets Field was filled to overflow. The building plan said 32,000 was capacity, but that day 36,775 New Yorkers and a few other types squeezed into the ballpark on Bedford Avenue. Before the game, Eddie Lopat sat with his pupil. "This is a small ballpark. One mistake can kill you. Your control has to be perfect." Ford had all the confidence in the world; Turner and Lopat knew that. He walked out to the mound in the bottom of the first, ready to conquer the world. But the world conquered him, instead. Jim Gilliam, leading off, hit a long fly to right field, where Hank Bauer made one of his rare miscues. He misjudged the ball, and it bounced for a ground-rule double. Then followed a single, wild pitch, walk, and a double by Snider, and Ford found himself three runs behind after the first inning. Stengel had seen enough. He conferred with Turner, and Ford did not go out for the second inning. He was through for the day, and so were the Yankees. Allie had gone down to the bullpen, but Casey was still saving Reynolds, and now followed four relievers who were touched up for four more runs. Meanwhile, Loes was holding the Yankees in check. He got some help from Clem Labine in the ninth, and the Dodgers held on for a 7–3 win, tying the Series at two games each, with one more left for the Dodgers at home. The bookmakers' odds now switched in favor of the streaking Dodgers.

Game Five was a gamble for both managers. Casey did not want to come back with Reynolds as a starter. He had an intuition that in a crunch, he would need him in a short burst and did not want to burn Allie out in a start. Dressen had a rested and eager Russ Meyer ready to go, but he played a hunch and went with twenty-year-old rookie Johnny Podres, a left-hander who went 9–4 during the season.

Turner had run out of options. His old men were willing but worn out; his youngster got shelled. Unlike 1951 when rain gave the Yankees a reprieve against the Giants, this series, like the year before, was played without interruption or days off. He turned to one of his second-liners, right-hander Jim McDonald, who had come to the Yankees in 1951 and had been barely a .500 pitcher since then. He was 9–7 this year, inconsistent and never fulfilling his promise. But he had six complete games and seemed to be able to throw all day long. He was also intelligent enough to listen to Allie and Vic when they went over the Dodger lineup with him.

McDonald was starting a game in front of the biggest crowd of his career. The Dodger management announced the exact same attendance for the second straight day: 36,775. That was the first miracle. The second was that McDonald threw the game of his life. Gene Woodling led off with a home run. The Dodgers had runners on the bases in the first and second inning but managed only one run. Dressen, after giving his rookie the start, had a relief pitcher warming up before the game began. The young rookie pitcher kept looking over his shoulder, while Russ Meyer threw more than 100 warm-up pitches over the first two innings. In the third, with the bases loaded, Dressen pulled Podres with the bases loaded, brought in the already worn-down Meyer, who proceeded to give up a grand slam home run to Mickey Mantle. The Yankees kept banging away, with Billy Martin adding a two-run homer and building a lead to 10–2. It looked like a cakewalk. But it was not to be.

In the bottom of the eighth the Dodger bats came alive. Three singles and Billy Cox's three-run home run closed the gap to 10–6. Casey came out, tapped his left arm, telling the umpire that he wanted left-hander Bob Kuzava to face George Shuba. As he walked back to the Yankee dugout, he stopped and turned to the bullpen, held up his right arm, and pointed with a bony finger. Tom Gorman, who had been warming up, sat down, and someone else stood up and took off the jacket. It was Allie.

In the Yankee ninth Gil McDougald homered off nearly forgotten Joe Black, making his only World Series appearance in 1953, the fourth Yankee home run of the game, making it 11–6. When the bottom of the ninth came, the overwhelmingly pro–Brooklyn fans, far from feeling defeated, rose as one and started screaming. Little Phil Rizzuto, standing out at shortstop, was almost disconcerted by the riotous racket. "It was something I will never forget." When the first hitter, Jim Gilliam, drove a Kuzava curveball into the left field seats, the place went berserk. Gilliam's shot set a record for home runs in a World Series game and made the score 11–7, with the heart of the batting order coming up. The Dodgers had come back before; they were a grand slam away from tying the game. Stengel felt the momentum building for the Dodgers. He had seen it happen before. The crowd didn't even let up when Reese made the first out, flying to left. When Snider singled to right center, Casey made his move. Jackie Robinson was moving to the plate. It was time for Reynolds. In the Dodger dugout, Campanella, looking at the figure walking in from the visitor's bullpen, muttered, "Christ, not him."

Casey was waiting for Allie on the mound to hand him the ball. He had to bellow to be heard above the roar of the crowd. "Have you thrown him a curveball yet?" Allie pawed the rubber to find a good spot. "No, not this series."

As Casey started walking back to the dugout, he turned to his pitcher. "Try a curveball, but keep it down."

Reese, the Dodger captain, exhorted his teammates. "This is not the same Wahoo. We've knocked him out once already. He's a cripple. Get in there and get him." They had two outs to do it.

On the first pitch Reynolds reached back and buzzed a fastball in and tight on Robinson, driving him out of the batter's box. Jackie did not get back in immediately; he took some dirt in his hands, looked around, pushing the screaming noise of the crowd out of his mind and trying to concentrate on his enemy out on the rubber who was waiting to throw another lethal pitch. Robinson was looking for the fastball, this time hittable, because Reynolds would not like to get behind 2–0. The pitch came, and broke sharply down and away: a curve. Robinson was helpless; he tapped a ground ball near second base, where Martin fielded it, flipped to Rizzuto, who fired to Collins at first. Double play, game over, 11–7 Yankee win. Save, Allie Reynolds. The crowd sat in stunned silence. The Dodgers had out-hit the Yankees, 14–11. But, in all of these Dodger-Yankee World Series going back to 1947, Robinson, Snider, Campanella and Hodges had a combined batting average against Reynolds of .124.

The Yankees had done what they had wanted to do: win a game at Ebbets Field. Now they were going back to the Stadium with a 3–2 lead in games, and one more win would give them what no other team had ever accomplished in baseball history: five consecutive World Series victories. The Dodgers were going back to Yankee Stadium determined to do what the Yankees had done the year before: win two games in enemy territory. They were ready. They had the better team, and they knew it. They had Erskine and Loes, both in their mid-twenties, who had already looked better than the fading Yankee aces Reynolds and Raschi. They also had to stop that pest Martin. The little bastard had ten hits already.

On the morning of October 5, Reynolds, Raschi and Lopat went to Turner to ask where they were best off, sitting on the bench or in the bullpen. "Sit with me," he told them. It would be easier to watch the kid. Ford would try to redeem himself in Game Six. He was pitching in Yankee Stadium, would get the breaks in the big outfield.[6] Lopat had sat with him already that morning, going over the Dodger batters. Reynolds and Raschi joined in. They liked Whitey from the beginning because he was a terrific listener. Wherever pitching was being discussed, Ford was never far away; not always talking, but within earshot, picking up comments, particularly from the three wise men and their coach. With Yogi, Whitey was different; they were friends, back when they were called Larry and Eddie, even before Carmen and Joanie became part of the foursome. They were peers and equals. With the three pitchers he was like a much younger brother whom they cared about, and with Casey and Turner, a much, *much* younger nephew. There were temperament differences, as well. Berra and Ford were stable, anchored in their families and reliable. They were also more easygoing and lacked the intensity of the older men. On the Yankees, no one trained as hard as these three. Pitchers were historically the worst conditioned athletes on any team; the position players on major league teams would ridicule their pitchers, not even dignifying them with the term "athlete." But on these Yankee teams, Allie, Vic and Eddie led the way. Everyone knew that they were also the most versatile athletes on the team. Basketball, track, football, golf, they excelled at everything. They brought intensity to everything they did. Ford was genuinely laconic, could walk away from a 1–0 loss and shrug it off. True, Whitey was part of the new Three Musketeers on the Yankees, an ensemble that George Weiss did not like: Mantle, Martin and Ford. There had already been incidents at Toots Shor's saloon that Casey overlooked, because he knew others would take care of them. Ford was mature enough to realize how far he could go in abusing his body. He had always been — even as a teenager — a pretty serious casual drinker. He liked the high life of New York City, but it never got out of control. Billy drank less, but lost his head quickly; Mickey was well on his way to becoming the alcoholic he was later in life.

On the day of the sixth game of the 1953 World Series, Whitey Ford was all business. He had listened well and would not make the same mistakes he committed in Game Four. When he walked to the mound in front of 62,370 fans, he was loose and had Lopat's words of advice ringing in his ears. They had talked about the powerful right-handed Dodger lineup for hours. Keep the ball in the park; don't let them hurt you with the long ball. When you start tiring, tell Jim right away; no heroics. Complete games don't mean a damn thing. Allie will be in pen without anyone telling him to go there. He'll know when.

Ford did exactly what he was supposed to do. Over seven innings he gave up five singles, two doubles and one run. The Yankees got to Erskine early; this would be no record-setting strikeout effort. By the end of two innings the Yankees had pecked away to a 3–0 lead. Erskine, in his third start in six days, was clearly not the same pitcher. His velocity was down, and his devastating curveball was hittable. By the end of four innings, he was through. He had walked four and given up six hits. Once again, Dressen could not manage his pitchers.

From the fifth inning on, Lopat, who with Turner was looking hard at every pitch that Ford threw, asked his pupil who sat down next to him, "How are you feeling?" Each time, Whitey, putting on his jacket, said, "Fine." In the Dodger sixth, Reese hit one 400 feet to Mantle in deep right center. When Robinson doubled down the left field line, four sets of eyes turned to Reynolds, who was already taking off his warm-up jacket. He went down the ramp to the trainer's room to start stretching. Robinson stole third without drawing a throw, and Campanella's ground ball to Rizzuto brought in the first Dodger run, cutting the Yankee lead to 3–1. Hodges, who did nothing all day long at bat, grounded out to end the inning. While the Yankees left the field, Allie walked out to the Yankee bullpen. Ford sat next to Lopat. "Keep an eye on me next inning."

In the Dodger seventh Ford fanned Snider for the third time leading off an inning. When Furillo went to a full count, Lopat got off the bench and stood with one foot on the steps, looking intently. But Whitey got him on a fly ball to Mantle in deep center. Eddie's concern grew to worry when Cox singled, bringing pinch-hitter Bobby Morgan to the plate. On the second pitch Morgan, not known for his power to the opposite field, hit a line shot toward right, heading for the stands. At the last minute, Bauer reached up and grabbed it for the third out. Turner and Lopat both looked at Stengel. The message was clear in their eyes: Whitey is finished. The big question in the minds of every Yankee was: how much did the Indian have left? In the bullpen, Allie threw his first pitch and winced. His arm felt tired, and his back muscles were in spasm.

Clem Labine came in to relieve Bob Milliken in the seventh, and the Yankees went down quickly. They took the field, but no pitcher came out of the Yankee dugout. Now all eyes sought out the figure coming in from the Yankee bullpen, as the crowd noise rose to a crescendo. As Allie Reynolds strode resolutely to the mound, his teammates stood alone with their own thoughts. Phil Rizzuto, who had played with Allie on the Yankees since 1947, was a worrier by nature. He worried for Reynolds. "The Super Chief," as the newspapermen liked to call him, was going on courage and intelligence. Phil knew what that bus accident had taken out of the pitcher. He had seen Reynolds lying for hours on the training table as his back was subjected to manipulation so painful that it had to be sprayed with a freeze so Allie could get up. There were times that he could barely walk. But, watching the Chief go past him, the emotional Rizzuto was almost overcome. "Stengel and Turner knew they could ring the bell and Reynolds would respond. The Cleveland team had said that Allie didn't have a big heart. When I saw him come in, I could feel *my* heart and it was telling me: this game is ours. As a friend of Allie's, I would never have asked him to pitch in this game, but I was glad that someone else had."

By the sound of the ball hitting Berra's glove as Reynolds threw his eight warm-up pitches, it was obvious that his velocity was down. He made an occasional grimace. He was in pain. The Dodgers had the top of the order up. Gilliam flied to Bauer. Reese flied to Bauer. Allie tried to get a pitch up and in on Robinson, but it stayed over the plate and Jackie drilled it to left for a single. The tying run was on base, Campanella the hitter. He thought of his friend Vic Raschi in Game Three. No fastballs for Campy this time. Allie struck him out on curveballs, down and away. The Yankees went quietly in the bottom of the eighth against Labine to set the stage for the last inning.

Vic had been watching Allie closely as they sat on the bench waiting for the Yankees to complete their at-bat. He knew his friend was in pain but would say nothing. He was only worried about location. Could Allie get the ball where he wanted it?

Gil Hodges got hold of Reynolds' fastball on the outside of the plate, but it was only another 400-foot out to Mantle. Allie could not feel the muscles in his back when Duke Snider drew a walk, his first time on base that day. Again the tying run came to the plate, this time Carl Furillo, the National League batting champ, who already had seven hits in the series. Raschi, on the bench, was thinking along with his friend: remember, Furillo is a good opposite field hitter. Don't give him something to hit that he can handle going the other way to right. Allie worked carefully until the count ran full. Vic was right alongside in Allie's thoughts, as he prepared himself for the 3–2 pitch. But, the two of them were not the only ones there. Furillo was thinking also: Reynolds uses the whole field, gives you something to hit 400 feet for an out. He'll give me the fastball, and I'm supposed to hit it to Mantle. Furillo had it figured out. Reynolds threw his best fastball over the outside corner. He got the location he wanted. But Carl, as Reynolds was completing his stretch and looking at first base to check the runner, had already moved his left foot a step closer to the plate and turned his left shoulder in. His body was aimed at right field.

Furillo got all of Allie's fastball. He hit it hard and far over Hank Bauer's head in right field. When it landed in the stands four rows deep, the game was tied at 3–3. The few thousand Dodger fans were on their feet, reborn and ready for the resurrection.

Ford, sitting in the Yankee dugout, did not care that he had lost the chance for his second World Series win. He was only thinking about this guy on the mound who had just given up a home run that lost the lead for the Yankees in the top of the ninth. Now what? Whitey was asking himself: How do we react or recover from this devastation? One pitch, one hit, could turn a team around completely. In the fourth game of the 1941 World Series between Brooklyn and New York, Tommy Henrich had struck out to end the game and give the Dodgers a win to tie the series. But Mickey Owen could not handle Hugh Casey's spitter, the ball got past Owen, and Henrich wound up at first. In the dugout, the normally tactical genius of Leo Durocher went into paralysis. The Yankees ran off two singles, a double and two walks and scored four runs to win the game. Durocher never came out of the dugout. He was frozen as his pitcher threw away the game and the World Series.

Here, thought Ford, we go again. What will the Chief do now? Would he blow up like that Dodger pitcher? Will Casey yank his meal ticket? He didn't have long to wait for an answer. As an octogenarian, Rizzuto recalled it clearly: "Then Allie did something that even makes me proud today. He struck out Cox and Labine." The Yankee bench leapt to greet their pitcher as he came into the dugout.

Turner asked Reynolds if he could go another inning, and Allie said he could, then added, "Let's end it now." Labine was still pitching for the Dodgers and walked Bauer to start the bottom of the ninth. After Berra lined out to right, Mantle, still playing on one good leg, hit a high chop between the pitcher and third. Racing with everything he had, he beat the throw, Bauer going to second. Now the pest came to bat, Billy Martin. The Dodger bench came alive with abuse, because they had developed a genuine hatred for the scrawny big mouth playing second base for the Yankees. He also was beating the hell out of them in this series. Martin came to the plate, with a faint smile of scorn on his lips, as he heard the insults coming from the Dodger dugout.

He hit the first pitch from Labine up the middle into center field, his twelfth hit; a World Series record for six games. When Bauer's foot touched home plate with the winning run, Vic and Eddie embraced their warrior friend sitting next to them on the bench. He would have given anything to save the game for the kid; instead, he had his seventh victory in World Series play, tying him with Red Ruffing for the most wins.

Roger Kahn was the *Herald Tribune* beat reporter covering the grim Dodger clubhouse after the game. "Duke Snider caught my eye: 'I still say we're the better team.' 'I know,' I said. 'That's the hell of it. That's the rottenest thing in this life, isn't it? The best team doesn't always win.'"

The Yankees had done it one more time, establishing a record for eternity.

That evening, the Yankees celebrated their historic accomplishment. The younger players were hooting and hollering, not completely in touch with what they had done. Most of the celebrants had not been with the team for those five years; not Whitey, Mickey, Billy. The mythical DiMaggio, not in attendance, had been part of this miracle for three of the five years. There were just nine who felt the total impact of this accomplishment, and only six had seen the five years of heroics on the mound and had watched the three pitchers excel, then grow old, and still persevere. Yogi knew most of all what they had done. The others included Woodling and Bauer, brought in as acolytes to discipline and control the younger players; Rizzuto, a veteran but perennial little kid in need of protection; Johnny Mize, who astonishingly won five World Series rings in the twilight of his career as perhaps the most valuable part-time player in history; and Charlie Silvera, Berra's backup who made rare appearances in games but understood deeply the character of these teams. A few others had sensed the commitment to the club that made their experience unique: Bobby Brown, Joe Collins, Gil McDougald, and Jerry Coleman understood the ethos, the heart of these teams. They knew who made it happen, and that it could not be replicated.

Allie, Vic and Eddie sat with their wives and enjoyed the satisfaction of knowing they had accomplished what no other team in the memory of baseball had done. In this fifth World Series, it had not been elegant. Eddie won his start with a complete game and gave up only two runs. Vic pitched well in his one start, but lost. For the first time in these five years, he came away without a win. Allie's ERA in the series had ballooned to 6.75, but he had pitched in three games, saved one and won another. The Dodgers hit .300 against the Yankee pitchers. Brooklyn had the better team, and they lost. Something else mattered.

Casey was now in a class by himself, even beyond his mentor John McGraw and the other Yankee icon, Joe McCarthy. They looked over at George Weiss, smiling as much as he was capable, sitting with Dan Topping and Del Webb. A reporter had quoted Weiss earlier, saying that changes had to be made, even if the Yankees had won their fifth consecutive championship. Weiss had said that there was too much complacency on the team, and that too many players had gotten rich at the expense of the Yankee organization.

The six friends spotted the target of Weiss's barbs. The only Yankees who had grown wealthy while Weiss watched were Casey Stengel, who came to his job a rich man and grew richer with his investments in oil and real estate, thanks to his smart wife, Edna; and Allie Reynolds, who literally struck oil in Oklahoma. But, they knew the object of Weiss' anger and resentment was Vic Raschi, who was stubborn, formal, argumentative, determined to make his point in heated discussions with the general manager and the winner in each negotiation, during which Stengel would intervene for his player. But now he would pay.

9

One by One

"George Weiss had a very short memory."—Vic Raschi

The Reynoldses quickly left New York City and returned to Oklahoma. Vic and Sally went back up to Conesus, New York, after visiting with Vic's family in Springfield; Eddie got ready to take the *Eddie Lopat All-Stars* barnstorming to Japan. Before splitting up, they sat down in the clubhouse to talk about aches, pains, and the future. Allie and Eddie knew that Vic would be the most vulnerable of the Yankees in dealing with Weiss's arithmetic: thirteen wins added up to a salary cut. But they would talk to Casey, and Casey had always be able to keep the general manager under control. Vic was to let them know when the contract offer arrived in the mail; then they would get busy. Allie, the businessman of the trio, thought that Weiss would probably try to get a small reduction in Vic's salary, which had reached $40,000. His 13–6 record wasn't that bad, and the fifth World Series had to be worth *something,* even in Weiss's stone heart. The Yankees made a lot of money this year; maybe Weiss will mellow a little. They said goodbye to one another, hoping that their optimism was justified. It wasn't.

Just after Thanksgiving, Vic was looking out over the snow-covered field near his house. He could see Conesus Lake, where he had lived since he and Sally were married. He loved the country near the Finger Lakes of New York; he liked being near Geneseo State College where he could work out with the teams, coach a little, and teach. He knew that this was where he would settle down permanently. Sally's people were from these parts; it's where she felt most at home, and so did Vic. He took another look at the printed form letter in his hand, to make sure he had read the typed-in number correctly where it said "Compensation for the 1954 season." The dollar figure read: "$25,000.00"— the maximum 25 percent cut. Before sending the unsigned standard one-page contract back, he wrote George Weiss a note and attached it. Vic argued that his performance did not warrant the maximum salary cut; going from $40,000 to $25,000 did not reflect what he thought was his value to the team. Vic's physical condition was a product of his effort and willingness to sacrifice and to play hurt, never missing a turn. "Mr. Weiss, I have made myself a cripple." He hoped that George Weiss would remember that. Vic signed the letter, put the unsigned contract in an envelope, and mailed it back to the New York Yankee organization, in care of George Weiss. He had no illusions. Before calling Allie, he told Sally Raschi, "Mom, we're gone."

When Reynolds heard from his friend that he had been given the maximum cut allowed, he reminded himself never to be put in that sort of situation with Weiss. He would take no such insult. Vic could use the money; Allie did not need his baseball salary. He would not negotiate with Weiss or try to convince him of his value to the team. Vic did that every year, and what did it get him? A salary cut that would hurt his pride, which is what Weiss wanted to do, to humiliate his players, particularly his stars, whom he was determined to take down more than just a peg. Well, he wasn't getting away with it this time, thought Allie. Reynolds called Casey Stengel right after he mailed his own unsigned contract back to the Yankees. Let them deal with both of us, he thought.

Stengel said he would talk to Topping and Webb first, but that he had to deal with Weiss. Don't worry, he told Allie, Weiss and I understand each other. Baseball people could not figure out how Casey and Weiss got along so well, indeed, had been friends and confidants for nearly thirty years. Their temperaments and personalities were polar opposites. The manager advised Allie to come to spring training unsigned. If he wanted to, he could still come to camp and deal with Weiss, who Casey knew had a high opinion of Reynolds. Stengel was sure that he could work things out. He wanted his old twin cobras back for a sixth title.

But Weiss was determined to win this one. On December 16, 1953, he announced a monster trade with the Philadelphia Athletics. The Yankees sent six players, including their hottest black prospect, Vic Power, to the A's for three marginal players, plus veteran first baseman Eddie Robinson, and — the prize in the package — twenty-eight-year-old right-handed pitcher Harry Byrd. Byrd had been the American League Rookie of the Year in 1952 with a good Philadelphia team that flopped miserably in 1953, and Byrd flopped with them, falling to 11–20. But, he was big and strong, threw hard, and Weiss wanted the word to get out that the Yankees turned around the mediocre careers of Reynolds and Lopat and they could find others and do it again. It was time to replace the old warhorses with new blood. Of course, they could stick around, but not at the same salary.

Weiss was playing hardball, and he did not care who knew it. Later that year he told a reporter, "We've made at least eight of our players independently wealthy and they were acting as if we had to get down on our hands and knees and beg them to play for us." Weiss started telling the beat reporters that the holdouts refused to talk to him. When Reynolds read this in the papers, he called Stengel again to tell Casey that the general manager was planting stories that were not true. When Eddie and Libby returned from the Japanese barnstorming trip, Allie spoke to his roommate. They wondered what was on Weiss's mind.

No one could have known. In his shrewd and calculating business head, George Weiss had come to an epiphany: *It might be better to lose in 1954.* It took a while for the working press to figure this out, but those who listened to him regularly finally understood. One *Sports Illustrated* article later in the year stated, "The Yankees Real Boss: He is a shrewd, practical businessman named George Weiss who would like to win the pennant, but won't be too disturbed if his team loses this year."

Weiss Makes His Move

> *"Mr. Weiss broke the spell. The magic was gone."*—Phil Rizzuto, on the sale of Vic Raschi

Vic was sitting on the porch of their rental house in St. Petersburg when the phone rang. He had arrived at camp with the other pitchers and catchers on time, a week before the position players were scheduled to show up. He had come without a contract, but his letter to Weiss in the winter was reasonably cordial. He didn't think a 25 percent salary cut was justified. Weiss had not gotten back to him. Vic thought he must be occupied with the dozen players who had not signed contracts.

He went inside to answer the phone. It was a photographer who worked for one of the newspapers covering the Yankees. He asked if he could take a picture of Vic in his new uniform. "What?" asked Raschi. "What do you mean?" The photographer said the Yankee front office had told his newspaper that Vic Raschi had been sold to the St. Louis Cardinals for $85,000.

In his heart, Vic knew that it would happen some day, and that George Weiss would make his threat come true, although Vic could not believe that he had had a bad year. Anyway, Weiss didn't want to talk about it. As it turned out, there was no negotiation. He just wanted Vic gone. Later, Weiss told the press that he needed to make an object lesson of some of the players. With a dozen holdouts, the situation was intolerable, and the players had to understand that the Yankee front office meant business. At a press conference he announced that the Yankee payroll had reached $750,000 a year, far from the $185,000 annual budget when Weiss took over. He had, Weiss informed the journalists, the complete authority to make necessary adjustments. A reporter had asked him, "How does Casey feel about losing one of his warhorses?" Weiss did not answer. Another journalist, close to the Yankee clubhouse, asked if Weiss received a percentage of the money that represented savings under a certain gross dollar amount that he had available for players. Weiss's eyes turned to slits, and he walked out.

It was February 23, 1954, and for the first time in his professional life, Vic Raschi was no longer a New York Yankee. The next day, before going over to the ball field to clean out his locker, he received the Western Union telegram. There was no salutation, just the following: "Your contract has been assigned outright to the St. Louis Cardinal National League Baseball Club. All good wishes for your future success. George Weiss." Those were the last words Vic Raschi ever got, either in writing or orally, from George Weiss. No call to have a drink or dinner after a lifetime as a Yankee. After telling his wife Sally that they would not have to move right away because the Cardinals also trained just across town, he called his mother in Springfield. She was delighted. She said that she never liked the Yankees.

When Stengel heard about the trade, he went into a public rage. Yet, it is difficult to believe that Weiss had not spoken to his close friend about his intentions. Many times over the past five years Casey had gotten the general manager to change his mind or to give a grudging salary increase. Stengel would work on Weiss until he got what he wanted. But, there were times when Casey could see that there would be no moving him. There was no going back now: Vic was gone. Stengel, always surrounded by reporters, told them that he was unhappy to lose Raschi. So he only won thirteen games. He brought more to the team than just wins, Casey told them; he was right, again.

In the clubhouse, Vic cleaned out his locker. The word raced through the knots of players, all pitchers and catchers. Weiss had done the deal before the other veterans had shown up. Now they could read about it in the newspapers and let it sink in: no one was untouchable. Allie sat on his stool, staring straight ahead, with his mouth tightly closed. When he spoke, all he said was, "If Weiss argues with me about salary, I'll retire right now. No matter what, this is it. No more."[1] Eddie Lopat came up to Raschi. "Is it true? Weiss traded you? Does he know what he's done?" Jim Turner came stalking in. He very rarely raised his voice or spoke harshly. "What the hell does Weiss know about a clubhouse? What does he know about what makes a team tick? He thinks we're great ballplayers because he's smart! We win pennants and World Series because of his brains! He has no idea how a clubhouse works." He was breathing very hard. Jim Turner loved the Yankees, was a loyal coach for Casey Stengel. But his dedication to his pitchers and particularly to these three men went beyond anything that he or they had experienced in years of playing baseball. Even their wives had seen this closeness evolve. It happens occasionally among men in bonding situations. It happened here with the Yankees, and they transmitted this experience to their teammates. This is what Eddie Lopat meant when said, "Does he know what he's done?"

Did George Weiss know what he had done? He and Stengel were accustomed to talking for hours on end about baseball strategy, spotting talent, individual players and their ability. They would talk candidly about trades, whom to keep, whom to shop around, whom to acquire. Weiss was at ease with Casey in hundreds of intimate conversations about the game they both loved. The only time Weiss shook his head impatiently was when Stengel started talking about how McGraw spotted the kind of character that some of his great leaders had, how Christy Mathewson could mold a team together out of twenty-five personalities. Weiss was not interested. Casey then would talk about "my three pitchers" and their coach. It was rare, he said, for pitchers to take that kind of role on a team. Matty did it, and my three horses do it, too. Stengel laughed when he told Weiss how the team's three young merry night wanderers would get ripped up and down by "the Chief" or see Whitey get taken off into a corner by Lopat, who would put an arm around his shoulder, put his mouth right next to Ford's ear, and shape him up. Mantle worshiped Reynolds; Ford listened to every word spoken by Lopat. Raschi would challenge Billy Martin to a sit-up competition, which would leave the second baseman holding his stomach in agony, or take on all of his teammates in a basketball shooting contest. They were always together, these three pitchers, these three great athletes and friends.

Weiss was not interested in mentoring or role models. These were professional athletes who drew a salary. He had private detectives to build character.

If Weiss wanted to deal a blow to the team, if he *really* did not want a sixth consecutive pennant, he had found a way to prevent it from happening.

An Empty Locker

> "We believed in each other. Every time one of us walked out on the mound, the others felt he would give 100 percent, and he would win."—Vic Raschi, on his friendship with Eddie Lopat and Allie Reynolds

Before leaving the clubhouse, the three men, all out of uniform, sat down for a final time as teammates. Turner was out on the field already, with Yogi. Now they sat in their corner just as they did when they were back at Yankee Stadium, three old warriors in a circle, sitting on stools. They talked in hushed tones while the other players—friends, rookies in high-numbered uniforms—

wandered out into the Florida sun. Vic's head was down, but he was talking, uncharacteristically. He was always the quietest of the three, often silent, introspective, and private, except with he took the ball and went to the mound. After this, there would be no more cheering for each other, no more visits from Vic's blind brother, Gene, no more shared battles. But they knew one thing: they would be friends forever.

When Vic got back to his house, there was a telegram waiting. It was from the St. Louis Cardinal Baseball Club, no salutation. Raschi wondered if the St. Louis general manager also counted words in telegrams. "St. Louis Cardinals acquired your contract this date. Please contact me by phone at St. Petersburg 70129. Dick Mayer, General Manager." Sally wanted Vic to be satisfied. He was a proud man and would not be treated the way George Weiss insisted on dealing with his players. Vic had always called him "Mr. Weiss," had always been formal, respectful and businesslike. Now he would have to deal with someone else. Sally told Vic that he should meet with the St. Louis management; then they would decide what to do. He still hadn't signed a contract. It certainly would be convenient. The Cardinals were training right there in St. Pete, practically next door. Vic went over to the St. Louis offices, met Dick Mayer and owner August A. Busch, Jr. Raschi was offered a contract at $40,000 — no cut from the previous year. He signed, went home to tell Sally, got his gear, and the next day reported to the St. Louis Cardinals.

In eight years with the New York Yankees, Raschi's record was 120–50, a winning percentage of .710. It has remained the best won-lost record in Yankee history to this day. In 1949, 1950, and 1951 he won twenty-one games in each season. In World Series competition he was 5–3; two of his losses were 1–0 and 3–2. His Series ERA was 2.24. He had been a big-game pitcher, winning the pennant clincher in the last game of the 1949 season and World Series final games in 1949 and 1951. There were other contributions that were not measured in any record book.

In the Yankee clubhouse, there was an empty locker.

The Season of 1954

"Loyalty was always a big thing in baseball. But there was a lot of loyalty broken after 1953." — Yogi Berra

Weiss was right about one thing: the unsigned players got the message, and within ten days after the arrival of the entire squad, every one of the holdouts had signed his contract. There was something else they talked about in the spring training clubhouse and out in the hot sun of St. Petersburg: it didn't make any difference if you were one of Casey's boys. There had been few illusions.

No one in the hardnosed world of professional baseball expected much sentimentality. Hell, they were ready to trade DiMaggio for Williams! In spite of
this, they knew that Stengel had gone to bat for them with Weiss and the owners. Vic was so important to each of them over these five years, part of the inner
core. Even the toughest of cynics, ex–Marines like Bauer and guys who always
played angry like Woodling, never expected that it would be a telegram that
just said, "You've been traded. Best wishes."

Stengel sensed the bitterness and had a team meeting. For the first time in
his years as Yankee manager he had to deal with the team's morale. Casey felt
a cynicism that disappeared when the team took the field, but Stengel and the
coaches knew it was just beneath the surface. These were professionals who
understood why they were being paid. But the manager knew that something
had been taken out of the heart of his team. Writer Peter Golenbock described
the atmosphere that spring "as an undefinable lassitude that ran through the
Yankee camp," one now deprived of the training ethic of the three older pitchers, the sight of them doing endless exercises or wind sprints, encouraging or
challenging their teammates. Lopat and Reynolds were there, together, but you
could see that their hearts just weren't in it. They were no longer "the Big
Three." Whitey might be the ace of the staff, but he was not a warrior to follow into battle, not someone who, like Vic Raschi, sat alone before he pitched
and looked into the volcano about to erupt within him.

Allie had told Lopat that he was through at the end of the year. He wouldn't
have come back if he had known about Vic. He would finish out the season,
and then it was back to Oklahoma—for good. Eddie, he knew, had to be more
cautious. If he wanted to stay in baseball, he would need Weiss perhaps to give
him a good push; that's why he never gave the general manager quite the same
hard time. Lopat kept it formal, always "Mr. Weiss" and fought for his salary,
but he never had Vic's bulldog tenacity when it came to dealings with this most
difficult of baseball executives.

There was one new pitcher in camp up from Binghamton, a big twenty-
four-year-old right-hander named Bob Grim, who reminded them of Vic.
Casey asked Allie to help him, and Reynolds, always generous to rookies,
worked with Grim. He had the equipment: good fastball, slider, and a sharp-
breaking curve. Allie worked with him on pitching inside and up in the strike
zone, the high hard one that in those bygone days was still called a strike by
umpires, who considered a fastball across the uniform letters part of the
pitcher's territory. Grim would put together a 20–6 season that earned him
Rookie of the Year honors in the American League.

The Yankees went on to win more games in 1954—103—than they ever
had in the five years when they won the world championships. But the Cleveland Indians compiled an astonishing 111–42 record, a winning percentage of

.721, and the Yankees finished eight games behind. No matter how many games they won, no one could convince the veterans that they would have lost if they had Vic Raschi for the big games.[2]

Allie couldn't wait for the season to end. Although Bob Grim had been a willing and enthusiastic pupil, the atmosphere was just not the same. It was obvious that Harry Byrd was not going to fill Raschi's shoes, and Allie could not forget Weiss's heartless treatment of his friend. He had told Earlene that Vic's departure was a personal loss that preyed on him. He could not get it out of his mind. He had learned a great deal about the art of pitching from Eddie Lopat; he had learned about character from Vic, from his relationship to his blind brother, Gene, and to the Raschi clan.

He was fortunately distracted by his dealings with major league owners concerning the pension plan and took out some of his hostility to that fight. Reynolds and Kiner were becoming formidable advocates for the players, and Vic's fate was never far from Allie's thoughts. Just before spring training they had met with management and demanded that the pension for five-year players be raised from $50 to $100 per month and to $150 for ten-year veterans. Reynolds and Kiner, smarter than many of the owners, also suggested that part of the television and radio revenues should go to the pension fund. The owners capitulated. The agreement signed in 1954 was the cornerstone of big changes to come.

Stengel wanted Allie as a starter and reliever, again. By this time, Jim Turner was looking out primarily for his pitchers and not the team, and he told the manager that Reynolds should not be exploited, because the damn owners would get rid of him if he were hurt. "Christ, Raschi pitched for a whole year with only three days rest, and what goddam good did it do him in the end? Sacrifice? Bullshit!" Allie's back still had spasms, but Earlene had worked all winter on his traction, and the pain had diminished. By the All-Star break, he was 9–1, the bone chips were rattling around but not causing much trouble, and Allie was selected for his fifth All-Star game as he approached his fortieth birthday.

Yet, nobody was catching the Indians. The Yankees won thirteen in a row, and Cleveland still held a 5 1/2 game lead. Harry Byrd could not put two wins back-to-back, and although Bob Grim added a great arm, the pitching staff was not coming together. Whitey was winning, but still not going the distance, which meant Reynolds or Sain had to come in more often.

There was something else that Allie was missing. Some fire had gone. He needed the companionship of someone who practiced his craft the same way he did, and felt emotionally about things the same way, as well. Both Allie and Vic had learned together to *despise* hitters, to conquer them, to intimidate and beat them into submission. Jim Turner taught this to Vic in Portland, and when

Allie came to the Yankees with the burden of a reputation that said he lacked courage and toughness, Turner worked his will with both of them until they became the two serpents that terrified Roger Kahn.

Eddie was different. He won because he *respected* hitters, knew how dangerous they were with a bat in their hands. Reynolds had learned to pitch the way Lopat did, but he loved to talk with Vic about *the enemy*, those battles with Robinson, Hodges, Rosen, Minoso, Zernial, the big right-handed sluggers; or the titanic confrontations with Ted Williams. He had told Roger Kahn in an interview in 1954, "As soon as my foot hits the mound, it's war." That's also how it was with Vic.

On September 26, the *New York Times* ran a small paragraph at the end of the story covering the final home game at Yankee Stadium, stating that there had been a brief ceremony before the game to award plaques honoring the members of the 1949–1953 Yankees. There were two members missing. Bobby Brown had started his medical residency. Vic Raschi did not attend. George Weiss thought to himself, "No one even missed him." He was wrong.

Allie finished his last season in professional baseball with his best major league winning percentage, .765, and a 13–4 record. He was no longer a starting pitcher, completing only five of eighteen; he had seven saves in eighteen relief appearances. Before he left New York for Oklahoma City, Allie told Casey and Jim Turner that he was through. Later, George Weiss asked to see him. Allie went to the Yankee offices for what he hoped would be a brief conversation. Weiss was friendlier than he had ever been, and then dropped a bombshell: how would Allie like to stay with the Yankee organization? It did not take Reynolds long to give an answer. He was eager to leave New York; his wife did not like the city, and they would spend their years together in Oklahoma. He shook hands with Weiss. "If you have a change of heart, let me know, Allie." Back in New Jersey, the Reynolds said goodbye to Eddie and Libby Lopat, to Yogi and Carmen Berra, and headed west.

Weiss, in his office, sat deep in thought. His star of the future had experienced another good year, but not the kind that DiMaggio had in his first four in the major leagues. Mickey Mantle had all the equipment, *more* than DiMaggio even. He terrified American League pitchers; they walked him 102 times! But a .300 batting average, twenty-seven home runs and 102 runs batted in was not an extraordinary year, not a superstar year, and for the Yankees to maintain their dominance in a league that would find Cleveland signing more black ballplayers, and perhaps other teams, as well, Weiss needed more out of Mantle. This hoped-for *Wunderkind*, fragile in body, more fragile in *mind*, needed to be disciplined and *watched*. Up until this year, his teammates kept him in check. Not even Casey could do it. Weiss, who was almost invisible in the clubhouse during the season, used a side door to see Stengel if he needed him, and had no idea what was going on among the players. There were others, Weiss had heard from Stengel, who held a grip on Weiss's prize ballplayers and problems: Ford and Mantle. But, Weiss had his eye on what he considered the *real* problem: that goddam Martin, Casey's pet. This year, discipline was more lax. They won games, but his "sources" had told him that Mantle and Ford had hitched up with Martin, who was in the army, for some big-time carousing. Mantle, he knew, came into the clubhouse hung over — and this year no one did anything about it. Then Mickey got hurt again. Something had to be done to gain control over these people. After another minute, Weiss thought he had found the solution. He picked up the phone to call up the private detective agency. He would get the evidence and confront them. Weiss knew there would be no trading of Mantle and Ford. But Martin could go, if it would help the other two. Weiss now knew that the discipline would come from the front office, and he was ready and eager.

Back home with Earlene, Reynolds worked in his thriving oil business. He had told Ralph Kiner that the Players' Association should start looking around for a replacement representative for the American League. But after Christmas, the warrior began smelling baseball. On a warm January day, he went out to the local high school field to try some jogging and sprints. He had not trained all winter, just played some golf. He wanted to ask his body to respond; it did not. He felt the spasms, and he knew that he could not go back. He told Earlene, who was happy to have him home permanently. On February 2, 1955, Allie Reynolds announced his official retirement from baseball.

Allie's career as a major leaguer was over. He had had *two* careers: the struggling years with the Indians, and his resurrection as a Yankee, where his record was 131–60. Altogether, Allie retired with a 182–107 record and forty-nine saves. He was the last modern pitcher to be both a starter and a reliever. As Stengel had said, he was the best *ever* two ways. Better than Mathewson. Better than Cy Young. "And I seen them both," said Casey.

Eddie Lopat, after the 1954 season, would be back. He had become the most successful once-a-week pitcher in baseball. At age thirty-six, with permanent tendonitis that left him unable to raise his left arm after pitching, he still had the guile and cunning to frustrate major league hitters. In 1954 the Junkman still beat Cleveland five times in five tries, even as the Indians were pulling ahead to their pennant. Lopat finished 12–4, made twenty-three starts, but completed only seven games. For the first time in five years, he was giving up more hits than innings pitched. In 170 innings, the opposition banged out 189 hits. Eddie knew that guys he had handled with ease were adjusting and punching his pitches. His ERA had jumped to 3.55.

But Lopat had already made a mental transition to coaching. He worked closely with Jim Turner. He also reconciled himself to the time he would no longer be a Yankee. That meant a trade, or at worst his outright release. Knowing Weiss, who always tried to get something for nothing, he expected that, like Vic, he would be sold. Weiss had a genius for selling damaged goods to unknowing customers.[3] Vic was a cripple. Eddie knew that he had slipped a disc in the winter while doing some physical education teaching at a local high school. Vic's back was in trouble, his knees were gone, he had a shrunken leg, and Weiss got $85,000 for him!

The barnstorming was getting a little arduous, and Eddie was ready for another entrepreneurial baseball activity. With Weiss's encouragement he opened up an instructional camp in Florida for young players and umpires. Eddie had been tinkering with the idea since 1949, when Yankee teammate George Stirnweiss got him interested. He would be able to stay in shape, Libby and the kids could have some winter vacation time, and he might make a few bucks. If Vic or Allie wanted to come in with him, he would be delighted. They spoke often over the telephone, kept in touch even by mail. In one letter, Eddie wrote to both of them, "I'm in trouble. With the two of you gone, I'm exposed!"

It had been a difficult year for Vic. Once he got over the shock of the trade, with Sally's help, he pulled himself together. "I'm certainly going to give the Cards my best," he told a reporter, but Raschi was not physically up to the grind. He worked extremely hard on conditioning his weakened knees and got off to a good start, winning his first five games. The Cardinals vaulted to first place late in May. But, Eddie Stanky brought all of his playing days' on-field intensity to managing the Cardinals, and, like Charlie Dressen, thought he knew everything about pitching. He used starters Harvey Haddix, Brooks Lawrence, and Gerry Staley as regular relievers, and blew them out. Raschi told Stanky that his arm took too long to loosen up for relief use, and Vic was spared. Nevertheless, in an early June game, pitching from a stretch motion, his back went out again, and he was finished as an effective starter. He ended up with an 8–9 record and an ERA of 4.73 for the sixth-place Cardinals. Stanky would last into 1955, when a player revolt got him fired early into the season. He returned in 1965 with the Chicago White Sox and managed for three more years and then was out of baseball.

In 1955, after pitching in only one game for the Cardinals, Vic was sold to the Kansas City A's, who had moved from Philadelphia with the franchise that year. Raschi had nothing left. After going 4–6 with an ERA of 5.44, at age thirty-six, he called Jim Turner and told him that he felt he was taking the place of somebody who might make a greater contribution to the team. Jim and Vic talked whenever Kansas City and the Yankees crossed paths. Always the loyal teammate, Raschi told Turner about some of the good young ballplay-ers on the A's, particularly little Bobby Shantz, whom people thought was washed up, but Vic saw life in his arm. Raschi also like a right-handed pitcher who could throw hard: Art Ditmar. Both eventually came to the Yankees.

In June, after a painful slip on the mound, Vic spoke first to Sally and then to manager Lou Boudreau and retired from baseball. His combined record for his last two years in baseball was 12–16. No amount of money could compen-sate for his pride. He had his dignity in tact and would not hang on just for a paycheck. "Baseball has been my whole life since I was nine years old. I put everything into it and got a lot out of it." That night he called Allie, Eddie, and Jim Turner. Next day, he left for Conesus, New York, to join Sally and the kids. A new life had begun for Vic Raschi.

Lopat was right about George Weiss getting *something* for as little as pos-sible. When the 1955 season began, Eddie knew that his time was limited. Weiss had re-acquired left-hander Tommy Byrne, who had finally discovered the loca-tion of home plate. With Ford and Byrne in the starting rotation, there was no room for a thirty-seven-year-old once-a-week left-hander with an arthritic arm. Weiss had made it clear first with Vic Raschi, then in 1954 with Gene Woodling, another of Casey's favorites, that a player would be dropped the minute his pro-duction goals and the general manager's expectations were not met. Eddie was struggling, with a 4–8 record, although he had a respectable 3.72 ERA. But he was superfluous, and Weiss had a way about him that eliminated any thought of sentimentality. On Oldtimers' Day, July 30, 1955, at Yankee Stadium, Sten-gel himself threw the switch.[4] He had learned from the experience with Vic Raschi that all a player left behind was bad feelings and trouble if he didn't do these things right. He called Eddie into his office in the clubhouse. Weiss was just leaving, and they nodded to each other. A shiver went up Eddie's spine. Stengel was sitting at his desk, but did not look Lopat in the eye. Eddie remem-bered that Vic told him that Weiss never could look directly at Raschi when they were talking salary. Now it was Casey's turn. "We made a deal for you. You're going to Baltimore. I enjoyed being with you and your playing for me. But you realize that these things happen." That was it. "Yes, Casey, I realize that these things have to come to an end somewhere along the line." He turned and left the office, closing the door behind him, feeling as if he had just died.

Two days later, he reported to manager Paul Richards in Baltimore. He finished the season with a 3–4 record, talked it over with Libby, and told Richards he would not be back next year. Eddie Lopat was the last of the three to go. He called his friends to give them the news. In two days, he was with Libby and the kids in the home they would keep for the rest of their lives in Hillsdale, New Jersey.

In a year, Eddie was back in baseball, managing the Yankees' Triple-A International League team in Richmond. He would remain part of the game he loved for the rest of his life.

In eight years with the Yankees, Eddie Lopat produced a 113–59 record, a .657 winning percentage and a 3.21 ERA. Even more than that, he had made a pitcher out of Whitey Ford and often played the tough cop when Mantle sulked after a strikeout or looked as if he had been out all night. Lopat would verbally hammer the kid before Allie would come up and put an arm around him.

Now they were all gone. Over the five triumphant years they had won 256 games in the regular season and sixteen in World Series play. Reynolds also made fifty-six relief appearances and recorded twenty-nine saves. Either Allie or Vic was the winning pitcher or got the save in the final game of each of the five World Series.

But those were only numbers.

Mantle's Yankees

> *"The thing I can understand even now more than I could while my husband and Ed and Allie were winning all those games is that they were not just pitching to win. They were pitching for the approval of Turner and the other two pitchers. All the million-dollar contracts will never make that magic happen again."*—Sally Raschi

> *"The idea of the game was to give yourself up for the team."*—Allie Reynolds

It was October 4, 1955, and Yogi sat alone in the Yankee Stadium clubhouse. His team had just lost the seventh game of the World Series, at home, to the Brooklyn Dodgers. Berra was trying to deal with feelings he had never experienced. Losing in seven games, in a World Series, to Brooklyn. Two years in a row, he would have to go back to Carmen and spend the winter dealing with defeat. He sat on his stool, in the same corner that he had occupied for six years, once surrounded by familiar faces of older men who had never lost a final World Series game to the Brooklyn Dodgers—or to anyone else. Now, they were no longer in this corner of the clubhouse. He thought of the ferocity of Raschi and Reynolds, the contempt they loved to show to the hitters, the terror that Allie could engender with that paralyzing fastball, and what Vic could do just with a glare. He smiled when he recalled the fury of Al Rosen or Ted Williams, who could be driven to despair by Eddie Lopat's gentle offerings and the general elation on the Cleveland ball club when the Junkman, with his 40–12 lifetime record against them, was let go by Weiss. There was something else, too.

Weiss had thought it would be easy to replace them. The Yankee farm system was a cornucopia of talent in all positions. The new first baseman, Bill

Skowron, looked like he would be around for a long time. A good guy, a tough, hard worker. Allie had spotted him the year before, took the rookie out for dinner and told him what it meant to be on a team like this. Yogi was sure this kid, called "Moose," had the right attitude, the sense of sacrifice. Lopat saw it one day, when Skowron, a big, strong right-handed hitter, came to the plate after Mantle had a lead-off double, and on the first pitch, tapped a weak grounder to second base that moved Mantle to third, from where he scored one out later. He had given himself up to move the runner one base so he could come home on a fly ball. These were instincts rarely found in a rookie. No one had told him to move Mantle over; he just knew what to do.

The first great Yankee black ballplayer came up in 1955. Elston Howard, who came up as an outfielder, was being groomed by Stengel as Berra's eventual replacement behind the plate. Like Skowron, he was willing to do anything to win, and his teammates took to him instantly. As the 1954 spring training camp broke and Eddie Lopat heard that Howard was being sent down to the minors again, he went to Stengel and for the first time in his baseball career told the manager what to do: keep Howard with the team; he can help us *now*. Casey had to explain that Howard needed more work behind the plate, but he would be back because he was a quick learner.

There were more big hitters in the Yankee system, and they would be coming up. The corps of experienced scouts could spot talent. What the scouts did not find, Weiss's shrewd trading eye would unearth: the hidden gems on rival teams or other leagues. This is where Weiss thought that he could excel. In November, 1954, he sent Woodling, the disappointing Harry Byrd, catcher Gus Triandos and others to the Baltimore Orioles for two strapping right-handers, Bob Turley and Don Larsen, both big, strong, flamethrowers who Weiss was certain would make the New York public forget those names of the past. Turley had all the talent in the world, won seventeen games for the Yankees in 1955, and with Ford and Byrne led the team to recapturing the American League pennant. But, at 6'2", 215 pounds, this bull of a pitcher managed to lose thirteen games and needed constant care from Berra. He lacked some concentration, was a worrier, and often frightened himself with his lack of control on his fastball. Yogi would be exhausted at the end of a game thrown by Bob Turley.

Larsen was another story. Mantle and Ford, free from constraints and barely in their mid-twenties, became the champions of a Yankee ethos that demonstrated to Stengel and Weiss a disturbing inclination to seek pleasure in the nightlife. When Billy Martin returned from his military service, the three of them became a force of nature that attracted others to them. They were good guys, good teammates, beloved, generous, young, and, in their own eyes, immortal and now unchallenged in their unwanted leadership roles. They assumed the burden reluctantly, because they also knew what temperamental limitations each had. Billy could get enraged with a teammate who committed a mental error. He was tough, ready for a fight at any time, and a natural leader without the natural talent of Mantle or Ford. Mickey and Whitey did not throw their weight around, but Ford could at least discipline himself; their nature was to live and let live, and to lead by the example of winning and giving 100 percent. With Gene Woodling gone, Hank Bauer attached himself to Mickey, as well. Don Larsen sized up matters the minute he arrived in the clubhouse. He had found some kindred spirits and was prepared to enjoy himself thoroughly. Larsen was physically a monster: 6'4", nearly 230 pounds and could throw a ball through a brick wall. But something was missing, and neither Turner nor Berra could find the button to release the latent talent in this gigantic body. He finished his first season with the Yankees at 9–2, pitched in only nineteen games even though he wasn't injured. He threw less than one hundred innings, and remained a puzzle during his entire Yankee career. He was a constant target of George Weiss's detectives.

Berra noticed that there was also something missing in the rookie pitchers. In his second year, Bob Grim suddenly lost all effectiveness. He hurt his arm in spring training, started only eleven times and wound up with a 7–5 record, having pitched only ninety-two innings. The best-looking prospect in camp was a twenty-one-year-old kid from Hoboken, New Jersey, named Johnny Kucks, who from time to time would join the night revelers on their rounds. He was spotted as a starter and reliever and produced an 8–7 record, but Berra thought he had the stuff to do better, if he could learn to concentrate.

In 1955 they had enough to put away the Cleveland Indians for the pennant. Facing a Dodger team that was clearly inferior to the Brooklyn entries of previous years, the pitchers did not deliver. Ford and Byrne performed admirably; the too-tight Turley and the too-loose Larsen were battered, each losing a game and posting series ERAs of 8.44 and 11.25. The mighty right-handed bats of the Dodgers, normally muted by Raschi and Reynolds, were kept in check this time by southpaws Ford and Byrne, but came alive against Turley, Larsen, Grim and Kucks. Even Johnny Sain was gone, released at the beginning of the year. Seemingly free from the tyranny of the past, Furillo, Campanella, and Hodges banged out twenty-two hits, mostly against the right-handed offerings, and Snider belted four home runs and hit .320.

Somehow, Yogi had seen it coming. He tried to find words in the vocabulary of his mind to explain it, this extraordinary sense of togetherness that had marked those five pennant-winning teams and carried them to World Series victories each time. Berra knew that the Yankees of those years were not an overpowering team with the best players in the majors, no less the league. Pieces just fit together: Woodling one day, Bauer the next, Bobby Brown, then

McDougald or Collins. Woodling, Collins and Brown never even got picked for the All-Star game! Mickey and Hank started only once; McDougald, who was selected as a reserve by Stengel, got in as a pinch-hitter.[5]

Berra, wiser than anyone had given him credit for, understood what was missing. He had seen something that hadn't existed on any team he had ever been with. Usually, the regular players who were out there day after day were the captains, the leaders. Shortstops like Boudreau, Reese, Alvin Dark, Marty Marion, they led. Not here. Here there had been three pitchers, terrific athletes, guys who worked harder, took regular batting practice, even pinch-hit once in a while. The Chief used to pinch-run! They had brought Yogi into their circle, made him one of them, and helped him grow as a catcher and a leader in his own right. For five years, they showed a durability and willingness *to lead* that pitchers normally didn't demonstrate. They had been able to communicate with everyone: rookies, veterans, the partygoers, and the physician. They were not like other pitchers. Although they were in a corner of the clubhouse together and lived near each other not far from Yogi and Carmen, they would eat after a game with the greenest rookie or join a mob of players for a drink.

And they were *smart*. Allie and Vic had graduated from college, and Eddie was just as wise. Vic was the quietest, and on game days everybody stayed away from him. They never made anyone feel dumb or less educated. They were *teammates* and would do anything to win. Nobody ever told Allie to go down to the bullpen. He would go down the day after he pitched a complete game. No one ever saw that before; and they talked baseball to everybody, especially to the other pitchers. But they would play hearts with anybody.

And their *wives*. They had made Carmen so comfortable. When Coleman went into the army, they kept in touch with *his* wife. You got to feel part of everyone's family. Vic used to bring his blind brother into the clubhouse, and everyone would go up to Gene.

There was something else, too, a *will to win every day* that they somehow made everyone in the clubhouse feel. Bobby Brown, who spread out his medical books when he was rooming with Yogi, said something that Yogi never forgot: "Winning is our religion, the clubhouse is our church." But the spiritual leaders of the congregation had moved on, and there was no one to replace them.

The clubhouse was empty. Yogi got up off the stool, undressed, and went toward the shower. Then, he remembered other words from the medical books that the then soon-to-be physician Brown had given him to explain what the Yankees were all about: *synergy and catalysts*. Yogi had even gone to look them up in the dictionary. It meant something about chemicals that came together and made a substance that was greater than the individual parts. That's what we were, thought Yogi: greater than the individual parts. Bobby said you needed something to make it happen. It had come to Berra. Now he understood. It was Allie, Vic, and Eddie who made it happen. They were the *catalysts;* and they were gone.

Weiss never found the elixir, the unique mixture of talent and temperament that had given him the greatest five years in his professional baseball career. He kept looking, but he never knew what he was looking *for.* He thought all he had to find was potential talent, the *physical* qualities in the ballplayer. Weiss remembered his first trade, for Eddie Lopat. He remembered how MacPhail had gotten Reynolds. Besides Turley and Larsen, over his last years as Yankee general manager he acquired veterans Ralph Branca, Jim Konstanty, Sonny Dixon, Ted Gray, Mickey McDermott, Gerry Staley, Sal Maglie, Virgil Trucks, Duke Maas, Murry Dickson, Art Ditmar and Bobby Shantz, looking for the gold strike, the lightning in the arms that Weiss had discovered in those earlier days. He was certain that he could find the right combination of pitchers. He never did.

To the rest of the baseball world, the Yankees still seemed relentlessly dominant. No one noticed that each new year of success resulted from a mix of different factors: a year of brilliance from one talent, then burnout; a trade, a sensational rookie season, then dramatic failure; a collapse in 1959 and the World Series lost in seven games in 1955, 1957, and 1960. The miraculous sustainability of an earlier era seemed impossible to repeat. The present foundation was built on three sets of different shoulders: The titanic Mickey Mantle, who matured *physically* and produced at least three years of legendary accomplishment, three times the Most Valuable Player; Yogi Berra, whose three-time Most Valuable Player career spanned this extraordinary period of success; and Whitey Ford, the one premier pitcher whom Stengel could rely on every year.

In 1956, Mantle had the greatest offensive year in Yankee history: fifty-two home runs, 130 RBIs, a .353 batting average for a Triple Crown MVP year that swept away the rest of the American League and took the Yankees again to a World Series against the Brooklyn Dodgers, in spite of erratic pitching during the season. Turley won only nine games, Larsen, eleven, but Kucks and Tom Sturdivant rose to the challenge. In a seven-game struggle, the Yankees triumphed when Turley and Larsen came alive. Don Larsen, knocked out in Game Two, came back in Game Five after an all-night drinking binge to pitch the only perfect game in World Series history. Johnny Kucks had his career year with an 18–9 record and continued that once-in-a-career excellence in Game Seven, when he clinched the World Series with a 9–0, three-hit shutout. The Yankees were back on top.

In 1957, they won the American League pennant again, built on a second consecutive Mantle MVP performance. He missed the Triple Crown, but put up an astounding .365 batting average with thirty-four home runs. He was walked a league-leading 146 times, which kept his RBI total to 94 in less than 500 at-bats.

The Yankees won more than anyone else, but this was a rollicking, often unstable bunch. Weiss would pour through the reports from the private detectives and grind his teeth. Mantle's talent was so enormous that nothing else seemed to matter. He drank, he womanized, he left his family, and he grew into a stature of enormous heroism, to his teammates and to his fan worshipers. The press protected him.

Weiss's practice was to get rid of people he did not like or want, especially if they were superfluous. Billy Martin almost fit perfectly into each category, but he had been productive and heroic enough to remain safe. Besides, Stengel loved him and protected him. But Martin's string had run out.

On the evening of May 15, 1957, Ford and Mantle had planned to celebrate Billy Martin's twenty-ninth birthday. The invitees, besides Mickey, Whitey and their wives, were the Bauers, Berras, and Kucks. Martin, already divorced, brought a date. There was dinner at a Manhattan restaurant. Then they hit the bright lights: first the floor show at the Waldorf Astoria, and then on to the Copacabana nightclub, mobbed with patrons, New York show business people, and newspaper columnists to see Sammy Davis, Jr., who was getting rave reviews. The Yankee party had already consumed considerable amounts of wine and spirits, and at the Copa got involved with a drunken member of a local bowling team who was heckling the black entertainer with racist remarks. The evening ended with the bowler out cold in the men's room and Bauer standing over him, with Ford and Berra holding him back.

Weiss saw the headlines the next morning in every New York newspaper. All the Yankees involved were fine, but Weiss had his mind made up, and this time Topping and Weiss agreed: Casey would have no say in this. Martin was gone.

The trade came exactly one month later, on June 15, 1957. Martin was sent to the Kansas City Athletics. He and his band of brothers wept. Even Casey cried, but he knew that his boy had to go. In the trade, the Yankees acquired a hard throwing right-handed relief pitcher with a drinking problem named Ryne Duren, who Weiss would have followed for the four years he pitched in New York. The Yankees won the American League pennant, and lost to the Milwaukee Braves, with Don Larsen losing the seventh game to former Yankee farmhand Lew Burdette, who had three World Series victories for the Braves. Yogi again sat alone in the Yankee Stadium clubhouse after Game Seven and thought back to a time when losing a seventh game at home was incomprehensible.

In 1958, the Yankees did it again with offense. Mantle, Berra, Skowron, Howard, and McDougald led an assault that banged out a league-leading 164 home runs, with Mantle again topping everyone in home runs (42) and walks (129). Only Turley and Ford had wins in double figures, and Turley put together his last great year of an erratic Yankee career, winning twenty-one and losing seven, with nineteen complete games. He stayed with the team until 1962, and never again won more than nine games. Ford went 14–7 with an ERA of 2.01. This year was Jim Turner's most challenging. He had eight pitchers with at least ten starts, a reliever in Ryne Duren who needed alcoholic treatment, but the Yankees won the pennant by ten games and went into the World Series against the repeating Milwaukee Braves, again led by two twenty-game winners, the ageless Warren Spahn and Lew Burdette. This time the Yankees prevailed, with Bob Turley performing the heroics with two wins and a save. The Yankees were down three games to one and all odds seemed stacked against them when Turley came alive. As he came in to pitch for the fourth time in a week in Game Seven to relieve Larsen, Casey turned to his friend and pitching coach Jim Turner. "Remind you of an Indian we knew?" For one series, Bob Turley brought to the mound the same electricity and self-assured authority that the Yankees had come to rely on some years earlier.

But it was all gone in 1959. The team collapse was total; Stengel and Weiss were in shock. Topping and Webb grumbled audibly. The team seemed to be divided between the all-night carousers, followed with worshipful adoration by those who loved Mickey and Whitey; and by a small group that Casey called "his malted milk drinkers." The Yankee farm system had produced a remarkable new double-play combination in shortstop Tony Kubek, at age twenty-two already in his third major league year, and Bobby Richardson, twenty-three, at second base. Both were agile hitters and rangy, gifted fielders. They were also church-going non-drinkers.[6] The Yankees now had two cultures. There was no friction between them, but they shared little in the way of values.

The Yankees lived and died with offense now, and with Mantle injured more often than not, the team did not have a chance. Berra and Bauer were aging. It was a club that desperately needed leadership, and there was none. On May 20 they were in last place for the first time since 1940. For the Yankees the season was over by August. They finished in third place, barely a .500 team at 79–75, fifteen games behind the "Go-Go" Chicago White Sox led by Al Lopez and the steady pitching of Early Wynn, Bob Shaw and Billy Pierce.

Weiss and Stengel, tied together by history, success, adversity and advancing age, were both worried. In good times, Dan Topping and Del Webb were jovial drinking buddies of Casey, bending an elbow at Toots Shor's with the boys. When the Yankees were losing, they were cold businessmen accustomed to getting rid of non-performers. The manager and general manager started looking over their shoulders. Casey was sixty-nine years old, Weiss approaching sixty-five. Topping and Webb were beginning to look at their investment.

Weiss had to show the baseball world that he still had the knack to acquire the hidden diamond at little cost. On December 11, 1959, he made what proved to be his last blockbuster trade, acquiring Roger Maris from Kansas City. Weiss had a mongoose's ability to hypnotize other general managers into believing that he was reluctantly parting with the crown jewels of the Yankees, where in reality Weiss was cutting his losses. Don Larsen never became the next Vic Raschi or Allie Reynolds, nor did Bobby Shantz fill the gap left by Eddie Lopat. In five seasons Larsen won forty-five games, and after a 6–7 season in 1959, Weiss dumped him. Hank Bauer was something else again. He had played on all nine of Stengel's pennant-winning teams and was a link to the five consecutive world championships. But he had reached old age for an outfielder at thirty-seven, was coming off his worst year as a Yankee, and Weiss thought that he was expendable. Stengel didn't fight him.

In exchange, the Yankees got one of the hottest hitting prospects in the American League in Roger Maris. For the next five years, Maris and Mantle, along with the aging Yogi Berra and Elston Howard, provided enough offensive punch to offset a pitching staff that featured one consistent starter: Whitey Ford. The Yankees put up extraordinary offensive numbers, highlighted in the historic 1961 season of the "M and M Boys," when Maris and Mantle hit an astonishing 115 home runs between the two of them, and the Yankees banged out 240 for an all-time record. This was an offensive juggernaut that appeared able to go on forever. But, Stengel and Weiss were not there to see it. At the end of the 1960 season, they both had been fired.

As the 1960 season began, the signs were there. Casey, spending more and more time with the writers at the hotel bars, was mouthing off at his players, yelling at Mantle and Ford for drinking too much, and at Richardson and Kubek for not drinking enough. He had a young third baseman named Clete Boyer who was a wizard with the glove, and Stengel thought he could make him a better hitter. He rode Boyer mercilessly, humiliating him in front of his teammates. Boyer developed a lifelong hatred of this wizened and now crotchety old man, who increasingly fell asleep on the bench.

Stengel was isolated from his players, seemed out of control, and didn't have Jim Turner anymore. At the end of the 1959 season, convinced that Turner had failed to develop sufficient pitching strength in the starting rotation and in need of a scapegoat, Weiss told Stengel to fire him. Casey, now uncertain of his own place in the order of things, was unwilling to look Weiss in the eye and tell him that he had failed to find suitable pitching replacements for the giants who had left. He also saw clearly that Weiss could make things tough for him, and Stengel decided not to defend his coach and right hand, and Turner was let go. He was ready. Jim knew that his experience in his first five years as Yankee pitching coach could never be replicated, because he would never find people like that again. Never would Turner find the combination of character, courage, ability, and willingness to sacrifice that made those five years special. He knew it; Berra knew it.

Ironically, Weiss had a glimmer of this. He tried to recapture the special quality he never wanted to acknowledge when Vic, Allie and Eddie were together with their coach, that band of four. To replace Turner, he asked Eddie Lopat to come in as pitching coach, and Casey agreed, hoping, too, that some of the magic would return. Lopat headed a pitching staff that was mediocre at best. Ford was hurt for most of the first three months of the season and journeyman Art Ditmar, acquired in one of the many trades with the Kansas City Athletics, led the team with fifteen wins. Yankee power propelled them through the 1960 season and they won the pennant easily over Paul Richards' Baltimore Orioles by eight games; the Yankee offensive machine entered the World Series as prohibitive favorites over the no-name Pittsburgh Pirates. Maris beat out Mantle for the first of his two consecutive MVP awards, and the Yankees seemed capable of winning with offense alone. But, Stengel, convinced that he knew his pitchers better than his pitching coach, set the rotation and made a terrible decision not to start Ford in Game One of the World Series. To the shock of the baseball world Pittsburgh beat the Yankees in seven games on Bill Mazeroski's walk-off home run in the bottom of the ninth off Ralph Terry. The Yankees won all the statistical battles: an incredible team batting average of .338 with ten home runs. The Pirates hit .256 and had four home runs. New York knocked in fifty-four runs, more than twice the number of Pittsburgh's twenty-six. The Pittsburgh pitching staff had a horrendous 7.11 ERA. Here was a Yankee team with great individual accomplishment and had lost the World Series in seven games for the third time in six years. They could still win pennants with overwhelming offensive power, but something was missing. The Yankee loss in the 1960 World Series was emblematic of what had changed from the late 1940s and early 1950s: the Yankees had become a team of great individual batting statistics, but they had not become a *team*. The chemistry had changed.

Topping and Webb had seen enough. The anger that had been building since the terrible 1959 season boiled over after the seventh game of the 1960 World Series. As they walked out of the owners' box in ancient Forbes Field in Pittsburgh, the playboy and the builder had made up their minds: the old men had to go. Webb had to return to Arizona immediately, and Topping told him he would handle things right away. When they got back to his hotel, Topping called his assistant to set up a press conference at the Savoy Hilton Hotel in New York City in five days. Then he reached for the phone to call Weiss and Stengel. He dropped the ax immediately.

The press conference in Le Salon Bleu at the Savoy Hilton in New York was jammed to the rafters. Topping and Stengel were there, but not Weiss, who had wept publicly in 1947 when MacPhail had almost gotten him fired. He did not want to give anyone the satisfaction of seeing him blubber, so he stayed at his home in Greenwich, Connecticut, with his wife, Hazel. Topping spoke first, and told the press that it was time for younger management to take over. He read from a prepared text, looking at his paper, and never actually said the words on the minds of everyone present. Then Stengel came to the microphone, also with a prepared statement that had been written by Topping's lawyer. Casey talked about the Yankee management youth program, getting some younger people into the dugout. "They have paid me off in full and told me that my services are not desired any longer by this club." Casey had barely put down his paper when a reporter shouted out, "Casey, tell us the truth. Were you fired?" The bitterness exploded. "Quit, fired, write whatever you want, I don't care!" That was all the press had to hear. With tears streaming down his face, he said, "I'll never make the mistake of being seventy again." He then waddled into the hotel bar, surrounded by a flock of loyal reporters hungry for the story they knew Stengel would spill. Topping was waiting for him in the hotel dining room.

Two weeks later, the newspapers reported that George Weiss, a member of the Yankee organization for nearly three decades, was retiring at age sixty-five.

The publicity that followed Stengel's departure was highly critical of the Yankees. Only a few journalists were sensitive enough to note that the players remained silent and would not even give off-the-record comments. When Ralph Houk was appointed manager, everyone cheered. Mantle, Ford, Richardson and Kubek were equally elated.

The Yankees were finished with Stengel and Weiss. Baseball was not. The National League finally agreed to bring an expansion franchise to New York City, to open in 1962. Until a stadium was completed in Flushing Meadows near the LaGuardia Airport, the New York National League team, called "The Mets," would play in the Polo Grounds, the former home of the departed New York Giants, now settled in San Francisco. On March 12, 1961, not quite six months after Topping fired him, George Weiss was introduced to the New York City media as the new president and head of baseball operations for the Metropolitan Baseball Club of New York City. On October 2 of that year, two days before the start of the World Series between the Yankees and the Cincinnati Reds, Weiss introduced the first manager of the New York Mets: seventy-one-year-old Casey Stengel. The Odd Couple were back in baseball. The press conference to announce Stengel's return was held in Le Salon Bleu of the Savoy Hilton Hotel. George Weiss never missed a chance to get even.

10

Friendship and Memory

Vic Raschi died on October 15, 1988, at the age of sixty-nine, on his favorite spot in all the world: the spacious lawn that stretched out from his carefully tended garden at the home that he and Sally had built in Conesus, New York, where they had spent most of their nearly forty-three years of married life. From that lawn Sally could look down the local golf course and see her own childhood home on Conesus Lake. It was a beautiful, peaceful view, and Vic loved his garden.

Vic and Sally had come home to this delightful region of New York state with their three children, and here is where they remained. While with the Yankees, he hated the limelight. He loved the tough games and the big crowds, but sought out his privacy as quickly as possible afterwards. More often victorious than not, he was followed by the writers right to his locker, but he had a reputation as one very tough interview.

Now Vic could find his privacy. He left behind the traveling, the painful knees and whatever bitterness he felt about his departure from the Yankees. It did not take long for the intensity of baseball competition to wind down; only former ballplayers who came to visit could see a hint of the inner fire and concentration that Vic stoked on a game day or the frightening stare that tyrannized the opposition players as well as his own teammates. Vic came away from baseball to find peace, and he did. His neighbors and local friends accepted the Vic Raschi they all knew: quietly reserved, always pleasant, wonderful with children, teenagers and college kids. He was a man comfortable in his own contentment.

The Colemans would visit; the Lopats came up from New Jersey. Yogi or Carmen would call. Once George Weiss was gone, Vic and Sally would occasionally drive down to New York for an Old-Timers' game. When some civic or Indian group out in Oklahoma honored Allie, Vic would attend. The pitchers talked regularly, with each other and their coach, Jim Turner. The three couples visited, spent time with each other, reminisced about the unforgettable five years, and boasted about their children and, later, grandchildren.

Family was at the heart of their lives. To be able to provide better than their fathers' could, this was the mantra of their generation. Their children went to college, but stayed close to the family. And the three men, growing older, stayed close to each other.

Vic and Sally loved to hear from Bobby Brown. As the years passed, Vic took particular pleasure in Brown's rising eminence, especially when he became president of the American League in 1984. Earlene, Libby and Sally kept in touch. The men spoke with Jim Turner, who stayed in baseball as a pitching coach until 1973. Eddie Lopat, like Turner, made his life in professional baseball, as a coach, manager and scout. He never missed an opportunity on his travels to get off the road at Conesus and see his friend.

When he was in his sixties, his hair almost completely white, Vic started getting phone calls from someone at the Baseball Hall of Fame in Cooperstown, where an intrepid young researcher, looking over individual statistics and information about team dynasties, came across the Yankees of Raschi's time and

At the New York Athletic Club ca. 1975: the friendship that never ended. Foreground, sitting, Allie Reynolds and his wife, Earlene; background, sitting, Vic Raschi and his wife, Sally, and Libby Lopat; in back, standing, Ed Lopat (Raschi Family).

noted the extraordinary performance of these three pitchers. His name popped up when the young man started looking at the highest winning percentages of all time, and Vic Raschi, with a 132–66 record and a percentage of .667, was fifth on this list for pitchers with more than one hundred wins. Vic was interviewed several times, especially after 1975, when he suddenly got thirty-seven votes for election to the Hall of Fame, after being virtually ignored for the previous decade. After that brief burst of modest attention, Vic Raschi's name faded from the ballot. It was all right with Vic.

He had saved his salary wisely, and he had his education. He looked for a small business that could provide a steady income and sufficient free time to involve himself in the educational activities he loved. Vic opened a liquor store in Conesus, which proved to be a solid investment. It left the Raschis comfortable. With Geneseo State College just around the corner, Vic found a ready outlet for physical education and coaching. From 1959 to 1961 he filled in as basketball coach, and then taught physical education before the inevitable: the college asked him to take over the baseball program. This became a lifelong pleasure for Vic and for a bunch of farm boys; he generally had no more than thirteen players on the roster (the entire male student population of Geneseo State was just over 200). Vic was a beloved coach and, of course, in a college with just over a thousand students, a reluctant celebrity.

Vic Raschi brought the same earnest modesty to his retirement life that he showed when pitching for the Yankees. A friend suggested that he use his name on the liquor store for recognition; he said no. But, the dedication to the task at hand was always present. He worked his baseball players all winter long, got them outdoors into the harsh Geneseo spring as soon as possible, and, bad knees and all, ran them into the ground. He conditioned them physically and mentally, and the players from this country community never forgot him. He would throw batting practice and give them just a small taste of what it was like in the big leagues. The president of the college used him as a goodwill ambassador and recruiter for the school, and he spent whatever free time he had in admissions.

In 1975, Geneseo State College dedicated the Victor J. Raschi Baseball Field.

As the October leaves were falling, Vic was planning a trip to see his old friends. Jim Turner had sent him, Allie and Eddie first-class airplane tickets to Nashville, where their pitching coach still lived. Jim had three bronze plaques made up, one each for his three pitchers, with their records over the five years between 1949 and 1953. In 1988, at age eighty-five, Jim didn't think there would be many more opportunities to get together with his three stalwarts. They met as often as possible, and always there was something special they knew belonged only to them, a record that would never be equaled. They would gather together on October 17, World Series time.

Vic had been having heart problems for the past ten years. Three days before he was scheduled to see his friends in Nashville, he died while mowing his lawn. Among the first people Sally called was Allie Reynolds and Libby Lopat.

The old *Herald Tribune* baseball writer Harold Rosenthal, when he heard of Vic's passing, remembered the interview with Casey when Stengel had said that Raschi was his best, because "he had it here, and here and here," pointing to his arm, his head, and finally his heart. He remembered at that moment something that Ted Williams had said to him nearly fifty years earlier: "Vic Raschi is the best pitcher alive. There just can't be anyone as good." Williams added as an afterthought, "Except maybe those other two sons-of-bitches." Rosenthal knew whom Williams meant: the three warriors, who made his life miserable, broke his heart, and whom he honored above all others.

Eddie had been right about Weiss. He had a feeling that when it came down to a crunch, the nasty general manager would give Lopat a break. As soon as Eddie was through with Baltimore in 1956, Weiss called him to manage at the Triple-A level with Richmond of the International League. In his first year he was a player-manager, went 11–6 with a 2.85 ERA. In 1960 Casey made him the Yankee pitching coach, replacing Jim Turner. Before taking the job, Eddie called Turner to make sure it was all right. The old coach said: Go for it. Just don't count on anything. Both Turner and Lopat had been around baseball long enough to know what he meant.

Eddie left after the 1960 season when Ralph Houk was picked to manage the Yankees. He liked Ralph, but with Houk managing at the Yankee Triple-A team in Denver and Lopat having done three years earlier with Triple-A Richmond, it was too obvious that they were in competition for the top job. When the Yankee management picked Houk, Eddie wanted to save him any embarrassment, so he stepped down as pitching coach.

He was not out of the game for long. When his long-time teammate Hank Bauer was named manager of the Kansas City Athletics in mid–1961, he turned right away to Eddie. At the end of the 1962 season management fired Bauer and turned to Lopat to manage. Eddie first called his former teammate. "Hank, they want me to take over. How do you feel about it?" Bauer told him to take it; he already had another offer.

So, for the 1963 season, Eddie Lopat had fulfilled another dream: he was managing in the big leagues, for Charley Finley, an insurance man-turned-baseball owner who hired and fired managers as if they were district managers who didn't meet their policy quotas. Eddie did not rebuild fast enough for Finley's taste, and in the middle of the 1964 season Finley pushed Lopat through the managers' revolving door and fired him. Libby, a veteran of baseball wanderings since their days together in the minor leagues, laughed when she told Earlene and Sally that they would never give up the house in New Jersey. The three good friends, all of whom had shared their husbands' lives in Single-A and Double-A leagues, knew how to make a family solid and stable. At this stage of their lives, Eddie might have to live the life of the bachelor from time to time, but he knew where he could get a good meal. Whenever Richmond had played Buffalo, Eddie spent time with the Raschis.

Even though Finley fired Lopat as his manager, he knew a first-rate baseball mind when he saw one; he asked Eddie to stay on as a scout, which he did, until the team moved to Oakland. For Lopat, that was too far from New Jersey.

Eddie never left the game. He stayed with the new Kansas City Royals franchise as a scout, and then went back to the Yankees and the new Montreal Expos before joining the Major League Scouting Bureau. As he grew older, he enjoyed the image of a baseball elder statesman. He talked hitting, he talked pitching, He loved to be with the old timers; he tried to get Vic and Allie to come more often to the reunions, but they preferred their own turf. The New York City kid loved the lights and action, and as long as Whitey Ford stayed active, through the late 1960s, people knew him as the guy who taught the Chairman of the Board how to pitch. From 1968 to 1972 Eddie would get the occasional Hall of Fame vote, never appearing on more than four ballots, then he disappeared from the voting. But, whenever a major league lefthander was having trouble with his off-speed pitches or needed another weapon in his arsenal, he was told to seek out the elderly gentleman with the slightly twisted arm —from throwing screwballs— in the Major League Scouting Bureau named Eddie Lopat. He'll know what to do.

While at the Major League Scouting Bureau, Eddie struck up a deep friendship with the commissioner of baseball, Fay Vincent, who was an astute baseball man besides serving as the game's chief administrator. Born in 1938 in Connecticut, he had grown up with Raschi, Reynolds and Lopat on the mound at Yankee Stadium or Fenway Park. Vincent, like his close friend and predecessor Bart Giamatti, was brought up in the cauldron of Red Sox-Yankee battles, loved to be with the old-time players, and his friendship with Eddie Lopat was a tribute to his teenage memories of the Bronx and Boston. He was a Yankee rooter. Giamatti, who had Vincent as his deputy during his time as commissioner, lived and suffered for the Red Sox. They both worshiped the warriors of those extraordinary battles from the 1940s and early 1950s.

Libby and Eddie remained close to the Reynolds, who stayed with them in their home in Hillsdale whenever they visited New York. Whenever they could, they saw Sally and Vic. These friendships ripened in the best of ways. In life as on the mound, they knew each other intimately, the six of them.

In 1990 Eddie was diagnosed with pancreatic cancer. He took treatment, went into remission for a while, but the cancer recurred. He and Libby went to stay with their son, John, in Darien, Connecticut, and on June 15, 1992, a week before his seventy-fourth birthday, Steady Eddie died in his sleep. Commissioner Vincent attended the funeral.

The first person Libby Lopat called was Sally Raschi. When Ted Williams heard that Eddie Lopat had died, he sat silently for a few minutes, then rose from his chair and slowly shuffled across the living room in his Florida home. He was seventy-three years old, struggling to walk, heavy in gait, no longer the slender Kid whose eyes, now dulled with age, could once sense a thrown baseball's rotation faster than any other human on earth. Williams picked up a thirty-four inch, thirty-three ounce Louisville Slugger bat that had been resting in the corner. He squeezed the handle and thought back to 1969, when he took over as manager of the Washington Senators. He needed a pitching coach, and there was only one man he wanted. He called Eddie Lopat.

Standing there alone in his living room, Ted Williams thought of the wonderful mind games that these two baseball warriors had once played with one another as they battled: the world's greatest hitter against a clever, cunning, good-humored opponent. Then, the old man slowly took his familiar batting pose. He looked into a mirror, and memory filled his mind. Then he muttered, "That fucking Lopat."

The Superchief

> "So who is this guy, and why is he almost forgotten today?"— Rob Neyer, on Allie, in Baseball Dynasties in 2000.

"How's our millionaire doing?" Eddie Lopat thought it might be time to lighten up a little after the tragedy. He took the joking tone, because he knew that Earlene and Allie had been, for the last six months, suffering terribly. Nothing could be worse for a family like the Reynolds than the loss of a child and a grandchild. On May 4, 1978, the Reynolds' oldest son, Allie Dale, and their grandson, Michael, were killed in the crash of a private plane. When Eddie had called a few months earlier, Allie had wept uncontrollably over the phone. Earlene, even then cool and under control, took the receiver from Allie and talked to the Lopats. They were getting along, but it's hard to forget. Thanks for thinking of us. Libby could hear the strength in Earlene's voice, and knew that she would pull the family through. No matter how much she felt the loss of her son and grandson, Earlene Reynolds was a nurturer and comforter. She would make others feel better. All three wives had this gift.

This tragedy had been the first dark cloud in their lives since Allie turned his back on New York City. As soon as he had returned to Oklahoma, he threw himself into the oil business, which was booming in the mid–1950s. Besides his other oil interests, Allie became the principal owner of the Atlas Mud Company, providing services to oil wells all over the state. He took to business with total dedication and enjoyed as much celebrity status among Oklahoman oil people as he did as a Yankee. He was a natural for honorary chairman of every charity drive in the state, and never refused. He got interested in mental health, Big Brothers, United Fund and the Oklahoma State Alumni Association. He and now-transplanted Oklahoman Warren Spahn, friends from their minor league days together, put on pitching exhibitions to raise money for the YMCA even before Allie had gotten out of baseball. He was a 32-degree Mason and a member of the Oklahoma City chapter of the National Football Foundation, which soon elevated him to their board of directors. His business sense was just as keen as it had been when negotiating with the major league owners, and he was asked to join the board of the Oklahoma Independent Oil Producers Association. In 1982, Oklahoma State University named the baseball field for him. When Vic had the same honor bestowed on him, the first person he called was Allie. "Too bad Eddie didn't go to college; we might have found a name for him, too," they laughed.

Baseball kept after him. Oklahoma City had a struggling franchise in the top minor league Pacific Coast League but was failing. The surest road to survival was to get Reynolds involved. First he became a stockholder, and, inevitably, president of the franchise, which he moved to the more suitable midwestern American Association. The franchise thrived under his leadership. In 1969 the league board of directors asked him to move to the top of the chain, and Allie Reynolds became president of the Triple-A American Association.

Baseball also had some memory. In 1963 *Sports Illustrated* named Allie to the Silver Anniversary team, and as late as 1974 he would receive at least 100 votes for election to the Hall of Fame in Cooperstown. He also had the Raschis and Lopats. Allie and Earlene did not like to travel back to New York often, but occasionally they would attend an Old-Timers' Day at Yankee Stadium with Vic and Sally, and Eddie and Libby. They would fly down to Nashville and visit with Jim Turner. They stayed in touch.

Allie's roots grew deeper into Oklahoma and into his Indian heritage as he grew older. He led fund-raising all over the state for Native American events. The Center of the American Indian in Oklahoma City asked him to be its president, and he accepted. Whenever there was an event, Allie would invite his Yankee teammates. Bobby Brown, Vic, Eddie, Hank Bauer, Gene Woodling and Jim Turner spent more time in Oklahoma than they every dreamed possible, and they loved it. Mickey Mantle as a star in his prime and as a much-in-demand celebrity in his retirement never forgot what Reynolds did for him when he was a rookie struggling to make his way in New York City.

Bobby Brown, at one of the testimonials for Reynolds that he attended, had called Allie "one tough Indian." But, his whole being was tied to his family. The death of his son and grandson was the beginning of some life-shattering experiences that drained him. As tough and resourceful as Allie was on the mound or in business, he depended on Earlene for stability. She held the family together after the tragic deaths. Allie disintegrated, but she pulled him together. When Earlene was diagnosed with cancer late in the 1970s, she told him not to worry, that they would battle this disease together. This great female athlete and lifelong partner did indeed fight bravely, but in vain. On October 28, 1983, Earlene Reynolds died. She and Allie had been married for forty-eight years. Allie had wept when his son and grandson had died; now he wept again.

Earlene was one of three extraordinary women who played more than a casual role in Yankee history, although few at the time understood what Allie Reynolds had told an interviewer who asked him about success in baseball. "First you need a good marriage," Reynolds had told the puzzled reporter, who never did understand. There were times in their minor league careers when Allie, Vic, and Eddie were ready to toss in the towel and give up. At such critical moments, Earlene, Sally and Libby steadied the ground underneath their wavering and discouraged men and kept them from quitting. When Earlene Reynolds died, something went out of Allie's life that could not be measured. His friends knew it, because they shared the same kind of marriages.

The honors kept coming, but they didn't mean much without Earlene. In 1986 Vic came out to celebrate another tribute for Allie. Although they would talk often, this was the last time the old teammates would be together again. Vic saw that Allie was much quieter, more thoughtful, a little sad. His brother, Jimmy, had been ill, and he just could not stop thinking about Earlene. When Jimmy died during surgery in 1987, Allie was now the last of the Reynolds family.

He soldiered on bravely, accepting awards but watching his friends pass away—first Vic, then Eddie. He saw Lopat for the last time when Allie traveled to New York City and Yankee Stadium in August, 1989, at age seventy-four, for the unveiling of a plaque in the new outfield museum in the Stadium on the wall in center field, near the original monuments to Ruth and Gehrig. Then he went home to Oklahoma to stay. On November 16, 1991, he was inducted into the Oklahoma Hall of Fame along with Gene Autry, who was the owner of the California Angels and the original "Singing Cowboy."

Allie had been suffering for years with "the Indian disease," diabetes, but in 1993 he was diagnosed with lymphoma. In December, 1994, he entered St. Anthony's Hospital in Oklahoma City and died the day after Christmas. He was seventy-nine years old. At the funeral, the oldest person in attendance was a ninety-one-year-old former major league pitcher and coach, who now buried the last of his boys. Jim Turner quietly mourned for his stalwart pitcher.

His teammate Bobby Brown spoke at the memorial service. "When we talked to him, we called him Allie. But, when he wasn't in the room, he was referred to as the Chief, because we felt he was the one at the top, the real leader."

Now, the corner of the clubhouse was silent. The three warriors were gone.

Times passes, memories fade, history is conveniently re-created. One century has ended, a new millennium has begun, and the New York Yankees have continued winning baseball games, pennants, and even some World Series. My college students, children of the Age of Free Agency, believe that players have always been greedy and with their avarice are ruining the game. They have no notion of baseball before the times of Marvin Miller, and no idea that management was tyrannical, greedy and avaricious for seventy-five years, and that the players have fifty years to catch up to gain parity in arrogance. Once liberated from the slavery of the reserve clause, players and their agents soon lost interest in preserving the character of a game that has the word "sacrifice" imbedded in its on-field strategy. The great Cincinnati catcher Johnny Bench, interviewed by former catcher Tim McCarver, said that the Big Red Machine teams of the 1970s should have won pennant after pennant, and World Series after World Series, but the chemistry broke down. The team had factions; manager Sparky Anderson had two sets of rules: one for the stars and one for the rest. Bench, Pete Rose, Joe Morgan, and Tony Perez could do as they pleased; Cooperstown was already in sight. The rest of the roster did what they were told. The pitchers were not part of the machine. There was no bonding leadership; just wonderful talent. It was not enough.

There is an intangible in baseball that often transcends the raw ability to execute, to perform. The Boston Red Sox of Williams, Doerr, Dom DiMaggio, Pesky, Parnell and Kinder arguably should have been the Team of Destiny in the post–World War II years, both in the American League and World Series competition. Instead, they were a study in futility that haunted the franchise until the improbable self-described "idiots" of 2004 reminded fans just exactly how important that intangible is. There will be no Cooperstown induction ceremonies for Mark Bellhorn, Jason Varitek, Kevin Millar, Johnny Damon, Bill Mueller, David Ortiz or Trot Nixon. Of the regular position players, only Manny Ramirez has a chance for the Hall of Fame. After the Red Sox made their supernatural comeback against the New York Yankees to win the American League pennant in Game Seven, after trailing three games to none, Derek Jeter, the most thoughtful and perceptive of the Yankees, gave the post-game interview to the media. "We were just not the same team," he said quietly. The reporters were all over him: What do you mean you're not the same team? You added the best ballplayer in the major leagues (Alex Rodriguez) to an already powerful roster. If anything, you have more talent than ever before. Jeter tried again, a little less patient. "We are still not the same team," then turned to walk back into the clubhouse. One of the older journalists turned to a younger colleague. "He means Paul O'Neill, Scott Brosius, Tino Martinez, and Joe Girardi. He means the chemistry." The younger reporter would not be put off. "Chemistry doesn't win you a pennant or a World Series," he insisted. The older man looked at the Red Sox lineup that had just beaten the Yankees, looked back at his youthful colleague, and walked away.

More than fifty years separate today's chroniclers from the 1949–1953 Yankees. It is easier to create a likely and convenient history than an accurate one. Baseball historian Glenn Stout, writing briefly about the five consecutive world champion teams, places the accomplishment firmly on the shoulders of DiMaggio and Mantle. "These teams lacked a prototypical number one starter,"[1] he writes. Stout, otherwise a very astute historian, had made arguably one of the most ill-informed observations in baseball history. *New York Times* columnist Lee Jenkins, describing the same five consecutive World Series victories by the Yankees, describes a "Golden Age in that magical moment when Joe DiMaggio relinquished the throne to Mickey Mantle and maintained that unique unbroken dominance for five unprecedented years."[2]

Even the eminent film documentarist Ken Burns had a lapse of accuracy in his monumental documentary *Baseball*, which premiered on public television in 1994 and reconnected memory with millions of young Americans in the year of the strike and the lost World Series. In the seventh segment, titled "The Capital of Baseball," he shows brief newsreel cuts of New York City baseball greats during the era when the Yankees, Giants and Dodgers dominated the baseball world, Roger Kahn's *Era*, from 1947–1957. With Yankee broadcaster Mel Allen as the voiceover, there is a shot of Eddie Lopat, described by Allen as "the Junkman," then a quick cut to Allie Reynolds, called "The Superchief" by the great Yankee announcer who gave Reynolds that name. There was no mention of Vic Raschi until the scenes of Brooklyn's only World Series triumph over the Yankees, in 1955. Then there was a newsreel shot with the voice of another announcer saying, "Vic Raschi gives up a home run to Roy Campanella in the 3–2 Dodger victory."

It was not 1955; this was Game Three of the 1953 World Series. Even the extraordinary Ken Burns did not know that Vic Raschi never played on a Yankee team that lost a World Series to Brooklyn — or to anyone.

Americans are not noted for having particularly good memories. In fact, *not* having memory is almost a national characteristic. That age of fifty years ago and its unique personality have faded, its values lost in an America so very distant from today. Almost all of those players had experienced the hardships of the Depression. Although racism kept the black ballplayers locked in their own leagues, in many ways the players of that generation — black, white, red, and brown — in the 1930s, 1940s and 1950s were more similar to each other than they are today, when millions of dollars create disparities and gulfs between teammates, who might insist on private transportation and separate road accommodations. In that world of fifty years ago, when the minimum salary for a ballplayer was $5,000, everyone worked at something year-round to make a living. In the Negro leagues, you played year-round, if you could. Major league ballplayers either barnstormed or took whatever job they could during the off-season. Mickey Mantle, after his rookie year in 1951, went back to the zinc mines that killed his father. Rizzuto and Berra had it easy: they sold suits. It was the rare star — DiMaggio, Williams, Musial, or Kiner — who could enjoy the luxury of an off-season, if he wanted to. Otherwise, players found a job.

Our most visible memory of integration, as we look back during solemn anniversaries, focuses on the martyrdom of Jackie Robinson in those first two years when he was muzzled by Branch Rickey. But, Jackie did not have a martyr's personality. When Robinson was unleashed, he reverted to a style that was just as tough as anyone's in the game, regardless of the color of his skin. It was Jackie who reminded Reynolds of his Indian heritage by calling him "Blanket Ass." Leo Durocher and Robinson, after Leo's move to the Giants, enjoyed a deep hatred for one another and shared a reputation as two of the loudest of the loudmouths. Durocher remembered Jackie's talent in the dugout; he would say anything about you, your mother, your wife. He was a tormenter, vicious, unmerciful. This, coming from perhaps the all-time most ferocious and vulgar bench jockey of any baseball generation, was said with almost professional admiration.[3]

There are few who remember the New York Yankee teams from 1949 to 1953, a band of generally ordinary baseball players who accomplished a feat unimaginable today. Like everyone else on the sixteen major league teams, they were grateful to be working at the highest level of professional baseball and at a game they loved. Many were war veterans, a very few were college-educated; there was an abundance of second generation Americans, the children of European-born immigrants. Some were ballplayers past their prime; others had not reached their potential. For the 1949 New York Yankees, things did not look promising if you just took a look at the talent. There were to be no offensive league leaders among them for all of these next five years, *not one in any offensive category*. Other teams were going to have the benefit of black players. In 1947 Jackie Robinson had transformed how the game was played and the National League was heading toward hegemony; in 1948 Larry Doby and Satchel Paige put the Cleveland Indians over the top to the world championship. But there would no black ballplayers on the Yankees of Topping, Webb and Weiss.

Other teams in the American League had some great veteran managers. Joe McCarthy, Lou Boudreau, and Bucky Harris had all won World Series; the Yankees, on the other hand, had signed on as manager a buffoon who had only worked in the National League and never took his teams higher than fifth place.

What made the miracle? More than fifty years later, why would the handful of living survivors of those five teams urge me, when I said that I wanted to write about three pitchers on their team, to tell their story? Those old athletes could close their eyes and see. Bobby Brown, Yogi Berra, Phil Rizzuto, Jerry Coleman, Hank Bauer, and Charlie Silvera — they remembered. Who else? A few old writers, baseball men, who sat in the press box for those years and watched with respectful admiration as history was created: Roger Kahn, Donald Honig, Dave Anderson, Robert Creamer. They would remember a moment in time when three pitchers, not quite forgotten yet, carried a team to immortality.

Chapter Notes

Introduction

1. Rickey's determination to integrate baseball in 1946 was more than a decade ahead of the times in this country, still racially fixated. In 1956, NBC made Nat "King" Cole the first black entertainer to have a weekly variety show on television. A year later, after an artistically successful run, Cole could still not find a regular sponsor, and quit. "Madison Avenue is still afraid of the dark," he said. Black entertainers working in Las Vegas as late as the early 1960s could not drink at a hotel bar or eat in a restaurant, much less sleep in the guest facilities. Professional tennis and golf were also for whites only.

1. The Players of the American Game: Ethnicity and Race

1. David Halberstam, *Teammates: Portrait of a Friendship* (New York: Hyperion Books, 2003), 36.

2. The insensitivity of ballplayers and fans, even in the modern era, could be extraordinary. Roger Kahn routinely heard shouts from the bleachers and dugouts: "Hey, ump! Who taught you to call pitches, Helen Keller? Who they got umpiring, Ray Charles?" Roger Kahn, *Boys of Summer* (New York: Harper Row, 1971), 9–10.

3. That is, "Tiny" Bonham, "Hippo" Vaughn, "Fat Freddie" Fitzsimmons.

4. Charles C. Alexander, *Breaking the Slump: Baseball in the Depression Era* (New York: Columbia University Press, 2002), 191–195.

5. Lawrence S. Ritter, *The Glory of Their Times* (New York: Collier Books, 1966), 164.

6. When black world heavyweight champion Jack Johnson knocked out "the Great White Hope" Jim Jeffries on July 4, 1910, in Reno, Nevada, race riots broke out all over the country, resulting in the deaths of at least thirty black people. *New York Times*, July 5, 1910, front page.

7. Paul Brown, owner of the professional football Cleveland Browns, played the role of Rickey, signing Marion Motley in 1946. The first black to play in an NBA game was Lloyd Cooper of the Washington Caps, on October 31, 1950, although the Boston Celtics' Red Auerbach deserves a seat of honor next to Rickey for drafting the first black hoopster, Chuck Cooper. Auerbach wanted Harlem Globetrotters center Nat "Sweetwater" Clifton, but the New York Knicks signed him first.

8. Jeffrey Powers-Beck, *The American Indian Integration of Baseball* (Lincoln, Nebraska: University of Nebraska Press, 2004).

9. Paul Adomites, ed., *The Cooperstown Review* (Pittsburgh: Sheridan, 1993), 122.

10. American journalism was of little help in addressing civil rights. A.J. Liebling, as a young copyreader for the *New York Times* sports desk in 1925, had included the scores of Morgan State and Virginia State football games, until his editor discovered that they were historically black schools and immediately dropped them from the listings. A.J. Liebling, *Just Enough Liebling* (New York: North Point Press, 2004), 42.

11. Aviva Kempner, *The Life and Times of Hank Greenberg*, Twentieth Century Fox Entertainment, 2001.

12. More than a hundred years after the Irish immigration, Ford held to his time-honored stereotypes in *The Quiet Man* (1952), where the Irish seem happy only when they are drunk and brawling. For this film he won his fourth Academy Award for best director.

13. Royse Parr and Bob Burke, *Allie Reynolds: Super Chief* (Oklahoma City: Oklahoma Heritage Association, 2002), 107.

14. Peter Golenbock, *Dynasty: The New York Yankees, 1949–1964* (Upper Saddle River, New Jersey: Prentice Hall, 1975), 89.

15. Although not a routinely depicted stereotype in films, Polish-Americans could

take little comfort in the picture of Stanley Kowalski, played by Marlon Brando in *A Streetcar Named Desire* (1951): inarticulate, carnal, and violent.

16. William Marshall, *Baseball's Pivotal Era* (Lexington, Kentucky: University of Kentucky Press, 1999), 295–296.

2. Getting There

1. Roger Kahn, *Memories of Summer* (New York: Hyperion, 1997), 65.

2. Volney Meece, "Allie's Still the Chief to Friends," *The Daily Oklahoman*, August 26, 1989.

3. Reynolds' birth year is listed in various sources as 1915 and 1917. When he turned professional relatively late in life, he opted for the later date, as did many other ballplayers, who were looking for a couple of extra years down the road. His hometown obituary listed him as seventy-nine years old when he died in 1994. That would make 1915 the accurate date.

4. The local papers also described him as a twenty-two-year-old rookie. It might have been around this time that Reynolds became sensitive to his age, which was actually twenty-four, considered somewhat old for a Class C league first-year professional. Bob Feller, already a four-year major league veteran, was still only twenty years old.

5. In the 1940s when a pitcher was handed the ball as a starter, he was expected to complete the game.

6. *Memories of Summer*, 110.

7. Lester, Bromberg, "Blind Brother Sees Own Goal in Raschi," *The Sporting News*, July 21, 1948, 3.

8. One more baseball accident in 1945 when Gene was fifteen left him completely sightless. He soon entered the Perkins School for the Blind in Waltham, Massachusetts. He died in 2003. Vic, while he was the Yankee star pitcher, never failed to visit the school and speak at chapel.

9. The Yankees were true to their word. It took Vic Raschi eleven years to complete his degree in physical education at William & Mary. The Yankee organization paid his tuition until he received his degree in 1949.

10. Vic would not have noticed that on August 12, 1941, Allie Reynolds, pitching in the Class B Three-I League for Cedar Rapids, struck out seventeen.

11. Charlie Silvera, the backup catcher to Berra during the great Yankee run, came up in 1949 but had known Dressen in the Pacific Coast League. His comment on Dressen as a pitching coach: "Dressen thought he knew

everything about pitching, and he knew nothing. He would stop and tell the pitchers what they were doing wrong. He almost ruined Reynolds." Interview August 19, 2004. Reynolds also had no use for Dressen: "Dressen would make himself look good by making you look bad." Phil Rizzuto and Tom Horton, *The October Twelve* (New York: Forge Book, 1994), 168. Ralph Branca, who pitched for Brooklyn when Dressen managed them in 1951, referred to him as "that piece of dreck Dressen," was using a very unflattering Yiddish expression. Branca was not Jewish, but found the appropriate word. Roger Kahn, *The Era, 1947–1957* (New York: Ticknor & Fields, 1993), 107.

12. Dom Forker, *The Men of Autumn* (Dallas: Taylor, 1989), 15.

13. Interview with Bobby Brown, June 21, 2004.

14. It was Raschi's "look" that took the place of actually pitching "up and in." Of the three Yankee greats, Vic hit the fewest batsmen in his career, a total of only twenty-six, far fewer than Allie's fifty-seven and even control pitcher Ed Lopat's forty-three. Reynolds would terrify opposing hitters with a fastball under the chin. Raschi would terrify them with his "look." Lopat plunked any hitter he thought was getting too smart for his own good. None of them approached someone like Don Drysdale, who delighted in hitting 154 batters in his career.

15. It was at a similar Ebbets Field tryout around that time that Dodger manager Casey Stengel, looking over a very diminutive infielder with another beat-up glove, told him to go home and get a shoeshine box: baseball was too rugged a game for such a little kid. That little kid's name was Phil Rizzuto. Neither of them ever forgot the incident.

16. This was another marriage for life, which ended with the passing of Ed Lopat in 1992.

17. His New York Yankee teammate Hank Bauer said that he hardly ever saw Lopat eat anything other than baby food and ice cream.

18. Interview with Ed Lopat, August 26, 1988, A.B. Chandler Oral History Project, University of Kentucky.

3. The Coming of Casey

1. Howard Bryant, *Shut Out: A Story of Race and Baseball in Boston* (New York: Routledge, 2002).

2. Weiss, among his other characteristics, was a racist as well as a snob. He told reporters that his carriage-trade clientele would not sit next to black fans. But, he was astute enough as a baseball man to know that Jackie Robin-

son, Larry Doby, and later Mays, Aaron, and Frank Robinson were going to bring a combination of power and speed that the major leagues had never seen. He instructed his scouts to look for white ballplayers who possessed black talent: speed and power. Tom Greenwade found one such kid in Oklahoma. His name was Mickey Mantle. His talent kept the Yankees white for nearly as long as the Red Sox.

3. Kahn, *The Era*, 89–90.

4. Golenbock, *Dynasty*, 5.

5. Kahn, *The Era*, 171.

6. Leonard Koppett, *The Man in the Dugout: Baseball's Top Managers and How They Got That Way* (Philadelphia: Temple University Press, 2000), 110.

7. Koppett, *The Man in the Dugout*, 120.

8. Bill James refers to this shape as the "Hack Wilson type body." Bill James, *The New Bill James Historical Baseball Abstract* (New York: The Free Press, 2001), 370. He mentions Kirby Puckett, Roy Campanella, and Smoky Burgess as other short-armed, short-stature, powerful hitters. Today, all-star catcher Ivan Rodriguez, at five-foot-nine and 200 pounds, is the current model, along with Miguel Tejada, who may become the best hitter in baseball. Weiss also knew that, with the right instruction, Berra would be a quick learner. He recognized Berra's quality of mind and saw through the press's mistake in selling him as a simple innocent and the butt of their humor.

9. Stengel showed little ability to spot young pitching talent. At Boston he dismissed two rookies, whom he said had no promise: Warren Spahn and Johnny Sain.

10. Interview with Jerry Coleman, June 15, 2004.

11. Rizzuto, *The October Twelve*, 155.

4. The Team Within the Team

1. On June 15, 1992, Sally Raschi, widowed for four years, received a phone call from Libby Lopat telling her of Ed's death that day from pancreatic cancer. Within the hour Sally was called by Allie, Bobby Brown, Jerry Coleman, and Yogi Berra.

2. David S. Neft, Richard M. Cohen, and Michael L. Neft, *Baseball* (New York: St Martin's, 2001), 278.

3. The Yankees, thanks to Weiss' inclinations, had more than their share of college-educated players on the roster.

4. In one of the few times he ever interfered with Weiss or Stengel, Topping told them to get rid of the fifteen-game winner in 1951 after another nerve-bending performance. As

hard as the general manager and field manager fought for Byrne, the owner had his way. Stengel got him back three years later.

5. Bobby Brown confessed, "I learned more about hitting from Eddie Lopat than I did from any batting coach in my career."

6. Interview, June 21, 2004.

7. It was Harold Rosenthal, writing in the *New York Herald-Tribune*, who began describing Stengel's use of alternating two players at one position, often during the same game, as "platooning." Robert W. Creamer, *Stengel: His Life and Times* (New York: Simon and Schuster, 1984), 228. No one could figure out what Stengel was doing at times, but he produced mystical results. Hank Bauer remembers from the 1949 season. "In the middle of one game, the old man put Cliff Mapes in right, moved me to left field, and we both threw a guy out at the plate." Dave Anderson, *Pennant Races* (New York: Doubleday, 1994), 193.

8. Yogi Berra and Dave Kaplan, *Ten Rings* (New York: HarperCollins, 2003), 40.

9. For all of his professional career and even as death neared, Ted Williams would only refer, with affection and admiration, to "that fucking Lopat." Williams included him in his list of the toughest five pitchers he ever faced. The other four — Ford, Lemon, Feller, and Wilhelm — are all in the Hall of Fame.

10. Looking back from the enormous achievement of the 2004 Red Sox in winning the World Series with a group of journeymen named Bellhorn, Damon, Millar, Varitek, Cabrera and Nixon, mixed in with three genuine all-stars such as Schilling, Martinez and Ramirez, there is little doubt that the Boston world champion team was not the most talented collection of Red Sox in history. That honor arguably would go to the 1949 club, from which some intangible was missing. The 2004 entry for Boston was just the second year of new management, the last vestiges of the Yawkey era having ended in 2002.

11. "Casey gave me carte blanche with the pitchers. I'd always take my list in there — so-and-so is pitching tomorrow, we've got so-and-so in the bullpen — and Casey never changed it one time in eleven years. He trusted me, and I had great respect for him because of that. We never had one cross word in eleven years." Ira Berkow and Jim Kaplan, *The Gospel According to Casey* (New York: St. Martin's, 1992), 61.

12. His career record against the Indians was 40–12.

13. Of Turner's black book, Rizzuto said that the coach used it to keep every bit of information about his charges in it. "He knew if one of them changed a blade in their razors." Rizzuto, *The October Twelve*, 20.

14. Golenbock, *Dynasty*, 6.

15. On September 4, 1949, Ed Sinclair wrote in the *New York Herald-Tribune*," Allie Reynolds, the Yankee pitcher who can be counted on to start a game but never to finish one, confounded his critics this afternoon."

16. Years later Reynolds admitted that he suspected that diabetes, "the Indian disease," often sapped his strength.

17. David Halberstam, *Summer of '49* (New York: William Morrow, 1989), 60.

18. Niarhos was traded to the Chicago White Sox on June 27, 1950, one of many catchers whose careers as Yankees ended with the success of the Berra "Project."

19. John P. Rossi, *A Whole New Game* (Jefferson, NC: McFarland, 1999), 62.

20. Roger Kahn perhaps best described the complicated personality of Joe DiMaggio in *The Era*, along with Richard Ben Cramer. Richard Ben Cramer, *Joe DiMaggio: The Hero's Life* (New York: Simon and Schuster, 2000).

21. Daniel Okrent and Harris Lewine, ed. *The Ultimate Baseball Book* (Boston: Houghton Mifflin, 1981), 229–230.

22. Anderson, *Pennant Races*, 202.

23. Kahn, *The Era*, 223.

24. Tommy Henrich, *Five O'clock Lightning* (New York: Carol, 1992), 256.

25. Forker, *The Men of Autumn*, 202.

26. Gene Woodling, a rookie in 1949, caught the spirit quickly. "If you fooled with Chief Reynolds, Vic Raschi, Lopat, Hank Bauer or me, you were in trouble. We were serious. And we got on each other. Casey sat over there and watched us do his job. We played tough baseball." Danny Peary, ed. *We Played the Game* (New York: Hyperion, 1994), 107.

27. There is some belated justice in that it was the St. Louis Cardinals of 1964 who represented the first truly integrated team in major league baseball, with Bob Gibson, Curt Flood, Lou Brock, and Bill White acknowledged as the recognized leaders on the team. David Halberstam, *October 1964* (New York: Villard Books, 1994).

28. Ironically, the black Dodgers had been told by the American League's Larry Doby that Reynolds threw at him routinely. Years later, Reynolds denied throwing in on Doby any more than he did on other American League sluggers whom he tried to push off the plate. Ralph Kiner, who became close friends with Reynolds when they were league representatives in negotiations with the owners, considered him one of the great gentlemen he met in baseball. He recalls Reynolds' vehement denial of these charges: "It didn't make any difference what color they were. I just protected my territory." Ralph Kiner, *Baseball Forever: Reflections*

on *Sixty Years in the Game* (Chicago: Triumph, 2004), 43. By 1949, nothing had changed in baseball's time-honored tradition of racial and ethnic bench-jockeying. Those close enough to hear the players heard words like "snow flake" and "blanket ass" coming out of the two dugouts.

29. Rizzuto, *The October Twelve*, 32. This was the nature of the mortal combat in baseball. "The object is to frighten the hitter, not necessarily to maim him" (Joe Black, Brooklyn Dodgers); "I've got a right to knock down anybody holding a bat" (Early Wynn, Cleveland Indians); "How do you pitch to him? Knock him on his ass. He don't like that" (Don Drysdale, Los Angeles Dodgers).

30. Reynolds' intention was not to hit; it was to terrify, to intimidate. Every major league batter understood, as Ralph Kiner makes clear in the pre-batting helmet age: "Pitchers threw at batters without restraint. Whether that is good or bad is debatable, but it was certainly part of baseball. The fear of being hit took away many players' confidence at the plate and ruined their careers." Kiner, *Baseball Forever*, 43. Everyone lived by the same rules. Red Sox infielder Johnny Pesky: "Allie Reynolds was a peach of a guy. Eddie Lopat, Vic Raschi, they were decent people. If they pitched you close, you didn't bother to look out there because they'd say, 'If you didn't like that one, how about this one?' And the next one would be even closer." Harvey and Frederic Frommer, *Red Sox vs. Yankees: The Great Rivalry* (New York: Sports Publishing, 2004), 90.

31. Donald Honig, *A Donald Honig Reader* (New York: Simon and Schuster, 1988), 382–383.

32. Tom Meany, *The Yankee Story* (New York: Dutton, 1960), 161–162.

33. Kahn, *The Era*, 240.

5. The Education of Whitey

1. Okrent, *The Ultimate Baseball Book*, 230.

2. Kahn, *The Era*, 110.

3. Whitey Ford with Phil Pepe, *Few and Chosen* (Chicago: Triumph Books, 2001), 168–169.

4. Creamer, *Stengel: His Life and Times*, 235.

5. Parr and Burke, *Allie Reynolds: Super Chief*, 172.

6. Rizzuto, *The October Twelve*, 84.

7. Reynolds told historian Dom Forker, "I roomed with Lopat for six years. He was very helpful. He could tell you what you were doing

wrong when you didn't know yourself. He had all the guts in the world. He was egotistical and intelligent. And he never threw a strike."

8. Larry Moffi, *This Side of Cooperstown* (Iowa City, University of Iowa Press, 1996), 85.

9. In his autobiography, Whitey Ford wrote, "I can't think of Hank Bauer without also thinking of Gene Woodling." Ford, *Few and Chosen*, 145.

10. It was around this time that the Cincinnati Reds, to avoid any possible displeasure of their fans, changed their name officially to the Redlegs. In California, an enterprising restaurant announced that it would no longer serve Russian dressing. Instead, with pickles cut in, salads were now covered by an unabashedly American Thousand Islands dressing.

11. Forker, *The Men of Autumn*, 6.

12. Whitey Ford and Mickey Mantle with Joseph Durso, *Whitey and Mickey* (New York, Viking Press, 1977), 55.

13. Ford, *Few and Chosen*, 146.

14. *New York Times*, September 12, 1950, 30.

15. *New York Times*, October 2, 1950, 28.

16. In *The Boys of Summer*, Roger Kahn refers to a standing joke around the league: "What has two arms, two legs, and no guts? The answer: Don Newcombe," 90.

17. Gene Woodling, one of the toughest of the Yankees who had some battles with his manager, picked up on Stengel's softness: "He and Edna didn't have children and he was very sentimental about kids." Peary, *We Played the Game*, 280.

18. Berkow and Kaplan, *The Gospel According to Casey*, 148.

19. Kahn, *Memories of Summer*, 174.

20. The 1950 games would be the last all-white World Series. There were no black ballplayers on either the Yankees or the Phillies.

21. Forker, *The Men of Autumn*, 6.

22. Red Smith had written about DiMaggio the next day in the *New York Herald Tribune*: "Doddering Joe DiMaggio, who'll hobble into his thirty-seventh year next month, was the feeblest Yankee of them all. Then he came up again in the tenth inning. Roberts threw him one pitch. Roberts said it was a fastball. Whatever it was coming, it was a fastball going." October 6, 30.

23. Parr and Burke, *Allie Reynolds: Super Chief*, 175.

24. Interview with Charlie Silvera, August 19, 2004.

25. Robert Shaplan, "The Yankees Real Boss," *Sports Illustrated*, September 20, 1954, 34–37.

6. *Eddie's Year*

1. Kahn, *The Era*, 189–190.

2. In his off moments, Weiss confessed his bigotry to many journalists. Roger Kahn, Peter Golenbock, Ira Berkow, Robert Creamer and others documented Weiss' intention. But, by 1954, he had to give in and invited the first black ballplayer to a Yankee spring training camp: Elston Howard.

3. Within a few years, Weiss' expectation was realized: Frank Robinson, Hank Aaron, Ernie Banks and Mays had transformed the National League into dominance over the American League.

4. Golenbock, *Dynasty*, 58. McDougald made the team because Billy Martin had already been drafted, but was soon released from the army because of family hardship and rejoined the Yankees for the rest of the season. Bobby Brown, interning at a San Francisco hospital, missed all of spring training and returned on April 24. Meanwhile, Stengel and Weiss continued to divest from McCarthy's team. On May 14, Billy Johnson was sent to the St. Louis Cardinals. A month later, the erratic Tommy Byrne was dealt to the St. Louis Browns, at the insistence of Dan Topping, followed at the end of July by Cliff Mapes.

5. Berra, *Ten Rings*, 93.

6. Adrian Burgos, Jr., "Caribbean Players in the Negro Leagues, 1910–1950." *Centro: Journal of the Center for Puerto Rican Studies*, vol. VIII, nos. 1–2, 129–149.

7. Minoso and Carrasquel, when they represented the left side of the White Sox infield, gave a hint of the Latino presence yet to come. "Chico" was succeeded by Luis Aparicio.

8. No one noticed it, perhaps, but this was the end of the dynasty that never materialized in Boston. Bobby Doerr played only 106 games with a bad back and retired at the end of the year. Dom DiMaggio soon followed, Pesky would be traded, and a lonely and bitter Ted Williams was left to play out his career, never again with a contending team, never tipping his hat.

9. Weiss had dealt dozens of Yankee prospects to other teams in trades, proud that he never let a really good talent escape. Burdette was the exception. When the Braves moved to Milwaukee in 1953 Burdette moved into Sain's slot as the right-handed ace of the staff, and in the 1957 World Series beat the Yankees three times with complete games.

10. DiMaggio later recalled the conversation for reporters: Rosen: "Joe, I think Phil's gonna bunt." DiMaggio: "He might, he might." Then DiMaggio took off for home.

11. Parr and Burke, *Super Chief*, 188.

12. Carmen Berra was listening to the game from a hospital bed, awaiting the delivery of her baby. Outside her room, a nurse and orderly heard a horrible cry of agony and rushed to the side of the expectant mother. "What's the matter?! What's the matter?!" Carmen, crying in her bed, replied, "My husband dropped the ball." The baby was delivered without event the next day.

13. Berra, *Ten Rings*, 96.

14. *The Sporting News*, October 10, 1951.

15. Besides finding form in stories handed down by generations of grandfathers, these playoff games were also shrouded in hilarious espionage intrigue, when in 2001 backup Giants catcher Sal Yvars revealed that during the streak, at Durocher's instruction, utility infielder Hank Schenz would sit in the center-field Giant clubhouse with powerful binoculars, stealing signals from the opposing catcher and by electric impulse send them to the Giant bullpen, where the stolen pitch sign would quickly be given to the batter. After reading Yvar's account, seventy-year-old Brooklyn Dodger fans were outraged. Bobby Thomson said that the stolen signals didn't help. No one in Brooklyn believed him.

16. The Chicago White Sox put Sam Hairston in the lineup for four games in July of 1951, but shipped him back to the minors. Here is a list of the first black player with each team and the date of his first game: Dodgers, Jackie Robinson, April 15, 1947; Indians, Larry Doby, July 5, 1947; Browns, Henry Thompson, July 17, 1947; Giants, Henry Thompson, July 8, 1949; Braves, Sam Jethroe, April 18, 1950; White Sox, Sam Hairston, July 21, 1951; Athletics, Bob Trice, September 13, 1953; Cubs, Ernie Banks, September 17, 1953; Pirates, Curt Roberts, April 13, 1954; Cardinals, Tom Alston, April 13, 1954; Reds, Saturnino Escalera, April 17, 1954; Senators, Carlos Paula, September 6, 1954; Yankees, Elston Howard, April 14, 1955; Phillies, John Kennedy, April 22, 1957; Tigers, Ossie Virgil, June 6, 1058; Red Sox, Pumpsie Green, July 21, 1959.

17. Fifty years later, three outstanding Atlanta Braves pitchers enjoyed the same kind of base hit rivalry: John Smoltz, Tom Glavine, and Greg Maddux.

18. Two years later, on August 4, 1953, Vic set a record for runs batted in by a pitcher when he drove in seven runs against the Detroit Tigers in a 15–0 romp. When he got back to his locker, Raschi discovered that his two pitching comrades had stuffed it full of Louisville Sluggers.

19. That winter Weiss agreed to sign five black ballplayers: Artie Wilson, Ruben Gomez, Vic Power, Frank Barnes and Elston Howard.

He traded Wilson, Gomez and Barnes almost immediately, and held on to Power and Howard. In 1953, Power hit .349 for Kansas City in the American Association and played a scintillating first base. He was exactly what the Yankees needed to solve their perpetual problem at that position. Instead, Weiss traded Power to the Philadelphia Athletics. Weiss put his public relations people to work, describing Power as flashy, mercurial, what players call "a showboat"; they also hinted that he dated white women. Weiss held on to Elston Howard, who would become the first black Yankee in 1955 and eventually Yogi Berra's replacement. Stengel, when he first saw Howard in spring training in 1954, said, "When I finally get one, he can't run."

20. DiMaggio had been humiliated by a magazine story that had appeared before the World Series. It was a scouting report on his diminished ability: "Cannot get around on a fastball, has only one throw per game in his arm."

7. Rickey's Dodgers

1. After O'Malley abandoned Brooklyn for Los Angeles in 1957, stories circulated all over the borough that there were priests available and willing to conduct a Black Mass to curse the eternal soul of this most hated of traitors. As of 2005, some elderly priests were apparently still available.

2. This was the early 1950s, when surgery meant the last desperate throw of the dice for a pitcher.

3. Creamer, *Stengel: His Life and Times*, 251.

4. There is little doubt that Roger Kahn saw it correctly when he suggested that Black was robbed of the Most Valuable Player award in the National League when a block of white baseball writers voted for the fifth-place Chicago Cubs' outfielder Hank Sauer, on the strength of his league-leading thirty-seven home runs and 121 RBIs. Kahn, *Memories of Summer*, 69. Black's complete-game clincher was also the last game played at Braves Field, Boston. For the 1953 season, the Braves moved to Milwaukee, the first franchise move in fifty years.

5. This was the pre–Cy Young Award era, which began in 1956. Reynolds came in third in the MVP voting in 1951, second in 1952.

6. In 1954, hotel management finally allowed the black ballplayers to stay at the Chase, but they could not use the dining facilities and had to eat in their rooms.

7. Some diehard Yankee writers found

hope in noting that 1952 was an unusual year for Brooklyn: they played .680 on the road and .577 at home.

8. Seeing the Finish Line: The Return of Whitey

1. Ford described Reynolds some years later to reporter Joe Pepe: "He was from Oklahoma and naturally everyone called him "Chief." And he was a chief in more ways than one. He was the boss. Everyone looked up to Reynolds. We were all afraid of him. I was and Mantle was and I think even Martin was. It got to the point that you wanted to do well if only to keep peace with the Chief."

2. The three pitchers were both "enforcers" and "protectors" on the Yankees. Stengel saw this clearly demonstrated in an early-season game against the St Louis Browns. With Reynolds pitching, the pugnacious catcher Clint Courtney was looking for a fight and steamed into second base with spikes high. He cut Rizzuto's leg, and by the time the dust had settled, Reynolds was off the mound, had grabbed Courtney and had beaten him into unconsciousness, before the other Yankees had a chance. Rizzuto, a twelve-year Yankee veteran and the smallest player on the field, never forgot Allie's charge to his defense.

3. Eventually, Allie received a $30,000 settlement from the bus company in 1957.

4. No one knew it at the time, but this was to be the last win for Vic Raschi in a Yankee uniform.

5. The curveball thrown directly overhand — from twelve o'clock to six o'clock — can be as devastating to the pitcher as it is to the hitter. It shortened the careers of both Erskine and Sandy Koufax. An exception was Warren Spahn, who also came directly over the top and pitched in the major leagues for twenty-one years and won 363 games.

6. Before the renovations to Yankee Stadium in the 1970s, it had an enormous outfield expanse, ranging to the 457-foot marker in center field, where DiMaggio and Mantle made catches around the monuments to Ruth, Gehrig and Miller Huggins.

9. One by One

1. Weiss gave Reynolds a raise to $41,500, making him the highest paid pitcher in Yankee history. It was Allie's last contract.

2. On September 12, the Yankees trailed Cleveland by six games and had a doubleheader in Municipal Stadium. There were more than 86,000 fans, 12,000 of whom were standing. The Yankees needed to win both. Lemon and Wynn beat Ford and Byrne in a twin loss for New York, and the season was effectively over.

3. This was before the age of deals made contingent upon passing a physical exam. There was a limited amount of honor among these devious general managers.

4. For some reason, Stengel dropped the bomb, releasing Phil Rizzuto also on Old-Timers' Day in 1956, this time with Weiss in the room for support.

5. Berra is referring only to the period between 1949 and 1953. Mantle was named to every All-Star roster from 1952 to 1968.

6. Richardson would eventually become a major figure in the Christian evangelical movement. In 1995, he sat at the bedside of the dying Mickey Mantle and later officiated at his funeral.

10. Friendship and Memory

1. Johnson and Stout, *A Yankee Century* (Boston: Houghton Mifflin, 2002), 252.

2. April 1, 2005.

3. Leo Durocher with Ed Linn, *Nice Guys Finish Last* (New York: Simon and Schuster, 1975), 203–212. Jackie's comments about Durocher's Hollywood wife, Laraine Day, sent Leo into a rage.

Bibliography

Books & Periodicals

Adomites, Paul. *The Cooperstown Review* (Premier Issue). Pittsburgh: Sheridan Publishers, 1993.

Alexander, Charles C. *Breaking the Slump: Baseball in the Depression Era.* New York: Columbia University Press, 2002.

Anderson, Dave. *Pennant Races.* New York: Doubleday, 1994.

Berkow, Ira, and Jim Kaplan. *The Gospel According to Casey.* New York: St. Martin's, 1992.

Berra, Yogi, and Dave Kaplan. *Ten Rings: My Championship Seasons.* New York: HarperCollins, 2003.

Bromberg, Lester. "Blind Brother Sees Own Goal in Raschi." *The Sporting News.* July 21, 1948, 3.

Bryant, Howard. *Shut Out: A Story of Race and Baseball in Boston.* New York: Routledge, 2002.

Burgos, Adrian, Jr. "Caribbean Players in the Negro Leagues, 1910–1950." *Centro: Journal of the Center for Puerto Rican Studies* (13:1–2), Spring 1996, 129–149.

Cramer, Richard Ben. *Joe DiMaggio: The Hero's Life.* New York: Simon and Schuster, 2000.

Creamer, Robert W. *Stengel: His Life and Times.* New York: Simon and Schuster, 1984.

Durocher, Leo, with Ed Linn, *Nice Guys Finish Last.* New York: Simon and Schuster, 1975.

Ford, Whitey, and Mickey Mantle with Joseph Durso. *Whitey and Mickey: An Autobiography of the Yankee Years.* New York: Viking Press, 1977.

Ford, Whitey, with Phil Pepe. *Few and Chosen: Defining Yankee Greatness Across the Eras.* Chicago: Triumph, 2001.

Forker, Dom. *The Men of Autumn.* Dallas: Taylor, 1989.

Frommer, Harvey, and Frederic J. Frommer. *Red Sox vs. Yankees: The Great Rivalry.* New York: Sports Publishing, 2004.

Golenbock, Peter. *Dynasty: The New York Yankees, 1949–1964.* Upper Saddle River, New Jersey: Prentice Hall, 1975.

Halberstam, David. *October 1964.* New York: Villard, 1994.

_____. *Summer of '49.* New York: William Morrow, 1989.

_____. *Teammates: Portrait of a Friendship.* New York: Hyperion, 2003.

Henrich, Tommy. *Five O'clock Lightning.* New York: Carol, 1992.

Honig, Donald. *A Donald Honig Reader.* New York: Simon and Schuster, 1988.

James, Bill. *The New Bill James Historical Baseball Abstract.* New York: The Free Press, 2001.

Johnson, Richard A., and Glenn Stout. *A Yankee Century.* Boston: Houghton-Mifflin, 2002.

Kahn, Roger. *Boys of Summer.* New York: Harper Row, 1971.

_____. *The Era, 1947–1957.* New York: Ticknor & Fields, 1993.

_____. *Memories of Summer.* New York: Hyperion, 1997.

Kempner, Aviva. *The Life and Times of Hank Greenberg.* Twentieth Century Fox Entertainment, 2001.

Kiner, Ralph, with Danny Perry. *Baseball Forever: Reflections on Sixty Years in the Game.* Chicago: Triumph, 2004.

Koppett, Leonard. *The Man in the Dugout: Baseball's Top Managers and How They Got That Way*. Philadelphia: Temple University Press, 2000.

Liebling, A.J. *Just Enough Liebling: Classic Work by the Legendary New Yorker Writer*. New York: North Point Press, 2004.

Marshall, William. *Baseball's Pivotal Era*. Lexington: University of Kentucky Press, 1999.

Meany, Tom. *The Yankee Story*. New York: Dutton, 1960.

Meece, Volney. "Allie's Still the Chief to Friends." *The Daily Oklahoman*, August 26, 1989.

Moffi, Larry. *This Side of Cooperstown*. Iowa City: University of Iowa Press, 1996.

Neft, David S., Richard M. Cohen, and Michael L. Neft. *Baseball*. New York: St Martin's, 2001.

Okrent, Daniel, and Harris Lewine, eds. *The Ultimate Baseball Book*. Boston: Houghton Mifflin, 1981.

Parr, Royse, and Bob Burke. *Allie Reynolds: Super Chief*. Oklahoma City: Oklahoma Heritage Association, 2002.

Peary, Danny, ed. *We Played the Game*. New York: Hyperion, 1994.

Powers-Beck, Jeffrey. *The American Indian Integration of Baseball*. Lincoln: University of Nebraska Press, 2004.

Ritter, Lawrence S. *The Glory of Their Times*. New York: Collier, 1966.

Rizzuto, Phil, and Tom Horton. *The October Twelve*. New York: Forge Books, 1994.

Rossi, John P. *A Whole New Game*. Jefferson, NC: McFarland, 1999.

Shaplan, Robert. "The Yankees' Real Boss." *Sports Illustrated*. September 20, 1954, 34–37.

Newspapers

New York Times.

Archives

Interview with Ed Lopat, August 26, 1988. A.B. Chandler Oral History Project, University of Kentucky.

Index